HENRY WARD BEECHER'S WRITINGS.

FREEDOM AND WAR.

1 vol. 12mo. $1.50.

EYES AND EARS:

1 vol. 12mo. $1.50.

LECTURES TO YOUNG MEN.

NEW AND REVISED EDITION.

1 vol. 16mo. $1.00.

TICKNOR AND FIELDS, Publishers.

FREEDOM AND WAR.

DISCOURSES

ON TOPICS SUGGESTED BY THE TIMES.

BY

HENRY WARD BEECHER.

BOSTON:
TICKNOR AND FIELDS.
1863.

UNIVERSITY PRESS:
WELCH, BIGELOW, AND COMPANY,
CAMBRIDGE.

EDITOR'S INTRODUCTION.

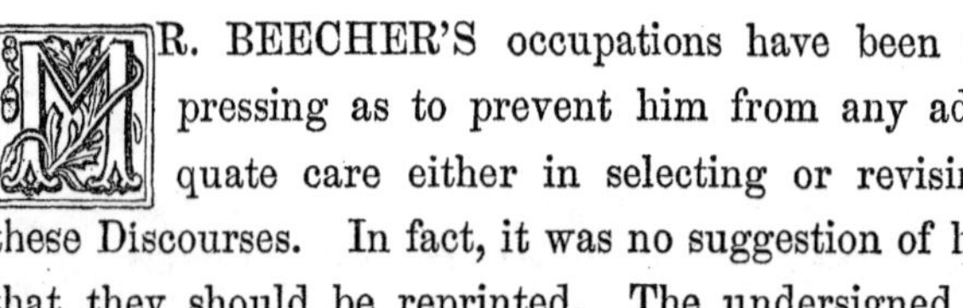

MR. BEECHER'S occupations have been so pressing as to prevent him from any adequate care either in selecting or revising these Discourses. In fact, it was no suggestion of his that they should be reprinted. The undersigned is responsible for the selection of all of them, and for the revision of all after the eighth. The first eight were hastily revised by Mr. Beecher.

The title sufficiently expresses the rule by which the selection was made. That rule was, to choose discourses on subjects of present interest, and which, at the same time, should as far as possible so handle those subjects as to have a more permanent value. They have also a certain significance from their order in time.

No other system will be found in the book, except a systematic purpose always to discuss the subject apparently most important at the time. Its general method is, to apply the principles of Christianity to the duties and circumstances of life; to insist on a sound and lofty and fearless Christian morality in whatever men do; and to show the increased importance of practising that morality in times like these. It is believed that, in seeking to do this, these Discourses are consistent and clear in teaching God's almighty supremacy and his goodness and wisdom, faith in humanity and its future, the absolute necessity of National Righteousness and of Christian Equality, the substantial truth and excellence of the frame of government of the United States, the substantial nobility and courage, justice and perseverance, of the real democracy of the country, and the certain and ineffable splendor of our future, if only we are true to ourselves, to humanity, and to God.

F. B. P.

CONTENTS.

I.

THE NATION'S DUTY TO SLAVERY.*

"Thus saith the Lord, Stand ye in the ways, and see, and ask for the old paths, where is the good way, and walk therein, and ye shall find rest for your souls. But they said, We will not walk therein. Also I set watchmen over you, saying, Hearken to the sound of the trumpet. But they said, We will not hearken. Therefore hear, ye nations, and know, O congregation, what is among them. Hear, O earth: behold, I will bring evil upon this people, even the fruit of their thoughts, because they have not hearkened unto my words, nor to my law, but rejected it." — Jer. vi. 16-19.

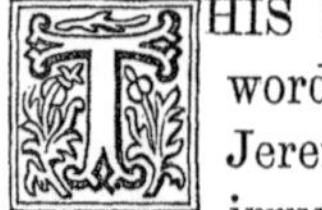HIS is a terrible message. It was God's word of old by the mouth of his prophet, Jeremiah. The occasion of it was a sudden irruption upon Judah of victorious enemies. God sent the prophet to reveal the cause of this disaster. The prophet declared that God was punishing his people because they were selfish and unjust and

* Preached October 30, 1859, while John Brown was in prison awaiting trial for his doings at Harper's Ferry. John Brown's raid took place while the country was just organizing for the campaign which resulted in the election of Mr. Lincoln. It was at once attempted to turn the occurrence against the cause of liberty, by representing it as a symptom and premature development of what was intended by the Republican party against the rights of the South. It was necessary that the friends of liberty should be vindicated, without at the same time taking part, or seeming to take part, against those in bonds.

covetous, and because the whole Church, with its ministry, was whelmed in the same sins. These mischiefs had been glossed over and excused and palliated and hidden, and not healed. There had been a spirit that demanded union and quiet rather than purity and safety. God, therefore, threatens further afflictions, because of the hardness of their hearts; and then, — for such always is the Divine lenity, — as it were, giving them another opportunity and alternative, he commands them to seek after God; to look for A BETTER WAY; to search for the old way, the right way, and to walk in it.

I need not stop to point out the remarkable pertinence which these things have, in many respects, to our nation in the past and to our times in the present. After a long silence upon this subject, I avail myself of the state of the public mind to make some observations on the present state of our land.

The surprise of a whole nation at a recent event is itself the best evidence of the isolation of that event. A burning fragment struck the earth near Harper's Ferry. If the fragment of an exploding aerolite had fallen down out of the air, while the meteor swept on, it would not have been more sudden or less apparently connected either with a cause or an effect!

Seventeen men, white men, without a military base, without supplies, without artillery, without organization more than as a squad of militia, attacked a State, and undertook to release and lead away an enslaved race! They do not appear to have been called by the sufferers, nor to have been welcomed by them. They volunteered a grace, and sought to enforce its acceptance. Seventeen white men held two thousand in duress. They barricaded themselves, and waited until the troops of two States, the *employés* of a great railway, and a portion of the forces of the Federal government could, travelling briskly night and day, reach them. Then, at one dash, they were snuffed out!

I do not wonder that Virginians feel a great deal of mortification! Everybody is sympathetically ashamed for them! It is quite natural that every effort should be made to enlarge the proportions of this escapade, that they may hide their weakness and incompetency behind a smartly upblown horror! No one doubts the bravery of Virginians! It needs no praising. But even brave men have panics. Courage is sometimes caught at unawares. Certainly it strikes us, at a distance, as a remarkable thing, that prisoners three to one more than their captors, and two thousand citizens, should have remained days and nights under the fear and control of seventeen white men. Northern courage has been at a discount in the South hitherto. It ought hereafter to rise in value, at least in Virginia!

The diligence which is now shown on the part of many public presses to inflame the public mind and infect it with fear is quite foolish. The inoculation will not take. The North may not be courageous, but it certainly is not silly. There is an element of the ludicrous in this transaction which I think will effectually stop all panic.

Seventeen men terrified two thousand brave Virginians into two days' submission, — *that* cannot be got over! The common sense of common people will not fail to see through all attempts to hide a natural shame by a bungling make-believe that the danger was really greater than it was! The danger was nothing, and the fear very great, and the courage none at all. And nothing can now change the facts! All the newspapers on earth will not make this case appear any better. Do what you please, — muster a crowd of supposed confederates, call the roll of conspirators, include the noblest men of these States, and exhibit this imaginary army before the people, and, in the end, it will appear that seventeen white men overawed a town of two thousand brave Virginians, and held them captives until the sun had gone laughing twice around the globe!

And the attempt to hide the fear of these surrounded men by awaking a larger fear will never do. It is too literal a fulfilment, not exactly of prophecy, but of fable; not of Isaiah, but of Æsop.

A fox having been caught in a trap, escaped with the loss of his tail. He immediately went to his brother foxes to persuade them that they would all look better if they too would cut off their tails. They declined. And our two thousand friends, who lost their courage in the presence of seventeen men, are now making an appeal to this nation to lose its courage too, that the cowardice of the few may be hidden in the cowardice of the whole community! It is impossible. We choose to wear our courage for some time longer!

As I shall not recur to this epic in Virginia history again to-night, I must say a word in respect to the head and heart of it. For it all stood in the courage of one man.

An old man, kind at heart, industrious, peaceful, went forth, with a large family of children, to seek a new home in Kansas. That infant colony held thousands of souls as noble as liberty ever inspired or religion enriched. A great scowling Slave State, its nearest neighbor, sought to tread down this liberty-loving colony, and to dragoon slavery into it by force of arms. The armed citizens of a hostile State crossed the State lines, destroyed the freedom of the ballot-box, prevented a fair expression of public sentiment, corruptly usurped law-making power, and ordained by fraud laws as infamous as the sun ever saw; assaulted its infant settlements with armed hordes, ravaged the fields, destroyed harvests and herds, and carried death to a multitude of cabins. The United States government had no marines for this occasion! No Federal troops posted by the cars by night and day for the poor, the weak, the grossly wronged men of Kansas. There was an army there that unfurled the banner of the Union, but it was on the side of the wrong-doers, not on the side of the injured.

It was in this field that Brown received his impulse. A tender father, whose life was in his son's life, he saw his first-born seized like a felon, chained, driven across the country, crazed by suffering and heat, beaten like a dog by the officer in charge, and long lying at death's door! Another noble boy, without warning, without offence, unarmed, in open day, in the midst of the city, was shot dead! No justice sought out the murderers; no United States attorney was despatched in hot haste; no marines or soldiers aided the wronged and weak!

The shot that struck the child's heart crazed the father's brain. Revolving his wrongs, and nursing his hatred of that deadly system that breeds such contempt of justice and humanity, at length his phantoms assume a slender reality, and organize such an enterprise as one might expect from a man whom grief had bereft of good judgment. He goes to the heart of a Slave State. One man, — and with sixteen followers! he seizes two thousand brave Virginians, and holds them in duress!

When a great State attacked a handful of weak colonists, the government and nation were torpid, but when seventeen men attacked a sovereign State, then Maryland arms, and Virginia arms, and the United States government arms, and they three rush against seventeen men.

Travellers tell us that the Geysers of Iceland — those singular boiling springs of the North — may be transported with fury by plucking up a handful of grass or turf and throwing it into the springs. The hot springs of Virginia are of the same kind! A handful of men was thrown into them, and what a boiling there has been!

But, meanwhile, no one can fail to see that this poor, child-bereft old man is the manliest of them all. Bold, unflinching, honest, without deceit or evasion, refusing to take technical advantages of any sort, but openly avowing his principles and motives, glorying in them in danger and death, as much as when in security, — that wounded old father is the most remarkable figure in this whole drama. The Governor, the officers of the State, and all the attorneys are pygmies compared with him.

I deplore his misfortunes. I sympathize with his sorrows. I mourn the hiding or obscuration of his reason. I disapprove of his mad and feeble schemes. I shrink from the folly of the bloody foray, and I shrink likewise from all the anticipations of that judicial bloodshed which doubtless erelong will follow,—for when was cowardice ever magnanimous? If they kill the man, it will not be so much for treason as for the disclosure of their cowardice!

Let no man pray that Brown be spared. Let Virginia make him a martyr. Now, he has only blundered. His soul was noble; his work miserable. But a cord and a gibbet would redeem all that, and round up Brown's failure with a heroic success.

One word more, and that is as to the insecurity of those States that carry powder as their chief cargo. Do you suppose that if tidings had come to New York that the United States armory in Springfield had been seized by seventeen men, New Haven, and Hartford, and Stamford, and Worcester, and New York, and Boston, and Albany would have been thrown into a fever and panic in consequence of the event? We scarcely should have read the papers to see what became of it. We should have thought that it was a matter which the Springfield people could manage. The thought of danger would not have entered into our heads. There would not have been any danger. But in a State where there is such inflammable stuff as slavery, there *is* danger, and the people of the South know it; and they cannot help it. I do not blame them so much for being afraid: there is cause for fear where they have such a population as they have down at the bottom of society. But what must be the nature of State and domestic institutions which keep brave men at the point of fear all their life long?

I do not propose, at this time, to express my opinion upon the general subject of slavery. I have elsewhere, and often, deliberately uttered my testimony. Reflection and experience only confirm my judgment of its immeasurable evils. It is double-edged evil, that cuts both ways, wounding master and slave; a pest to good morals; a consumption of the industrial virtues; a burden upon society in its commercial and economic arrangements; a political anomaly; and a cause of inevitable degradation in religious ideas, feelings, and institutions. All other causes of trouble derived from the weakness or the wickedness of men put together are not half so mischievous to our land as is this gigantic evil.

But it exists in our land, and with a wide-spread and a long-established hold. The extent of our duties toward the slave and toward the master is another and separate question. Our views upon the nature of slavery may be right, and our views of duty toward it may be wrong. At this time it is peculiarly necessary that all good men should be divinely led to act with prudence and efficient wisdom.

Because it is a great sin, because it is a national curse, it does not follow that we have a right to say anything or do anything about it that may happen to please us. We certainly have no right to attack it in any manner that may gratify men's fancies or passions. It is computed that there are four million colored slaves in our nation. These dwell in fifteen different Southern States, with a population of ten million whites. These sovereign States are united to us not merely by federal ligaments, but by vital interests, by a common national life. And the question of duty is not simply what is duty toward the blacks, not what is duty toward the whites, but what is duty to each and to both united. I am bound by the great law of love to consider my duties toward the slave, and I am bound by the great law of love also to consider my duties toward the white man, who is his master! Both are to be treated with Christian wisdom and forbearance. We must seek to benefit the slave as much as the white man, and the white man as really as the slave. We must keep in mind the interest of every part, — of the slaves themselves, of the white population, and of the whole brotherhood of States federated into national life. And while the principles of liberty and justice are one and the same, always and everywhere, the wisest method of conferring upon men the benefit of liberty and justice demands great consideration, according to circumstances.

How to apply an acknowledged principle in practical life is a task more difficult than the defence of the principle. It is harder to define what would be just in certain emergencies than to establish the duty, claims, and authority of justice.

Can any light be thrown upon this difficult path? Some light may be shed; but the difficulties of duty can never be removed except by the performance of duty. But some things may be known beforehand, and guide to practical solutions.

I shall proceed to show the wrong way and the right way.

1. First, we have no right to treat the citizens of the South with acrimony and bitterness, because they are involved in a system of wrong-doing. Wrong is to be exposed. But the spirit of rebuke may be as wicked before God as the spirit of the evil rebuked.

Simplicity and firmness in truth are more powerful than any vehement bitterness. Speaking the truth in love is the Apostle's prescription. Some men so love that they will not speak painful truth, and some men utter truth so bitterly as to destroy love; and both are evil-doers. A malignant speech about slavery will not do any good; and, most of all, it will not do those any good who most excite our sympathy, — the children of bondage. If we hope to ameliorate the condition of the slave, the first step must not be taken by setting the master against him. We may be sure that God will not employ mere wrath for wisdom; and that he will raise up and send forth, when his day comes, fearless men, who shall speak the truth for justice, in the spirit of love. Therefore it is a matter not merely of political and secular wisdom, but of Christian conscience, that those that have at heart the welfare of the enslaved should maintain a Christian spirit. This can be done without giving up one word of truth or one principle of righteousness. A man may be fearless and plain-spoken, and yet give evidence of being sympathetic and kind-hearted and loving.

2. The breeding of discontent among the bondmen of our land is not the way to help them. Whatever gloomy thoughts the slave's own mind may brood, *we* are not to carry disquiet to him from without.

If I could have my way, every man on the globe should be a freeman, and at once! But as they cannot be, will not be, for ages, is it best that bitter discontent should be inspired in them, or Christian quietness and patient waiting? If restlessness would bring freedom, they should never rest. But I firmly believe that moral goodness in the slave is the harbinger of liberty! The influence of national freedom will gradually reach the enslaved, it will surely inspire that restlessness which precedes development. Germination is the most silent, but most disturbing, of all natural processes. Slaves cannot but feel the universal summer of civilization. In this way they must come to restless yearnings. We cannot help that, and would not if we could. It is God's sign that spring has come to them. The soul is coming up. There must be room for it to grow. But this is a very different thing from surly discontent, stirred up from without, and left to rankle in their unenlightened natures. The time is rapidly coming when the Southern Christian will feel a new inspiration. We are not far removed from a revival of the doctrines of Christian manhood and the divine rights of men. When this pentecost comes, the slaves will be stirred by their own masters. We must work upon the master. Make him discontented with slavery, and he will speedily take care of the rest. Before this time comes, any attempt to excite discontent among the slaves will work mischief to *them*, and not good. And my experience — and I have had some experience in this matter — is, that men who tamper with slaves and incite them to discontent are not themselves to be trusted. They are not honest men, unless they are fanatical. If they have their reason, they usually have lost their conscience. I do not know why it is so, but my experience has taught me that men who do such things are crafty, and untrustworthy. Conspirators, the world over, are bad men. And if I were in the South, I should, not from fear of the master, but from the most deliberate sense of the injurious effects of it to the slave, never by word nor act do anything to excite discontent among those who are in slavery. The condition of the slave must be changed, but the change cannot go on in one part of the community alone. There must be change in the law, change in the Church, change in the upper classes, change in the middle and in all classes. Emancipation, when it comes, will come either by revolution or by a change of public opinion in the whole community. No influences, then, are adequate to the relief of the slave, which are not of a proportion and power sufficient to modify the thought and the feeling of the whole community. The evil is not partial. It cannot be cured by partial remedies. Our plans must include a universal change in policy, feeling, purpose, theory, and practice in the whole nation. The application of simple remedies to single spots in this great body of disease will serve to produce a useless irritation: it will merely fester the hand, but not cure the whole body.

3. No relief will be afforded to the slaves of the South, as a body, by any individual; or by any organized plan to carry them off, or to incite them to abscond.

The more enlightened and liberty-loving among the Southern slaves bear too much of their masters' blood not to avail themselves of any opening to escape. It is their right; it will be their practice. Free locomotion is an incident of slave property, which the master must put up with. Nimble legs are of much use in tempering the severity of slavery. If, therefore, an enslaved man, acting from the yearnings of his own heart, desires to run away, who shall forbid him? In all the earth, wherever a human being is held in bondage, he has a right to slough his burden and break his yoke if he can. If he wishes liberty, and is willing to dare and suffer for it, let him! If by his manly courage he achieves it, he ought to have it. I honor such a man!

Nay, if he has escaped and comes to me, I owe him shelter, succor, defence, and God-speed to a final safety. If there were as many laws as there are lines in the Fugitive Slave Law, and as many officers as there were beasts in Daniel's lions'-den, I would disregard every law but God's, and help the fugitive! A man whose own heart has inspired a courage sufficient to achieve what he desired, shall never come to my door, and not be made as welcome as my own child. I will adopt him for God's sake, and for the sake of the Christ who broods over the weak and perishing. Nor am I singular in such feelings and purposes. Ten thousand men, even in the South, would feel and do the same. A man who would not help a fellow-creature flying for his liberty must be either a villain or a politician.

I stand on the outside of this great cordon of darkness, and every man that escapes from it, running for his life, shall have some help from me, if he comes forth of his own free accord; yet I would never incite slaves to run away, or send any other man to do it. We have no right to carry into the midst of slavery exterior discontent; and for this reason: *that it is not good for the slaves themselves.* It is short-sighted humanity, at best, and poor policy for both the blacks and the whites. And I say again,

I would not trust a man that should do it. It would injure the blacks chiefly and especially. How it would injure them will appear when I come to speak positively of what is the right way to promote the liberty of the enslaved. I may say here, however, that the higher a man is raised in the scale of being, the harder it will be to hold him in bondage and to sell him; while the more he is like an animal, the easier it will be to hold him in thrall and harness. The more you make slaveholders feel that when they oppress and sell a man they are oppressing and selling God's image, the harder it will be for them to continue to enslave and traffic in human beings. Therefore, whatever you do to inspire in the slave high and noble and godlike feelings tends to loosen his chains, and whatever shall inspire in him base, low, and cruel feelings tightens them.

Running away is all fair for single cases. It is God's remedy for all cases of special hardship. It is the natural right of any slave who has manhood enough to resent even tolerant bondage. We are not speaking of the remedy for individuals, — but the remedy for the whole system. Four million men cannot run away, until God sends ten Egyptian plagues to help them. And those who go among the slaves to stir up discontent will help the hundreds at the expense of the millions. Those left behind will be demoralized, and, becoming less trustworthy, will grow sullen under increased severity and vigilance.

4. Still less would we tolerate anything like insurrection and servile war. It would be the most cruel, hopeless, and desperate of all conceivable follies, to seek emancipation by the sword and by blood. And

though I love liberty as my own life, though I long for it in every human being, though if God, by unequivocal providences, should ordain that it should come again as of old, through terrible plagues on the first-born, and by other terrors of ill, I should submit to the Divine behest; yet, so far as human instrumentality is concerned, by all the conscience of a man, by all the faith of a Christian, and by all the zeal and warmth of a philanthropist, I protest against any counsels that lead to insurrection, servile war, and bloodshed. It is bad for the master, bad for the slave, bad for all that are neighbors to them, bad for the whole land, — bad from beginning to end!

The right of a race or nation to seize their freedom is not to be disputed. It belongs to all men on the face of the globe, without regard to complexion. A people have the right to change their rulers, their government, their whole political condition. This right is neither granted nor limited in the New Testament. It is left, as are the functions of life, and even existence itself, as a thing not requiring commands or legislation. But, according to God's Word, so long as a man remains a servant, he must obey his master. The right of the slave to throw off the control of his master is not abrogated. The right of the subject to do this is neither defined nor limited. But the use of this right must conform to reason, and not to mere impulse. The leaders of a people have no right to whelm their helpless followers in terrible disaster by inciting them to rebel, under circumstances that afford not the slightest hope that their rebellion will rise to the dignity of a successful revolution. The nations of Italy are showing great wisdom and fitness in their leaders for their work, in that they are quelling fretful and irregular outbreak, and holding the people steadfast till success shall surely crown uprising revolution. This has been the eminent wisdom of that Hungarian exile, KOSSUTH. In spite of all that is written and said against this noble man, I stand to my first full faith in him. The uncrowned hero is the noblest man, after all, in Europe! And his statesmanship has been shown in this: that his burning sense of the right of his people to be free has not led him to incite them to premature, partial, and easily overmatched revolt. A man may give his own life rather than abide in servitude, but he has no right to lead a whole people to slaughter, without the strongest probabilities of success.

If nations were all armed men, it would be different. Soldiers can die. But a nation is made up of other materials than armed men; it includes women and children and youth. These are to be considered, and not merely men of muscle and knuckle and bone.

Now, if the Africans in our land were intelligent, if they understood themselves, if they had self-governing power, if they were able first to throw off the yoke of adverse laws and institutions, and afterwards to defend and build themselves up in a civil state, then they would have just the same right to assume their independence that any nation has.

But does any man believe that this is the case? Does any man believe that this vast horde of undisciplined Africans, if set free, would have cohesive power enough to organize themselves into a government, and maintain their independence? If there be men who believe this, I am not among them. I certainly think that even slaves would be made immeasurably better by liberty; but I do not believe they would be made better by liberty gained by insurrection or rebellion in the peculiar circumstances which surround them at the South. A regulated liberty; a liberty possessed with the consent of their masters; a liberty under the laws and institutions of the country; a liberty which should make them common beneficiaries of those institutions and principles which make us wise and happy, — such a liberty would be a great blessing to them. Freedom, with law and government, is an unspeakable good, but without them it is a mischief. And anything that tends to incite among men a vague insurrectionary spirit is a great and cruel wrong to them.

If, in view of the wrongs of slavery, you say that you do not care for the master, but only for the slave, I reply, that you *should* care for both master and slave! Though you do not care for the fate of the wrong-doing white man, I do! But even though your sympathy were only for the slave, then for his sake you ought to set your face against anything like an insurrectionary spirit.

Let us turn from these specifications of the wrong way to some considerations relating to the right way.

1. If we would benefit the African at the South, we must *begin at the North.* This is to some men the most disagreeable part of the doctrine of emancipation. It is very easy to labor for the emancipation of beings a thousand miles off; but the practical application of justice and humanity to those about us is not so agreeable. The truths of God respecting the

rights and dignities of men are just as important to free colored men as to enslaved colored men. The lever with which to lift the load of Georgia is in New York. I do not believe the whole free North can tolerate grinding injustice toward the poor, and inhumanity toward the laboring classes, without exerting an influence unfavorable to justice and humanity in the South. No one can fail to see the inconsistency between our treatment of those amongst us who are in the lower walks of life and our professions of sympathy for the Southern slaves. How are the free colored people treated at the North? They are almost without education, and with but little sympathy for their ignorance. They are refused the common rights of citizenship which the whites enjoy. They cannot even ride in the cars of our city railroads. They are snuffed at in the house of God, or tolerated with ill-concealed disgust. Can the black man be a mason in New York? Let him be employed as a journeyman, and every Irish lover of liberty that carries the hod or trowel would leave at once, or compel him to leave! Can the black man be a carpenter? There is scarcely a carpenter's shop in New York in which a journeyman would continue to work, if a black man was employed in it. Can the black man engage in the common industries of life? There is scarcely one from which he is not excluded. He is crowded down, down, down, through the most menial callings, to the bottom of society. We tax them, and then refuse to allow their children to go to our public schools. We heap upon them moral obloquy more atrocious than that which the master heaps upon the slave. And, notwithstanding all this, we lift ourselves up to talk to the Southern people about the rights and liberties of the human soul, and especially the African soul! It is true that slavery is cruel. But it is not at all certain that there is not more love to the race in the South than in the North. We do not own them, so we do not love them at all. The prejudice of the whites against color is so strong that they cannot endure to ride or sit with a black man, so long as they do not own him. As neighbors, they are not to be tolerated, but as property they are most tolerable in the house, the church, the carriage, the couch! The African owned, may dwell in America; but unowned, he must be expatriated. Emancipation must be jackal to colonization. The choice given to the African is plantation or colonization. Our Christian public sentiment is a pendulum swinging between owning or exporting the colored poor in our midst.

Whenever we are prepared to show toward the lowest, the poorest, and the most despised an unaffected kindness, such as led Christ, though the Lord of Glory, to lay aside his dignities, and to take on himself the form of a servant, and suffer an ignominious death, that he might rescue men from ignorance and bondage, — whenever we are prepared to do such things as these, we may be sure that the example of the North will not be unfelt at the South. Every effort that is made in Brooklyn to establish schools and churches for the free colored people, and to encourage them to educate themselves and to become independent, is a step toward emancipation in the South. The degradation of free colored men in the North will fortify slavery in the South!

2. We must quicken all the springs of feeling in

the Free States in behalf of human liberty, and create a public sentiment, based upon truths of Christian manhood. For if we act to any good purpose on the minds of the South, we must do it through a salutary and pure public sentiment in the North. When we have corrected our own practice, and set an example of the right spirit, then we shall have a position from which to exert a beneficial public influence on the minds of Southern slaveholders. For this there must be full and free discussion. Under our institutions, public opinion is the monarch; and free speech and debate form public opinion.

The air must be vital with the love of liberty. Liberty with us must be raised by religion from the selfishness of an instinct to the sanctity of a moral principle! We must love it for ourselves and demand it for others. Since Christ took man's nature, human life has a divine sanctity. We must inspire in the public mind a profound sense of the rights of men founded upon their relations to God. The glory of intelligence, refinement, genius, has nothing to do with men's rights. The rice slave, the Hottentot, are as much God's children as Humboldt or Chalmers. That they are in degradation only makes it more imperative upon us to secure to them the birthright which in their ignorance they sell for a mess of pottage.

These things must become familiar again to our pulpits. Our children must be taught to glow again in our schools over the heroic ideals of liberty. Mothers must twine the first threads of their children's life with the golden threads of these divine truths, and the whole of life must be woven to the heavenly pattern of Liberty!

What can the North do for the South, unless her own heart is purified and ennobled? When the love of liberty is at so low an ebb that churches dread the sound, ministers shrink from the topic; when book-publishers dare not publish or republish a word on the subject of slavery, cut out every living word from school-books, expurgate life-passages from Humboldt, Spurgeon, and all foreign authors or teachers; and when great religious publication societies, endowed for the very purpose of speaking fearlessly the truths which interest would let perish, pervert their trust, and are dumb, first and chiefly, and articulate only in things that thousands of others could publish as well as they, — what chance is there that public sentiment, in such a community, will have any power with the South?

But the end of these things is at hand. A nobler spirit is arising. New men, new hearts, new zeals, are coming forward, led on by all those signs and auspices that God foresends when he prepares his people to advance. This work, well begun, must not go back. It must grow, like spring, into summer. God will then give it an autumn — without a winter. And when such a public sentiment fills the North, founded upon religion, and filled with fearless love to both the bond and the free, it will work all over the continent, and nothing can be hid from the shining thereof.

3. By all the ways consistent with the fearless assertion of truth, we must maintain sympathy and kindness toward the South. We are brethren; and I pray that no fratricidal influences be permitted to sunder this Union. There was a time when I thought

the body of death would be too much for life, and that the North was in danger of taking disease from the South, rather than they our health. That time has gone past. I do not believe that we shall be separated by their act or ours. We have an element of healing, which, if we are true to ourselves and our principles, and God is kind to us, will drive itself further and further into the nation, until it penetrates and regenerates every part. When the whole lump shall have been leavened thereby, old prejudices will be done away, and new sympathies will be created.

I am for holding the heart of the North right up to the heart of the South. Every heart-beat will be, erelong, not a blow riveting oppression, but a throb carrying new health. Freedom in the North is stronger than slavery in the South. We are yet to work for them as the silent spring works for us. They are a lawful prey to love. I do not hesitate to tell the South what I mean by loving this Union. I mean liberty, I mean the decay of slavery, and its extinction. If I might speak for the North, I would say to the South: "We love you, and hate your slavery. We shall leave no fraternal effort untried to deliver you, and ourselves with you, from the degradation, danger, and wickedness of this system." And for this we cling to the Union. There is health in it.

4. We are to leave no pains untaken, through the Christian conscience of the South, to give to the slave himself a higher moral *status*. I lay it down as an axiom, that whatever gives more manhood to the slave slackens the bonds that bind him, and that whatever lowers him in the scale of manhood tightens those

bonds. If you wish to work for the enfranchisement of the African, seek to make him a better man. Teach him to be an obedient servant, and an honest, true, Christian man. These virtues are God's step-stones to liberty. That man whom Christ first makes free has a better chance to be civilly free than any other. To make a slave morose, fractious, disobedient, and unwilling to work is the way to defer his emancipation. We do not ask the slave to be satisfied with slavery. But, feeling its grievous burden, we ask him to endure it while he must, "as unto God, and not unto man"; not because he does not love liberty, but because he does love Christ enough to show forth His spirit under grievous wrong. Bad slaves will never breed respect, sympathy, and emancipation. Truth, honor, fidelity, manhood, — these things in the slave will prepare him for freedom. It is the low animal condition of the African that enslaves him. It is moral enfranchisement that will break his bonds.

The Pauline treatment is the most direct road to liberty. No part of the wisdom of the New Testament seems to me more divinely wise than Paul's directions to those in slavery. This is the food that servants need now at the South, everywhere, the world over! If I lived in the South, I should preach these things to slaves, with a firm conviction that so I should advance the day of their liberty! I should feel that I was carrying them further and further toward their emancipation. There is no disagreement between the true spirit of emancipation and the enforcement of every single one of the precepts of the New Testament respecting servants.

5. The things which shall lead to emancipation are not so complicated or numerous as people blindly think. A few virtues established, a few usages maintained, a few rights guaranteed to the slaves, and the system is vitally wounded. The right of chastity in the woman, the unblemished household love, the right of parents in their children, — on these three elements stands the whole weight of society. Corrupt or enfeeble these, and there cannot be superincumbent strength. Withhold these rights from savage people, and they can never be carried up. They are the integral elements of associated human life. We demand, and have a right to demand, of the Christian men of the South, that they shall revolutionize the moral condition of the slaves.

I stand up in behalf of two million women who are without a voice, to declare that there ought to be found in Christianity, somewhere, an influence that shall protect their right to their own persons, and that their purity shall stand on some other ground than the caprice of their masters! I demand that the Christian Church, both North and South, shall bear a testimony in behalf of marriage among the slaves, which shall make it as inviolable as marriage among the whites. It is not to be denied that another code of morals prevails upon the plantation than that which prevails in the plantation mansion. So long as husband and wife are marriageable commodities, liable to be sold apart, to form new connections, there can be no such thing as sanctity in wedlock.

Let it be known in New York that a man has two wives, and there is no church so feeble of conscience that they will not instantly eject him; and the law will promptly visit him with penalties. But the communicants of slave churches not only live with a second while their first companion is yet alive, but in succession with a third and fourth; nor is it any disqualification for church-membership. The Church and the State wink at it. It is the commercial necessity of the system. If you will sell men, you must not be too nice about their moral virtues.

A wedding among this unhappy people is but a name, — a mere form to content their conscience or their love of imitating their superiors. Every auctioneer in the community has the power to put asunder whom God has joined. The bankruptcy of their owner is the bankruptcy of the marriage relation in half the slaves on his plantation.

Neither is there any gospel that has been permitted to rebuke these things. There is no church that I have ever known in the South that bears testimony against them. Neither will the churches in the North, as a body, take upon themselves the responsibility of bearing witness against them.

I go further. I declare that there must be a Christian public sentiment which shall make the family inviolate. Men sometimes say, "It is rarely the case that families are separated." It is false! It is false! There is not a slave-mart that does not bear testimony, a thousand times over, against such an assertion. Children are bred like colts and calves, and are dispersed like them.

It is in vain to preach a gospel to slaves that leaves out personal chastity in man and woman, or that leaves their purity subject to another's control; that leaves out the sanctity of the marriage state, and the unity and inviolability of the family. And yet no gospel has borne such a testimony in favor of them as to arouse the conscience of the South! If ministers will not preach liberty to the captive, they ought at least to preach the indispensable necessity of household virtue! If they will not call upon the masters to set their slaves free, they should at least proclaim a Christianity that protects woman, childhood, and household!

The moment that woman stands self-poised in her own purity, the moment man and woman are united together by bonds which cannot be sundered during their earthly life, the moment the right of parents to their children is recognized, — that moment there will be a certain sanctity and protection of the eternal and Divine government resting upon father and mother and children, and the death-blow of slavery will have been struck! You cannot make slavery profitable after these three conditions are secured. The moment you make slaves serfs, they are no longer a legal tender, and are uncurrent in the market; and families are so cumbrous, so difficult to support, so expensive, that owners are compelled, from reasons of pecuniary interest, to discontinue the system.

Therefore, if you will only disseminate the truths of the Gospel, if you will put timid priests out of the way, and lying societies whose cowardice slanders the Gospel which they pretend to diffuse, and if you will bring a whole solar flood of truth to bear upon the practical morals of the slave, you will begin to administer a remedy, if God designs to cure it by moral means, which will inevitably heal the evil.

6. Among the means to be employed for promoting

the liberty of the slave we must not fail to include the power of true Christian prayer. When slavery shall cease, it will be by such instruments and influences as shall exhibit God's hand and heart in the work. Its downfall will have been achieved so largely through natural causes, so largely through reasons as broad as nations, that it will be apparent to all men that God led on the emancipation; man being only one element among the many. Therefore, we have every encouragement to direct our prayers without ceasing to God, that he will restrain the wrath of man, inspire men with wisdom, overrule all evil laws, and control the commerce of the globe, so that the poor may be protected, that the bond may become free, that the ignorant may become wise, that the master and slave may respect each other, and that at length we may be an evangelized and Christian people. May God, in his own way and time, speed the day!

II.

AGAINST A COMPROMISE OF PRINCIPLE.*

"And there was delivered unto him the book of the prophet Esaias. And when he had opened the book, he found the place where it was written, The Spirit of the Lord is upon me, because he hath anointed me to preach the Gospel to the poor; he hath sent me to heal the broken-hearted, to preach deliverance to the captives, and recovering of sight to the blind, to set at liberty them that are bruised, to preach the acceptable year of the Lord." — Luke iv. 17 - 19.

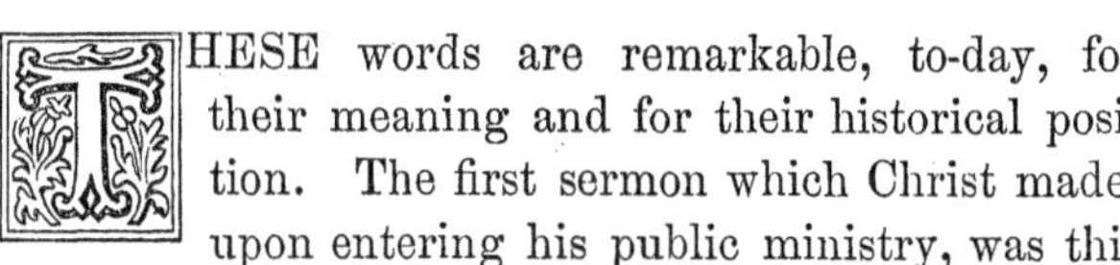

THESE words are remarkable, to-day, for their meaning and for their historical position. The first sermon which Christ made, upon entering his public ministry, was this one at Nazareth, where he had been brought up. That he chose these words in entering upon his mission — these words, of all the Law, of all the Psalms, and of all the Prophets — gives them peculiar significancy. And, when we consider their contents, they become yet more memorable, since they were the charter and index of his mission, — the text not only of his sermon, but of his life. Christ came to save the world, — not laws, not governments, not institutions, not dynasties, but the *people*. The fulfilment of his mission is to be looked for in the condition of nation-

* Thanksgiving Day, November 29, 1860.

alities and the character of peoples. Though peace breathe balm over all the world, and every law is obeyed, and every government rides among the people, as a man-of-war dressed for holiday, upon a tranquil sea, there is no reason for rejoicing if the people are ignorant and their capacities are undeveloped, if they are mean and sordid, and their morals, like a Chinese foot, are cramped too small to walk upon. But though there be wars and rumors of war, revolutions and tumults, the world is prosperous if by these convulsions the race is freed from oppression, thoroughly aroused, and incited to bolder enterprise and to nobler moral character.

We are, then, to study the advance of Christ's kingdom in the whole aspect of the world. The Church is of the people. God's Church includes the whole human race. Our separate churches are but doors to the grand spiritual interior. The good men who love God and man with overruling affection, of all nations, and of every tongue, are the true Church.

To-day we are assembled to give thanks for national mercies. I need not remind you of the year that is closing. Who knew, when January set her cold, calm face toward the future, that she was the herald of such a summer? When was there ever a year so fertile? so propitious to all industry? It has been a procession of rejoicing months, flower-wreathed and fruit-laden, — a very holiday year!

The soil awoke with new ardor; everything that lived by the soil felt the inspiration. Every root, and every blade, and every stem, and every bough has this year tasked itself for prodigal bounty. Except a narrow strip, this continent has been so blessed with husbandry as to make this year memorable even among years hitherto most eminent. The meadow, the tilled fields, the grazing pastures, the garden, the vineyard, the orchard, the very fence-row berry-bushes and wild wall-vines, have been clothed with unexampled bounty and beauty. Nature seems to have lacked messengers to convey her intents of kindness, and the summer, like a road surprised with quadruple freights, has not been able to find conveyance for all its treasures. The seas have felt the divine ardor. The fisherman never reaped such harvests from the moist furrows of the ocean as this year. These husbandmen of the sea, who reap where they have not sowed and grow rich upon harvests which they have not tilled, have this year put in the crooked hook for their sickle with admiring gladness for the strange and unwonted abundance of the deep.

All the sons of God rejoice, and all good men rejoice. It needs but one element to complete the satisfaction. If we could be sure that this is God's mercy, meant for good, and tending thereto, we should have a full cup to-day. That satisfaction is not denied us. The Mayor of New York, in a public proclamation, in view of this prodigal year, that has heaped the poor man's house with abundance, is pleased to say that there is no occasion apparent to him for thanksgiving. We can ask no more. When bad men grieve at the state of public affairs, good men should rejoice. When infamous men keep fast, righteous men should have thanksgiving. God reigns and the Devil trembles. Amen. Let us rejoice! *

* Mayor Fernando Wood's proclamation is such a curiosity of wickedness, even in the annals of New York city, that we append it: —

But it is not now to these topics that I shall confine my remarks. I propose to glance at other reasons for thanksgiving.

1. The advantage and increasing influence of nations which, in the main, tend to conserve human liberty, and the decadence and dwindling of those nations that have flourished by exaction and tyranny, is matter of gratulation. It should make good men glad when wicked men and wicked nations grow weak.

2. The emergence of the common people to that degree of political power that makes it necessary now for the whole of Western Europe to ask their permission for the establishment of any throne or monarchy is cheering and auspicious. Crowns were once made of gold beaten out on the people's backs. Now the strongest crowns are made of paper, — the paper votes of the common people. Therein we rejoice, and will rejoice.

"Mayor's Office, New York, November 24, 1860.

"Proclamation. — In accordance with custom and the proclamation of the Governor of the State, it becomes my duty, as Mayor, to recommend to the people of this city the observance of THURSDAY, the 29th inst., as a day of 'Thanksgiving and Prayer.'

"While in my judgment the country, either in its political, commercial, or financial aspect, presents no features for which we should be thankful, we are yet called upon by every consideration of self-preservation to offer up to the Father of all mercies devout and fervent prayer, for his interposition and protection from the impending evils which threaten our institutions and the material interests of the people.

"Therefore, acknowledging our dependence on Almighty God, and deeply sensible of our own unworthiness, let the day set apart as Thanksgiving be observed by the people of this city as one of humiliation and supplication, — not omitting in our prayers the expression of the hope that those who have, in violation of the Federal compact, unpatriotically and unwisely inflicted these injuries upon us, may be the only sufferers by their own wickedness and folly.

"[L. S.] Given under my hand and seal, the day and year aforesaid.

"FERNANDO WOOD, Mayor."

3. The resurrection of Italy is another memorable event of the year. I see as many tokens of a Divine presence in Italy as of old there were in the emancipation and conduct of the Israelites from Egypt. That such a conjunction of events should have taken place; that such a monarch as Victor Emanuel, who almost reconciles republicans to kings, should have sat waiting; that such a consummate statesman, of noblest patriotism, as Cavour, should have been prepared and waiting; that such a hero, simple, true, pure, disinterested, self-sacrificing, skilful, and lion-like, as Garibaldi, should have come at the hour, are marks of the planning of God. Men never devise such combinations. It would have been significant had either of these men come singly. That all should have come together, — a soldier to beat down the old despotism, a statesman to organize the new liberty, a just and patriot king to preside over the people's government, and a people, divided for centuries, but now at last united, — this reveals the mind and will of God. Let us rejoice!

4. The growing moderation of the Russian monarchy, the quiet improvement of the people, the emancipation of the serfs, ought to engage the attention and receive the sympathy of every Christian people. There is a great work begun in Russia. This gigantic nation, the antithesis of America politically and geographically, is, like her, almost half a globe of herself. The end we cannot now even suspect. Prophets are dead. God no longer tells beforehand what he is going to do. But, by the clearing that has been made for the foundations, by the materials that are gathering, and by the workmen that are employed, we judge

that no mean structure is about to arise to the glory of God. There is an immense History now in birth. Let us hope that the unmeasured future will be for Humanity, Justice, and Piety!

5. In the rest of the world there are signs, but more remote, of good. Heathen nations are growing weaker, Christian nations are growing stronger. The nations of Heathenism are imbecile. The nations of Christianity are of vigorous stock, and have a future. Already Christian nations rule the world. Who may war, how long, for what, with whom, depends upon the will of Christian peoples. There is a Christian police around this globe!

6. Our own land has not been behind. In this march of nations our country has kept step. We know it by the victory of ideas, by the recognition of principles instead of mere policies, by the ascendency of justice, and by the witnessing and ratifying rage of all who love oppression and oppressors.

To-day should not be profaned by partisan congratulations; but we should be ungrateful to God, who has guided us through peril and darkness, and at length brought us forth into illustrious victory, if we did not to-day remember, with profound gratitude and devout thanksgiving, the resurrection of the spirit of liberty from the graves of our fathers!

The tree of life, whose leaves were for the healing of the nations, has been evilly dealt with. Its boughs have been lopped, and its roots starved till its fruit is knurly. Upon its top had been set scions of bitter fruits, that grew and sucked out all the sap from the better branches. Upon its trunk the wild boar of the forest had whetted his tusks.

But now again it blooms. Its roots have found the river, and shall not want again for moisture; the grafts of poisonous fruits have been broken off or have been blown out; mighty spearmen have hunted the wild swine back to his thickets, and the hedge shall be broken down no more round about it. The air is fragrant in its opening buds, the young fruit is setting. God has returned and looked upon it, and behold, summer is in all its branches!

To some it may seem that the light in this picture is too high, and that the background is not dark enough. I do not wish you to think that the background is not dark; for it is. There is excitement. There is brewing mischief. The clouds lie lurid along the Southern horizon. The Caribbean Sea, that breeds tornadoes and whirlwinds, has heaped up treasures of storms portentous, that seem about to break. Let them break! God has appointed their bounds. Not till the sea drives back the shore, and the Atlantic submerges the Continent, will this tumult of an angry people move the firm decrees of God. He who came to open prison doors, to deliver captives, to loose those that are bound, — he it is that is among us. We are surrounded by airy hosts greater than those which the prophet of old saw filling the mountains. God is with us. The very rage of wickedness shows his presence.

While we tremble, then, let us rejoice; not triumph, nor boast, nor make invidious comparisons, nor throw fuel of passions into the flames already too hot. But, with a sober, temperate, and beneficent joy, let us give thanks to God, that he has begun to recall this nation from a course that would have wrought utter destruction; and that now, though waves are beating, and the tempest is upon the ship, she has changed her course, and heads right away from the breakers and the sand!

But be sure that, in these times, there can be no safe navigation except that which clings to great universal principles. Selfish interests, if they are our pilots, will betray us. Vainglory will destroy us. Pride will wreck us. Above all, the fear of doing right will be fatal. But justice and liberty are pilots that do not lose their craft. They steer by a divine compass. They know the hand that holds the winds and the storms. It is always safe to be right; and our business is not so much to seek peace as to seek the causes of peace. Expedients are for an hour, but principles are for the ages. Just because the rains descend and winds blow, we cannot afford to build on shifting sands. Nothing can be permanent and nothing safe in this exigency that does not sink deeper than politics or money. We must touch the rock, or we shall never have firm foundations.

I. Our prosperity had its beginning and continuance in Natural Laws. God's will in nature and in human society is the source of human strength and human wisdom. No matter how many are with you, if your councils are in the face of divine principles. Peace, regardless of equity, is a treacherous sleep, whose waking is death. It is not half so necessary to have a settlement as it is to have a *right* settlement. In the end, right political economy will work out prosperous national economy; and if for want of faith in the safety of rectitude you abandon sound and proved principles, or let them go by default, all your good intentions will not save you from national misrule and national wasting and destruction. The mariner who should take refuge in the Maelstrom, thinking it a safe harbor, would learn quickly that good intentions are good follies when men run against natural law. And for men to think that this nation has been prospered on account of the skill, the wisdom, or the arrangements or combinations of men, is the worst of infidelities. While papers and parties are in full outcry, and nostrums are advertised, and scared politicians are at their wits' ends, (without having gone far, either,) and men of weak minds are beside themselves, and imbeciles stand doubting in the streets, know ye that the way of peace is simple, accessible, and easy! Be still. Stand firm. Have courage to wait. Money is insane. Fear is death. Faith in Justice, and in Rectitude, and Trust in God, will work out safety. The worst is over. Our Northern apathy to freedom and our greed of commerce are a thousand times more dangerous than Southern rage and threat. Moral bankruptcy will ruin us all. No other bankruptcies will harm us!

Let us have firm courage, kindness of temper, willingness to make concessions in things of mere policy, but no concession of principles, no yielding of moral convictions, no paltering with our consciences. Thirty pieces of silver bought Christ and hung Judas. If you sell your convictions to Fear, you give yourself to a vagabond. If you sell your conscience to Interest, you traffic with a fiend. The fear of doing right is the grand treason in times of danger. When you consent to give up your convictions of justice, humanity, and liberty, for the sake of tranquillity, you are like men who buy a treacherous truce of tyrants by giving up their weapons of war. Cowards are the food of despots.

When a storm is on the deep, and the ship labors, men throw over the deck-load; they cast forth the heavy freights, and ride easier as their merchandise grows less. But in our time men propose to throw overboard the compass, the charts, the chronometer, and sextant, but to keep the freight!

For the sake of a principle our fathers dared to defy the proudest nation on the globe. They suffered. They conquered. We are never tired of praising them. But when *we* are called to stand firm for principle, we tremble, we whine, we evade duty, and shuffle up a compromise, by which we may sell our conscience, and save our pocket.

It is rank infidelity, and, at such a time as this, stupendous infatuation, to suppose that the greatness of this nation ever sprung from the wisdom of expediency, instead of the power of settled principles. Your harbor did not make you rich; you made the harbor rich. Your ships did not create your commerce; your commerce created your ships; and you created your commerce. Your stores did not make traffic. Your factories did not create enterprise. Your firms, your committees, your treaties, and your legislation did not create national prosperity. Our past greatness sprung from our obedience to God's natural and moral law. We had men trained to courage, to virtue, to wisdom. And manhood, — *manhood*, — MANHOOD, — exercised in the fear of God, has made this nation. Men are God's vicegerents; and if they will govern as he governs, then they shall be creators, too, in this world. The reason we have prospered in days past is not that we have known how to duck and dodge and trim; it is not that we have known all the minute ways of microscopic statesmanship: it is because we have known just enough to see the way in which natural law and God's kingdom were going, and to follow them. It is a simple thing; it is no secret; and accursed be he that counsels the people to seek peace and prosperity by abandoning the causes of it, and that leads them into destruction by leading them into the arms of a tinselled folly!

II. Let no man be foolishly fearful of EXCITEMENT. Our age marks the growth of the world by this: that excitement is now wholesome. When men low down in the scale begin to be stirred, the most active part is excited, which is passion. But when men have outgrown barbarism, and live in moral and intellectual elements, then excitement rouses up the higher nature. Among a savage people, excitement works downward and rages; among a Christian and civilized people, it works upward and toward peace. Excitements among a thinking people tend to clearer convictions, to surer intuitions, to more heroic purposes, and loftier enthusiasms. Do not be afraid because the community teems with excitement. Silence and death are dreadful. The rush of life, the vigor of earnest men, the conflict of realities, invigorates, cleanses, and establishes truth. Our only fear should be lest we refuse God's work. He has appointed this people, and our day, for one of those world-battles on which ages turn. Ours is a pivotal period. The strife is between a dead past and a living future; between a wasting evil and a nourishing good; between *Barbarism* and *Civilization*.

The condition of the common people always measures the position of any nation on the scale of civilization. The condition of Work always measures the character of the common people. It is not where the head is, but where the feet are, that determines a nation's position. By ascertaining where the working people are in the North and in the South, you can determine the respective positions of these two sections of our country. I need not tell you what is the relative position of these two extremes and opposites on any scale of Christian civilization.

The Southern States and the Northern alike found poisonous seed sown in colonial days. The North chose to weed it out. The South determined to cultivate it, and see what it would bear. The harvest-time has now come. We are reaping what we sowed. They sowed the wind, and they are about to reap the whirlwind. Let us keep in view the causes of things. Our prosperity is the fruit of the seed that we sowed, and their fears, their alarms, their excitements, their fevers, their tumults, and their rages are the fruit of the seed that they sowed. Ours is wholesome; theirs is poisonous. All, now, that we demand is, *that each side shall reap its own harvest.*

It is this that convulses the South. They wish to reap fruits of liberty from the seed of slavery. They wish to have an institution which sets at naught the laws of God, and yet be as refined and prosperous and happy as we are, who obey these laws; and since they cannot, they demand that we shall make up to them what they lack. The real gist of the controversy, as between the greatest number of Southern States and the North, is simply this.

The South claims that the United States government is bound to make slavery as good as liberty for all purposes of national life. That is the root of their philosophy. They are to carry on a wasting system, a system that corrupts social life in its very elements, to pursue a course of inevitable impoverishment, and yet, at every decade of years, the government is, by some new bounty and privilege, to make up to them all the waste of this gigantic mistake! And our national government has been made a bribed judge, sitting on the seat of authority in this land, to declare bankruptcy as good as honesty; to declare wickedness as good as virtue; and to declare that there shall be struck, from period to period, a rule that will bring all men to one common municipal and communal prosperity, no matter what may be the causes that are working out special evils in them.

The Southern States, then, have organized society around a rotten core, — slavery: the North has organized society about a vital heart, — liberty. At length both stand mature. They stand in proper contrast. God holds them up to ages and to nations, that men may see the difference. Now that there is a conflict, I ask which is to yield? Causes having been true to effects, and effects true to causes; these gradually unfolding commercial and political and moral results having been developed in the two great opposing extremes of this country, the time has come in which they are so brought into contact that the principle of the one or the principle of the other must yield. Liberty must discrown her fair head; she must lay her opal crown and her diamond sceptre upon the altar of Oppression; or else Oppression must shrink, and veil its head, and depart. Which shall it be? Two queens are not to rule in this land, one black and the other white; one from below and the other from above. Two influences are not to sit in culminated power at the seat of influence in this nation, one dragging and pulling toward the infernal, and the other drawing and exciting toward the supernal. No nation could stand the strain to which it would be subjected under such a state of things.

There is a Divine impulsion in this. Those who resist and those who strive are carried along by a stream mightier than mere human volition. Whether men have acted well or ill, is not now the question; but simply this: *On which side will you be found?* This controversy will go on. No matter what *you* do, God will carry out his own providences with you or without you, by you or against you. You cannot hide or run away, or shift the question, or stop the trial. Complaints are useless, and recriminations foolish and wicked.

The distinctive idea of the Free States is Christian civilization, and the peculiar institutions of civilization. The distinctive idea of the South is barbaric institutions. In the North mind, and in the South force, rules. In the North every shape and form of society in some way represents liberty. In the South every institution and element of society is tinged and pervaded with slavery. The South accepts the whole idea of slavery, boldly and consistently. The North will never have peace till she with equal boldness accepts liberty.

While liberty and slavery are kept apart, and only run upon parallels, there may be peace. But there is no way in which they can be combined; there is no unity made up of these deadly antagonisms. And all devices, and cunning arrangements, and deceitful agreements, are false and foolish.

The truth that men cannot hush, and that God will not have covered up, is the irreconcilable difference between liberty and slavery! Which will you advocate and defend?

There are three courses before us: —

1. To go over to the South.

2. To compromise principles.

3. To maintain principles upon just and constitutional grounds, and abide the issue.

1. Shall we, then, obliterate from our statute-books every law for liberty? Shall we rub down and efface every clear and distinctive feature of liberty? Shall we assume that one is just as good as the other, — slavery and freedom? Are we, for the sake of peace, to go over to the South, yield our convictions, and our moral influences, and our whole soul and body of teaching and conviction?

This course is not to be thought of for a moment, whatever it may be theoretically considered. As a matter of fact, you know, and I know, and everybody knows, that there will be no change in the convictions of the North. We have reaped too bountifully from the seed we have sown to change. Our method of moral and political tillage will be the same as heretofore.

2. Shall we then compromise? We are told that Satan appears under two forms: that when he has a good fair field, he is out like a lion, roaring and seeking whom he may devour; but that when he can

do nothing more in that way, he is a serpent, and sneaks in the grass. And so, it is slavery open, bold, roaring, aggressive, or it is slavery sneaking in the grass, and calling itself compromise. It is the same devil under either name.

If by compromise is only meant forbearance, kindness, well-wishing, conciliation, fidelity to agreements, a concession in things, not principles; why, then we believe in compromise, — only that is not compromise, interpreted by the facts of our past history! We honestly wish no harm to the South or its people: we honestly wish them all benefit. We wish no harm to their commerce; none to their manufactures; none to their husbandry; none to their schools and colleges; none to their churches and families; none to their citizens, who are bone of our bone and blood of our blood, and who are in many eminent respects united to us in a common historic glory. We are far from wishing them diminution or feebleness; so far from it, we most heartily and sincerely, and with much more earnestness than they reciprocate, wish them riddance of their trouble. We neither envy nor covet their territory. We are not jealous of their honors. We would that they were doubled, and doubly purified. All that belongs to the South; all that with liberalest construction was put in the original bond, shall be hers. Her own institutions were made inviolate in all her States. The basis of representation in the South was made broader than in the North, and property, as well as citizens, sends representatives to Washington. We will not complain. The common revenue and the common force of the nation protect them against intestine revolt. Let it be so. The

Constitution gives them liberty to retake their fugitive slaves wherever they can find them. Very well. Let them. But when the *Congress* goes beyond the Constitution, and demands, on penalty, that citizens of free States shall help, and render back the flying slave, we give a blunt and unequivocal refusal. We are determined to break any law that commands us to enslave or re-enslave a man, and we are willing to take the penalty. But that was not in the original bond. That is a parasitic egg, laid in the Constitution by corrupt legislation or by construction.

We do not ask to molest the South in the enjoyment of her own institutions. But we will not be made constables to slavery, to run and catch, to serve writs, and return prisoners. No political hand shall rob her. We will defend her coast; we will guard her inland border from all vexations from without; and in good faith, in earnest friendship, in fealty to the Constitution and in fellowship with the States, we will, and with growing earnestness to the end, fulfil every just duty, every honorable agreement, and every generous act, within the limits of truth and honor; all that, and no more, — *no more*, though the heavens fall, — *no more*, if States unclasp their hands, — *no more*, if they raise up violence against us, — NO MORE!

We have gone to the end. There is no need of compromise in this matter, then. It is a plain, simple matter. It is never mystified except when bad men have bad ends to accomplish, and bring up a mist over it.

Let us look things right in the face, then, and speak some plain truths. We are approaching times when men will not hear what they will listen to now; so let us drop the seed beforehand.

1. The secret intentions of those men who are the chief fomenters of troubles in the South cannot in anywise be met by compromise. They dread as much as we hate it. What do those men that are really at the bottom of this conspiracy mean? Nothing more or less than this: Southern empire for slavery, and the reopening of the slave-trade as a means by which it shall be fed. Free commerce and enslaved work is their motto. They will not yet say it aloud. But that is the whispered secret of men in Carolina, and men outside of Carolina. Their secret purpose is to sweep westward like night, and involve in the cloud of their darkness all Central America, and then make Africa empty into Central America, thus changing the moral geography of the globe. And do you suppose any compromise will settle that design, or turn it aside, when they have made you go down on your knees, and they stand laughing while you cry with fear because you have been cozened and juggled into a blind helping of their monstrous wickedness?

They mean slavery. They mean an Empire of Slavery. They don't any longer talk of the *evil* of slavery. It is a virtue, a religion! It is justice and divine economy! Slaves are missionaries. Slave-ships bring heathen to plantation-Christianity. They imagine unobstructed greatness when servile hands shall whiten the plains from the Atlantic to the Pacific with cotton. Carolina despises compromise. She means no such thing as liberty. She does not believe in the word. It is rubbed out. It is gone from her constitution and from her Bible. Its spirit is departed from her legislature and her church.

And do you think, poor simple peeping sparrow, that you can build your poor moss and hair nest of compromise on the face of the perpendicular cliff, that towers a thousand feet high, with the blackness of storms sweeping round its top, and the thunder of a turbulent ocean breaking upon its base, — and God, more terrible than either, high above them, meaning Justice and Retribution!

2. But in so far as those States are concerned that are contiguous to Carolina, and do not mean these things, even for them compromise can never reach, nor even any longer mollify, the causes of complaint; for I hold that the causes are inherent in them, not in us. And they are endless. If you cure one, another will spring up in its place. You cannot compromise with them except by giving up your own belief, your own principles, and your own honor. Moral apostasy is the only basis on which you can build a compromise that will satisfy the South!

No compromise will do good that does not go back to the nature of things, and change moral qualities. To be of any use, compromise must make the slaves contented, slavery economical, Slave States as prosperous as Free States. Compromise must shut the mouth of free speech, or it will send the shafts of truth vibrating into the midst of slavery. Compromise must cure the intolerance of the plantation, the essential tyranny of slave-owners. It must make evil as prosperous as good, enforced drudgery as fruitful as free labor.

What compromise can there be between sickness

and health? Between violence and peace? Between speech for liberty and speech for despotism? There may be peace between opposites, but no harmony, no compromise. If the South is fixed in her servile institutions, the North must be equally firm in her principles of liberty.

You cannot prevent, in the present state of this land, the departure of the children of oppression. You might as well attempt to prevent the tides of the Atlantic ocean. You might as well attempt to prevent vegetation in the tropics. Till the heavens be no more, and their orbs cease to draw, men will aspire, and will follow aspiration. There is too much light in the North, and even in the darkness of the plantation, to keep men in slavery. When one man gains his freedom, twenty men will know it, and to gain theirs will do what he did. Every hour there will be men who will take their life in their hands and risk all for liberty. It is of no use to tell the South that it shall not be so. It is of no use to whisper to them, and say, "Your trouble shall cease; we will fix this matter to your satisfaction." God never made brick or trowel by which to patch up that door of escape. By night and by day slaves will flee away and escape.

Compromise is a most pernicious sham. To send compromises to the South would be like sending painted bombs into the camp of an enemy, which, though harmless in appearance, would blow up and destroy them. Suppose you tell the people there that when their fugitives come North they shall be surrendered? Will you not please to catch them first? You know you cannot. There are five hundred men that run through the Northern States where there is one that stops or is turned back. They know it, you know it, we all know it! The radical nature of the feelings of the North is such that they will hurry on the black man and trip his hunter. If the managers of parties, the heads of conservative committees, say to the South, "Be patient with us a little longer, do not punish us yet, let down the rod and the frown, spare us for a short season, and we will see that your slaves are returned to you," do you suppose there will be a fulfilment of the promise? You know there will not. I know there will not. I would die myself, cheerfully and easily, before a man should be taken out of my hands when I had the power to give him liberty, and the hound was after him for his blood. I would stand as an altar of expiation between slavery and liberty, knowing that through my example a million men would live. A heroic deed, in which one yields up his life for others, is his Calvary. It was the lifting up of Christ on that hill-top that made it the loftiest mountain on the globe. Let a man do a right thing with such earnestness that he counts his life of little value, and his example becomes omnipotent. Therefore it is said that the blood of the saints is the seed of the Church. There is no such seed planted in this world as good blood.

I see that my words are being reported; and as free speech may get into Charleston, some men there may see what I say; and let me say this to my Southern brethren: We mean to observe the Constitution, and keep every compact into which we have entered. There are men that would deceive you. They are your enemies and ours alike. They would tell lies to you, but we will not stand up and indorse them. I tell you that as long as there are these Free States; as long as there are hills in which men can hide, and valleys through which they can travel; as long as there is a loaf in the cabin, and water in the cruse; as long as there is blood in the veins, and humanity in the heart, — so long the fugitive will not want for sympathy and help to escape!

I say, again, that we are bound, as men of truth and conscience, to look this matter in the face, and ask, "Is there any benefit to be expected from compromises?" My friends, we are not reasoning about a matter of which we have had no experience. From the beginning we have been living on compromises. Now there is a history, and we can make scientific inductions from facts, and know the results of certain courses. Do you suppose that, if, knowing what you know now, you had sat in the original Convention to frame the Constitution, you would have made compromises? Persons say, "Are you wiser than your fathers?" Yes! A man that is not wiser than his father, ought not to have had such a father, if his father was wise! Our fathers, when they laid the foundations of that structure, did the best that the wisdom of that time would enable them to do; and they were wise men, — much wiser, doubtless, for their time, than we are for ours. But, nevertheless, we may know now, better than they did then, what their wisest course would have been. When Carolina refused to come into the Confederacy except on the ground of certain favors to slavery, then was the time to have said to her, "Stay out."

Do you suppose that when Carolina infamously said, "I will not come in unless you will give me leave to traffic in slaves from 1790 till 1808," — do you suppose that then it was wise for our fathers to give her what she demanded? I do not blame them; they acted up to the best light they had; but if we, knowing the facts that we know now, had done what they did, we should have been infamous.

When, later, the compromise of 1850 was set on foot, there were not wanting, as there are not wanting now, men who lifted up their voices in favor of compromise; and I think that very few who saw the effects of compromise at that time believe it to be a cure. They promised finality. They took renewed courage, and with a strong arm of injustice destroyed a compromise still anterior to theirs, — namely, the Missouri Compromise, — itself a wickedness only paralleled by that which destroyed it. It ought not to have been made; but after it was made, it should have been removed only for purposes of liberty, and not for purposes of oppression. We sold our birthright for a mess of pottage, and the pottage was then stolen!

We have had, then, a long experience of the virtues and merits of compromise; and what has been the result, except growing demands, growing impudence, growing wickedness, and increasing dissatisfaction, until at last excitements that used to come once in twenty years began to come at every ten, and now once in four years, and you cannot elect a President strictly according to constitutional methods, without having this nation imperilled, banks shaken, stores overturned, panics created, and citizens terrified? You have come to that state in which the whole nation is turmoiled, and agitated, and driven hither and thither, on account of the evil effects of compromise.

It is asked, "What shall we do?" We should speak the truth about our feelings, and about our intentions. The North should have nothing to do with half-way measures or half-way men. A whole man is good if he is imperfect; but a half-way man has no place in heaven, he has no place in hell, and he is not wanted on earth! We do not want half-way measures, nor half-way men. We want true men, who will say to the South: "The North loves liberty, and will have it. We will not aggress on you. Keep your institutions within your own bounds: we will not hinder you. We will not take advantage to destroy, or one whit to abate, your fair political prerogatives. You have already gained advantages of us. These we will allow you to hold. You shall have the Constitution intact, and its full benefit. The full might and power of public sentiment in the North shall guarantee to you everything that history and the Constitution give you. But if you ask us to augment the area of slavery; to co-operate with you in cursing new territory; if you ask us to make the air of the North favorable for a slave's breath, we will not do it! We love liberty as much as you love slavery, and we shall stand by our rights with all the vigor with which we mean to stand by justice toward you."

In short, the North cannot love slavery or cease to love liberty; she cannot conceal her sentiments or restrain their moral power; she cannot prevent the irritating contrast between Free States and Slave States; she cannot prevent the growing intelligence of slaves, nor their love of liberty, nor their disposition to seek it, nor the sympathy that every generous soul must feel, nor the humane and irresistible wish that they may succeed in obtaining freedom; we cannot sympathize with the hounds that hunt them, nor with the miscreants employed to witness against them, nor with the disgraced Federal officers that are bribed with double fees to convict them: the North cannot either permit her own citizens — colored men, Christians, honest and industrious, and many of them voters a thousand times better fitted for the franchise than the ignorant hordes of imported white men that have cheated their way against law and morals to the exercise of the vote — to be subject to seizure as slaves under the odious and ruthless provisions of an insulting Fugitive Slave Law, without providing for them State protection; we will not assist in inflicting upon free territory an evil which we abhor, and which we believe to be the greatest blight that can curse a people; we will not accept the new-fangled and modern doctrine that slavery is national and universal instead of the doctrine of our fathers of the Revolution and of the Federal Constitution, who regarded slavery as local, existing not in the right of a national law, but only by force of special law: certainly we will not apostatize from the faith of our fathers only for the sake of committing disgraceful crimes against liberty!

Let not the South listen to any man who pretends that the North will look kindly or compromisingly upon slavery. In every other respect we may be depended upon for all sympathy, aid, and comfort. In this thing we shall give the strictest and most literal obedience to those constitutional requirements which we hate while we obey, and beyond bare and meagre duty we will not go a step.

Now, can any man believe that peace can come by *compromise?* It is a delusive hope. It is a desperate shift of cowardice. It will begin in deceit and end in anger. Compromises are only procrastinations of an inevitable settlement with the added burden of accumulated interest. Our political managers only renew the note with compound interest, and roll the debt over, and over, until the interest exceeds the principal. It is time for a settlement. We may as well have it now as ever. We shall never be better prepared. It will never be so easy as now. It would have been easier ten years ago, and yet easier ten years before that. Like an ulcer, this evil eats deeper every day. Unless soon cauterized or excised, it will touch the vitals, and then the patient dies!

The supreme fear of Northern cities is pecuniary. But even for money's sake, there should be a settlement that will stay settled. Compromises bury troubles, but cannot keep down their ghosts. They rise, and walk, and haunt, and gibber. We must bury our evils without resurrection. Let come what will,—secession, disunion, revolted States, and a ragamuffin empire of bankrupt States, confederated in the name of liberty for oppression, or whatever other monstrosity malignant fortune may have in store,—nothing can be worse than this endless recurring threat and fear,—this arrogant dragooning of the South,—this mercantile cringing in the North. Every interest cries out for Rest. It scarcely matters how low we begin. We have a recuperative enterprise, a fertile industry, a wealth of resources, which will soon replace any waste. Let the gates of a permanent settlement be set up in bleak and barren granite, and we will speedily cover them with the evergreen ivy of our industry. But perpetual uncertainty is destructive of all business. That is not a settlement that only hides, that adjourns, that trumps up a compromise against the known feelings of both parties, and which must inevitably fall to pieces as soon as the hands that make it are taken off. Shall every quadrennial election take place in the full fury of Southern threats? Is the plantation-whip to control our ballot-boxes? Shall Northern sentiment express itself by constitutional means, at the peril of punishment? Must panic follow elections? and bankruptcy follow every expression of liberty? And what are the precious advantages which the North reaps, which make it worth her while to undergo such ignominy and such penalty?

Every advantage that can be reckoned belongs to the North. Ours is the population. Ours is free labor. Ours is a common people not ashamed of toil, and able to make Work a badge of honor. Ours is popular intelligence, competitive industry, ingenuity and enterprise. We put the whole realm and wealth of Freedom and Civilization against Slavery and Barbarism, and ask what have we to fear? If secession and separation must come, — which God forbid! — which can best bear it, freedom or slavery?

The North must accept its own principles and take the consequences. Manliness demands this, — Honor demands it. But if we will not heed worthier motives, then Interest demands it. If even this is not strong enough for commercial pusillanimity, then Necessity, inevitable and irresistible, will drive and scourge us to it!

When night is on the deep, when the headlands are obscured by the darkness, and when storm is in the air, that man who undertakes to steer by looking over the side of the ship, over the bow, or over the stern, or by looking at the clouds or his own fears, is a fool. There is a silent needle in the binnacle, which points like the finger of God, telling the mariner which way to steer, and enabling him to outride the storm, and reach the harbor in safety. And what the compass is to navigation, that is moral principle in political affairs. Whatever the issue may be, we have but one thing to do, and that is to look where the compass of God points, and steer that way. You need not fear shipwreck when God is the pilot.

The latter-day glory is already dawning. God is calling to the nations. The long-oppressed are arousing. The despotic thrones are growing feeble. It is an age of liberty. The trumpet is sounding in all the world, and one nation after another is moving to the joyful sound, and God is mustering the great army of liberty under his banners! In this day, shall America be found laggard? While despotisms are putting off the garments of oppression, shall she pluck them up and put them on? While France and Italy, Germany and Russia, are advancing toward the dawn, shall we recede toward midnight?

From this grand procession of nations, with faces lightened by liberty, shall we be missing? While they advance toward a brighter day, shall we, with faces lurid with oppression, slide downward toward the pit which gapes for injustice and crime?

Let every good man arouse and speak the truth for liberty. Let us have an invincible courage for liberty.

Let us have moderation in passions, zeal in moral sentiments, a spirit of conciliation and concession in mere material interests, but unmovable firmness for principles; and — foremost of all political principles — for Liberty!

III.

OUR BLAMEWORTHINESS.*

"And there arose a great storm of wind, and the waves beat into the ship, so that it was now full. And he was in the hinder part of the ship, asleep on a pillow: and they awake him, and say unto him, Master, carest thou not that we perish? And he arose and rebuked the wind, and said unto the sea, Peace, be still. And the wind ceased, and there was a great calm." — Mark iv. 37 - 39.

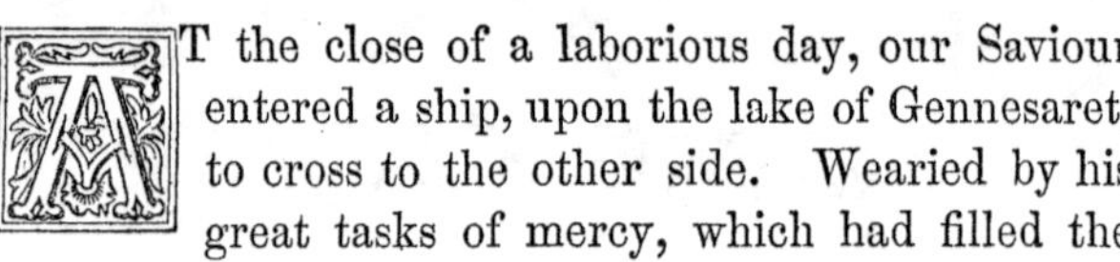

AT the close of a laborious day, our Saviour entered a ship, upon the lake of Gennesaret, to cross to the other side. Wearied by his great tasks of mercy, which had filled the day, he fell asleep. Meantime, a sudden and violent wind, to which that lake is even yet subject, swept down from the hills, and wellnigh overwhelmed them. They were not ignorant of navigation, nor unacquainted with that squally sea. Like good men and true, doubtless, they laid about them. They took in sail, and put out oars, and, heading to the wind,

* During the winter of 1859 - 60 the South and its Democratic allies at the North were industriously charging the unhappy state of the country upon the Republican party, and imputing it to excesses and fanaticisms in the name of liberty. This sermon was preached January 4, 1861, the Fast Day appointed by President Buchanan. It was intended to show that, while the nation undoubtedly had ample reason for fasting, humiliation, and confession, this reason was, not that too much had been done for liberty, but too little.

valiantly bore up against the gale, and thought nothing of asking help till they had exerted every legitimate power of their own. But the waves overleaped their slender bulwarks, and filled the little vessel past all bailing.

Then, when they had done all that men could do, but not till then, they aroused the sleeping Christ and implored his succor. Not for coming to him did he rebuke them, but for coming with such terror of despair, saying to them, Why are ye so fearful? How is it that ye have no faith? He outbreathed upon the winds, and their strength quite forsook them. He looked upon the surly waves, and they hasted back to their caverns. There is no tumult in the heavens, on the earth, nor upon the sea, that Christ's word cannot control. When it pleases God to speak, tempestuous clouds are peaceful as flocks of doves, and angry seas change all their roar to rippling music.

This nation is rolling helplessly in a great tempest. The Chief Magistrate in despair calls us to go to the sleeping Saviour, and to beseech his Divine interference. It may be true that the crew have brought the ship into danger by cowardice or treachery; it may be true that a firm hand on the wheel would even yet hold her head to the wind, and ride out the squall. But what of that?

Humiliation and prayer are never out of order. This nation has great sins unrepented of; and whatever may be our own judgment of the wisdom of public men in regard to secular affairs, we cannot deny that in this respect they have hit rarely well. Instead of finding fault with the almost only wise act of many days, let us rather admire with gratitude this unexpected piety of men in high places.

This government is in danger of subversion; and surely, while the venerable Chief Magistrate of this nation, and all the members of his Cabinet, are doubtless this day religiously abstaining from food, according to the proclamation, and humbly confessing their manifold sins, it would ill become us to go unconcerned and negligent of such duties of piety and patriotism. Nor need we be inconveniently frank and critical. What if some shall say that fasting is a poor substitute for courage, and prayer a miserable equivalent for fidelity to duty? What if the national authorities have not only appointed the Fast, but afforded sufficient material in their own conduct for observing it? It is all the more necessary on that account that we should pause, and humble ourselves before God, and implore his active interference.

But however monstrous the pretence of trouble may be, the danger is the same. Government is in danger of subversion. No greater disaster could befall this continent or the world; for such governments fall but once, and then there is no resurrection. Since there is no famine in the land, no pestilence, no invasion of foreign foe, no animosity of the industrial classes against each other, or against their employers, whence is our danger? from what quarter come these clouds, drifting with bolts of war and destruction? Over the Gulf the storm hangs lurid! From the treacherous Caribbean sea travel the darkness and swirling tornadoes!

What part of this complicated Government has at last broken down? Is it the legislative? the judicial? the executive? Has experience shown us that this costly machine, like many another, is more ingenious than practicable? Not another nation in the world, not a contemporanous government, during the past seventy-five years, can compare, for regularity, simplicity of execution, and for a wise and facile accomplishment of the very ends of government, with ours. And yet, what is the errand of this day? Why are we observing a sad Sabbath? a day of humiliation? a day of supplication? It is for the strangest reason that the world ever heard. It is because the spirit of liberty has so increased and strengthened among us, that the Government is in danger of being overthrown! There never before was such an occasion for fasting, humiliation, and prayer! Other nations have gone through revolutions to find their liberties. We are on the eve of a revolution to put down liberty! Other people have thrown off their governments because too oppressive. Ours is to be destroyed, if at all, because it is too full of liberty, too full of freedom. There never was such an event before in history.

But however monstrous the pretence, the danger is here. In not a few States of this Union reason seems to have fled, and passion rules. To us who have been bred in cooler latitudes and under more cautious maxims, it seems incredible that men should abandon their callings, break up the industries of the community, and give themselves up to the wildest fanaticism, at the expense of every social and civil interest, and without the slightest reason or cause in their relations to society and to the country, past or future.

Communities, like individuals, are liable to aberrations of mind. Panics and general excitements seem to move by laws as definite as those which control epidemics or the pestilence. And in one portion of our land such an insanity now rules. Cities are turned into camps. All men are aping soldiers. For almost a thousand miles there is one wild riot of complaint and boasting. Acts of flagrant wrong are committed against the Federal Government. And these things are but the prelude. It is plainly declared that this Government shall be broken up, and many men mean it; and that the President elect of this great nation shall never come to the place appointed by this people. Riot and civil war, with their hideous train of murders, revenges, and secret villanies, are gathering their elements, and hang in ominous terror over the capital of this nation.

Meanwhile, we have had no one to stand up for order. Those who should have spoken in decisive authority have been — *afraid!* Severer words have been used: it is enough for me to say only that in a time when God, and providence, and patriotism, and humanity demanded courage, they had nothing to respond but fear. The heart has almost ceased to beat, and this Government is like to die for want of pulsations at the centre. While the most humiliating fear paralyzes one part of the Government, the most wicked treachery is found in other parts of it. Men advanced to the highest places by the power of our Constitution, have employed their force to destroy that Constitution. They are using their oath as a soldier uses his shield, to cover and protect them while they are mining the foundations, and opening every door, and unfastening every protection by which colluding traitors may gain easy entrance and fatal success. Gigantic dishonesties, meanwhile, stalk abroad almost without shame. And this Puritan land, this free Government, these United States, like old Rome in her latest imperial days, helpless at the court, divided among her own citizens, overhung by hordes of Goths and Barbarians, seems about to be swept with the fury of war and revolution.

If at such a solemn crisis as this men refuse to look at things as they are; to call their sins to remembrance; to confess and forsake them; if they shall cover over the great sins of this people, and confess only in a sentimental way, (as one would solace an evening sadness by playing some sweet and minor melody,) then we may fear that God has indeed forsaken his people. But if we shall honestly confess our real sins; if we propose to cleanse ourselves from them; if we make prayer not a substitute for action, but an incitement to it; if we rise from our knees this day more zealous for temperance, for honesty, for real brotherhood, for pure and undefiled religion, and for that which is the sum and product of them all, regulated liberty to all men, then will the clouds begin to break, and we shall see the blue shining through, and the sun, erelong, driving away the tumultuous storm, shall come back in triumph.

1. It is well, then, that every one of us make this day the beginning of a solemn review of his own life, and the tendencies of his own conduct and character. A general repentance of national sins should follow, rather than precede, a personal and private conviction of our own individual transgressions. For it has been found not difficult for men to repent of other people's sins; but it is found somewhat difficult and onerous

to repent of one's own sins. We are all of us guilty before God of pride, of selfishness, of vanity, of passions unsubdued, of worldliness in manifold forms, and of strife. We have been caught in the stream, and swept out into an ocean of thoughts and feelings which cannot bear the inquest of God's judgment-day. And we have lived in them almost unrebuked. Each man will find his own life full of repentable sins unrepented of.

2. We should take solemn account of our guilt in the great growth of social laxity and vice and crime in our great cities. We have loved ease rather than duty. Every American citizen is by birth a sworn officer of state. Every man is a policeman. If bad men have had impunity, if the vile have controlled our municipal affairs, if by our delinquencies and indolence justice has been perverted, and our cities are full of great public wickedness, then we cannot put the guilt away from our own consciences. We have a partnership in the conduct of wicked men, unless we have exhausted proper and permissible means of forestalling and preventing it. Every citizen of such a city as this, looking upon intemperance, upon lewdness, upon gambling, upon the monstrous wickednesses that ferment at the bottom of society, or beat in its arteries, should feel that he has some occasion to repent of his own delinquency and moral indifference. We are responsible for existing evils in such a nation as ours, in as far as they might have been prevented or limited by our resolute influence.

3. We may not refuse to consider the growth of corrupt passions in connection with the increase of commercial prosperity. Luxury, extravagance, osten-

tation, and corruption of morals in social life, have given alarming evidence of a premature old age in a young country. The sins of a nation are always the sins of certain central passions. In one age they break out in one way, and in another age in another way; but they are the same central sins, after all. The corrupt passions which lead in the Southern States to all the gigantic evils of slavery, in Northern cities break out in other forms, not less guilty before God, because of a less public nature. The same thing that leads to the oppression of laborers among us leads to oppression on the plantation. The grinding of the poor, the advantages which capital takes of labor, the oppression of the farm, the oppression of the road, the oppression of the shop, the oppression of the ship, are all of the same central nature, and as guilty before God as the more systematic and overt oppressions of the plantation. It is always the old human heart that sins, North or South; and the natures of pride and of dishonesty are universal. We have our own account to render.

4. There is occasion for alarm and for humiliation before God, in the spread of avarice among our people. The intense eagerness to amass wealth; the growing indifference of morals as to methods of acquisition; the gradual corruption of the moral sense, so that property and self-interest dominate the conscience and determine what is right and wrong; the use of money for bribery of electors and elected; the terrible imputations which lie against many of our courts, that judges walk upon gold in securing place, and then sit upon gold in the judgment-seat; the use of money in legislation; and the growing rotten-

ness of politics from the lowest village concern to matters of national dimension, from constables to the Chief Magistrate of these United States; — is this all to be confessed only in a single smooth sentence?

Such is the wantonness and almost universality of avarice as a corrupting agent in public affairs, that it behooves every man to consider his responsibilities before God in this matter. The very planks between us and the ocean are worm-eaten and rotting, when avarice takes hold of public integrity; for avarice is that sea-worm, ocean-bred, and swarming innumerable, that will pierce the toughest planks, and bring the stoutest ships to foundering. Our foundations are crumbling. The sills on which we are building are ready to break. We need reformation in the very beginnings and elements of society. If in other parts of our land they are in danger of going down by avarice in one form, we are in danger of going down by avarice in another form.

Our people are vain, and much given to boasting; and because they love flatteries, those deriving from them honor and trust are too fond of feeding their appetite for praise. Thus it comes to pass that we hear the favorable side of our doings and character, and become used to a flattering portrait. Men grow popular who have flowing phrases of eulogy. Men who speak unpalatable truths are disliked; and if they have power to make the public conscience uncomfortable, they are said to abuse the liberty of free speech, — for it is the liberty of fanning men to sleep that is supposed to be legitimate; the liberty of waking men out of sleep is supposed to be license! And yet we shall certainly die by the sweetness of flattery; and if we are healed, it must be by the bitterness of faithful speech. There is tonic in the things that men do not love to hear; and there *is* damnation in the things that wicked men love to hear. Free speech is to a great people what winds are to malarial regions, which waft away the elements of disease, and bring new elements of health. Where free speech is stopped, miasma is bred, and death comes fast.

5. But upon a day of national fasting and confession, we are called to consider not alone our individual and social evils, but also those which are national. And justice requires that we should make mention of the sins of this nation on every side, past and present. I should violate my own convictions, if, in the presence of more nearly present and more exciting influences, I should neglect to mention the sins of this nation against the Indian, who, as much as the slave, is dumb, but who, unlike the slave, has almost none to think of him, and to speak of his wrongs. We must remember that we are the only historians of the wrongs of the Indian, — we that commit them. And our history of the Indian nations of this country is like the inquisitor's history of his own trials of innocent victims. He leaves out the rack, and the groans, and the anguish, and the unutterable wrongs, and puts but his own glozing view in his journal. We have heaped up the account of treachery and cruelty on their part, but we have not narrated the provocations, the grinding intrusions, and the misunderstood interpretations of their policy, on our part. Every crime in the calendar of wrong which a strong people can commit against a weak one has been com-

mitted by us against them. We have wasted their substance; we have provoked their hostility, and then chastised them for their wars; we have compelled them to peace ignominiously; we have formed treaties with them only to be broken; we have filched their possessions. In our presence they have wilted and wasted. A heathen people have experienced at the hands of a Christian nation almost every evil which one people can commit against another.

Admit the laws of race; admit the laws of advancing civilization as fatal to all barbarism; admit the indocility of the savage; admit the rude edges of violent men who form the pioneer advance of a great people, and the intrinsic difficulties of managing a people whose notions and customs and laws are utterly different from our own, and then you have only explained how the evil has been done, but you have not changed the fact nor its guilt. The mischief has been done, and this is simply the excuse. It is a sorry commentary upon a Christian nation, and indeed upon religion itself, that the freest and most boastfully religious people on the globe are absolutely fatal to any weaker people that they touch. What would be thought of a man who, when he became converted to Christianity, was dangerous to the next man's pocket? What would be thought of a man who grew dangerous in the ratio of his moral excellence? And what must be the nature of that Christianization which makes this Republic a most dangerous neighbor to nations weaker than itself? We are respectful to strength, but thieves and robbers to weakness. It is not safe for any to trust our magnanimity and generosity. We have no chivalry. We have avarice; we have haughty arrogance; we have assumptive ways; and we have a desperate determination to live, to think only of our own living, and to sweep with the besom of destruction whatever occupies the place where we would put our foot.

Nor is this confined to the Indian. The Mexicans have felt the same rude foot. This nation has employed its gigantic strength with almost no moral restriction. Our civilization has not begotten humanity and respect for others' rights, nor a spirit of protection to the weak. Nor can we excuse ourselves by declaring that these wanton cruelties have been inspired by Southern counsels, and perpetrated by Southern influence, and that they are the legitimate fruit of that unholy system of slavery which for fifty years has swayed the government of this nation. These facts are undoubtedly true. But we must not forget that we permitted the outrages. Resistance was feeble. Protests were mild. We preferred to suffer such wrongs upon the weak, rather than imperil our peace and commercial prosperity by a resolute resistance.

It is quite in vain to say that the land from which we sprung did the same that we are doing. A wicked daughter is not excused because she had a wicked mother. We boast of the Anglo-Saxon race; and if bone and muscle, an indomitable sense of personal liberty, and a disposition to do what we please, are themes for Christian rejoicing, then the Anglo-Saxon may well rejoice. There are sins that belong to races; there are sins that belong to peoples; there are sins that belong to generations of the same people; and the sins that I have enumerated are sins that belong to our stock.

But God never forgets what we most easily forget. Either moral government over nations is apocryphal, or judgments are yet to be visited upon us for the wrongs done to the Indian, and to our weak and helpless neighbors.

6. But I am now come to the most alarming and most fertile cause of national sin, — slavery. We are called by our Chief Magistrate to humble ourselves before God for our sins. This is not only a sin, but it is a fountain from which have flown so many sins that we cannot rightly improve this day without a consideration of them.

In one and the same year, 1620, English ships landed the Puritans in New England and negro slaves in Virginia, — two seeds of the two systems that were destined to find here a growth and strength unparalleled in history. It would have seemed almost a theatric arrangement, had these oppugnant elements, Puritan liberty and Roman servitude, — (for, whatever men may say, American slavery is not Hebrew slavery: it is Roman slavery. We borrowed every single one of the elemental principles of our system of slavery from the Roman law, and not from the old Hebrew. The fundamental feature of the Hebrew system was that the slave was a man, and not a chattel, while the fundamental feature of the Roman system was that he was a chattel, and not a man. The essential principle of the old Mosaic servitude made it the duty of the master to treat his servants as men, and to instruct them in his own religion, and in the matters of his own household; while the essential principle of Roman servitude allowed the master to treat his servants to all intents and purposes as chattels, goods), — it would have seemed, I say, almost a theatric arrangement had these oppugnant elements, Puritan liberty and Roman servitude, divided the land between them, and, inspiring different governments, grown up different nations, in contrast, that the world might see this experiment fairly compared and worked out to the bitter end.

But it was not to be so. The same government has nourished both elements. Our Constitution nourished twins. It carried Africa on its left bosom, and Anglo-Saxony on its right bosom; and these two, drawing milk from the same bosom, have waxed strong, and stand to-day federated into the one republic. One side of the body politic has grown fair and healthy and strong; the other side has grown up as a wen grows, and a wart, vast, but the vaster the weaker. We have yielded new territory to this terrible disease. They have demanded, and we have permitted, concessions, legislative compromises, constructions. Peace and friendship have been the ostensible pleas. The ambition of political parties and the short-sighted interests of commerce have been the real and active motives of this wicked consent!

We who dwell in the North are not without responsibility for this sin. Its wonderful growth and the arrogance of its claims have been in part through our delinquency. As our business to-day is not to find fault with the South, I am not discussing this matter with reference to them at all, but only with reference to our own individual profit. Because the South loved money, they augmented this evil; and because the North loved money, and that quiet which befits industry and commerce, she has refused to insist upon her moral convictions, in days past, and yielded to every demand carrying slavery forward in this nation. You and I are guilty of the spread of slavery unless we have exerted, normally and legitimately, every influence in our power against it. If we have said, "To agitate the question imperils manufacturing, imperils shipping, imperils real estate, imperils quiet and peace," and if, then, we have sacrificed purity and honesty,—if we have bought the right to make money here by letting slavery spread and grow there,—we have been doing just the same thing that they have. It has been one gigantic bargain, only working out in different ways, North and South. It is for us just as much as for them that the slave works; and we acquiesce. We clothe ourselves with the cotton which the slave tills. Is he scorched? is he lashed? does he water the crop with his sweat and tears? It is you and I that wear the shirt and consume the luxury. Our looms and our factories are largely built on the slave's bones. We live on his labor. I confess I see no way to escape a part of the responsibility for slavery. I feel guilty in part for this system. If the relinquishment of the articles which come from slave labor would tend even remotely to abridge or end the evil, I would without hesitation forego every one; but I do not see that it would help the matter. I am an unwilling partner in the slave system. I take to myself a part of the sin; I confess it before God; and pray for some way to be opened by which I may be freed from that which I hate bitterly.

But this state of facts makes it eminently proper for us to confess our sin, and the wrong done to the slave. All the wrongs, the crimes of some, the abuse of others, the neglect, the misuse, the ignorance, the separations, the scourgings, — these cannot be rolled into a cloud to overhang the South alone. Every one of us has something to confess. Those who have been most scrupulous, if God should judge their life, their motives, and their conduct, would find that they, too, had some account in this great bill of slavery. The whole nation is guilty. There is not a lumberman on the verge of Maine, not a settler on the far distant northern prairies, not an emigrant on the Pacific shore, that is not politically and commercially in alliance with this great evil. If you put poison into your system in any way, there is not a nerve that is not affected by it; there is not a muscle that does not feel it; there is not a bone, nor a tissue, nor one single part nor parcel of your whole body, that can escape it. And our body politic is pervaded with this deadly injustice, and every one of us is more or less, directly or indirectly, willingly or unwillingly, implicated in it. We have a great deal to confess before we cast reproaches upon the South. And while I hold Southern citizens to the full and dreadful measure of their guilt before God, and would, if I were settled there, tell them their sin as plainly as I tell you your sin, it is for us to-day, and here, to consider our own part in this matter; and to that I shall speak during the residue of my remarks.

Originally, we were guilty of active participation in slavery. It seems very strange to take up the old Boston books and read the history of slavery in Boston. We of the North early abandoned the practice of holding slaves. But it is said that ours is a cheap philanthropy; that, having got quit of our slaves by selling them, we turn round and preach to the South about the sin of holding theirs. There is nothing more false than such a charge. There is nothing more illustrious in the history of the State of New York, and of the Northern States generally, than the method by which they freed themselves from slavery. This State decreed liberty at a certain period, making it an offence, the penalty attached to which no one would willingly inherit, for a man to convey away, or in any manner whatsoever to sell out of the State, a person held as a slave; and if a man, anticipating the day of emancipation, wished to make a journey to the South with his slaves, he had to give bonds for their return before he went away, and an account when he came back, if they did not come with him. Nothing could have been more humane than the provision that the slave should not be sold out of the State of New York, but should be emancipated in it. And what is true of New York in this respect, is true of the States generally that emancipated their slaves.

But we of the North participated in the beginnings, and we are in part guilty of the subsequent spread of the system of slavery. When our government came into our hands, after the struggle of the Revolution, we had gone through such a schooling, that the head, the conscience, and the heart of this nation, in the main, were right on the subject of human liberties. And at the adoption of the Federal Constitution, nearly seventy-five years ago, it might be said that, with local and insignificant exceptions, there was but one judgment, one wish, and one prophetic expectation; namely, that this whole territory should be dedicated to liberty, and that every compliance or compromise was not to be made in the interest of oppression, but was to be made only to give oppression time to die decently. That was the spirit and intent of every concession or compromise that was made.

The schools, the academies, the colleges, the intelligence, the *brain* of this nation, at that time, were in the North, — and in the North I include all the territory north of Mason and Dixon's line. Churches, religious institutions, those moral elements that always went with the posterity of the Puritans, were then also in the North. When our Constitution was adopted, — when the wheels of our mighty Confederacy were adjusted, and the pendulum began to swing, — at that time the public sentiment was in favor of liberty. All the institutions were prepared for liberty, and all the public men were on the side of liberty. And to the North, because she was the brain, — to the North, because she was the moral centre and heart of this Confederacy, — was given this estate; for in the first twenty-five or thirty years the North predominated in the councils of the nation, and fixed its institutions, as the South has fixed its policy since. What, then, having this trust put into her hands, is the account of her stewardship which the North has to render? If now, after three quarters of a century have passed away, God should summon the North to his judgment-bar, and say, "I gave you a continent in which, though there was slavery, it was perishing; I gave you a nation in which the sentiment was for liberty and against oppression; I gave you a nation in which the tendencies were all for freedom and against slavery; I gave you the supreme intelligence;

I gave you the moral power in a thousand pulpits, a thousand books, a thousand Bibles, and said, 'Take this nation, administer it, and render up your trust'"; —if now, after three quarters of a century have passed away, God should thus summon the North to his judgment-bar, what would be the account which she would have to render? — the North, that was strongest in the head and in the heart, and that took as fair a heritage as men ever attempted to administer? To-day liberty is dishonored and discrowned, and slavery is rampant, in this nation. And do you think to creep out of the responsibility and say, "We are not to blame"? What have you been doing with your intelligence, your books, your schools, your Bibles, your missionaries, your ministers? Where, where is the artillery that God Almighty gave you, park upon park, for use in this contest, provided and prepared for that special emergency? Much as I love the North, — and I love every drop of Puritan blood that the world ever saw, because it seems to me that Puritan blood means blood touched with Christ's blood, — I take to myself part of the shame, and mourn over the delinquency of the North, that, having committed to it the eminent task of preserving the liberties of this nation, it has suffered them to be eclipsed. For to-day there are more Slave States than there were States confederated when this nation came together. And instead of having three or four hundred thousand slaves, we have more than four millions; instead of a traffic suppressed, you and I are witnesses to-day of a traffic to be reopened, — of rebellion, treasonable war, bloodshed, separate independence, for the sake of reopening the African slave-trade. So came this country into the hands of the North in the beginning, and so it is going out of her hands in the end. There never was such a stewardship; and if this Confederacy shall be broken up, if the Gulf States shall demand a division of the country, and the intermediate States shall go off, and two empires shall be established, no steward that has lived since God's sun shone on the earth will have such an account to render of an estate taken under such favorable auspices, as the North will have to render of this great national estate which was committed to her trust. It is an astounding sin! It is an unparalleled guilt! The vengeance and zeal of our hearts toward the South might be somewhat tempered by the reflection that we have been so faithless and so wicked.

That is not the worst. That is the material side. We have stood with all the elements of power, boasting of our influence, and really swaying, in many respects, the affairs of this continent; and yet we have not only seen this tremendous increase of slavery, but we have permitted the doctrines of liberty themselves to be stricken with leprosy. And to-day, *to-day*, TO-DAY, if you were to put it to the vote of this whole people, I do not know that you could get a majority for any doctrine of liberty but this: that each man has a right to be himself free. The great doctrine of liberty is concisely expressed by the Declaration of Independence; and it is this: that all men are free, born with equal political rights, of life, liberty, and the pursuit of happiness. And there is no true right that is not founded on this doctrine: That liberty which is good for me is indispensable for everybody. A right love of liberty inspires a man to say, "I will have it, and everybody shall have it." That is a poor love of liberty that makes a man a champion for the liberty of those that are capable of asserting their own liberty. But I doubt whether you could get a popular vote for the liberty of all men, if the Africans were known to be included. Why should you? I am ashamed of what I must speak. The pulpit has been so prostituted, and so utterly apostatized from the very root and substance of Christianity, that it teaches the most heathen notions of liberty; and why should you expect the great masses of men to be better informed on this subject than its preachers are? Do you believe that George Washington, were he living, would now be able to live one day in the city of Charleston, if he uttered the sentiments that he used to hold? He would be denounced as a traitor, and swung up on the nearest lamp-post. Do you suppose that one single man that signed the Declaration of Independence, if living, could go through the South to-day repeating the sentiments contained in that document? The lives of the signers of the Declaration of Independence would not be worth one day's lease in Alabama, Louisiana, Carolina, or Florida, if they were there to say the things plainly which they said when they framed this government, so utterly have the South vomited up their political views; so radically have they changed their notions. Was this country committed to our care? and is such the lesson that we have taught our pupils? Shall the schoolmaster render back the scholars that he undertook to teach, with their minds debauched, and say that he was not responsible for what they learned? And if any part of the country was responsible for the education of the whole, it was the free-schooled, million-churched North. The result of our instruction is this: slavery has spread gigantically, and the doctrine of liberty is so corrupted, that to-day nothing is more disreputable in the high places of this nation than that very doctrine. And at last, when the sleeper, long snoring, having been awaked, raised himself up, and, like all new zealots, somewhat intemperately made crusade for liberty, the land was so agitated, and with such surprise was this expression of the public sentiment of the North received, that the Chief Magistrate of this nation has declared that the advocates of the old colonial, original, constitutional doctrines of human rights were the cause of all the trouble!

But this is not all. The most serious, the most grievous charge, is yet to be made upon the North. So far have we been delinquent in the trust that God committed to us, that from the very fountain out of which flowed, as from the heart of Christ, the first drops that were to cleanse men from oppressions, has been extracted in our day, and in our North very largely, the whole spirit of humanity which breathes freedom.

It ill becomes, I think, one profession to rail against another, or the members of the same profession to rail against each other. I have no accusations to make against any; but I will forsake my profession, for the time being, and stand as a man among men, to lift up my voice, with all my heart and soul, against any man who, professing to be ordained to preach, preaches out of Christ's Gospel the doctrines of human bondage. If the Bible can be opened that all the fiends of hell may, as in a covered passage, walk through it to do mischief on earth, I say, blessed be infidels! If men can make the Bible teach me to disown childhood; if men can make the Bible teach me that it is lawful to buy and sell men, that marriage is impracticable between slaves, that laws cannot permit any custom which would hinder the easy sale of such property; if the Bible can be made the sacred document and constitutional guaranty of a system which makes it impossible that a man should receive education, because intelligence is costly, and swells the slave to a stature not convenient for selfish economy; if a man can take the Bible and lay it in the path over which men are attempting to walk from Calvary up to the gate of heaven; — then I declare that I will do by the Bible what Christ did by the temple: I will take a whip of cords, and drive out of it every man that buys and sells men, women, and children; and if I cannot do that, I will let the Bible go, as God let the temple go, to the desolating armies of its adversaries. And I do not wonder that, after so long an experience of the world, men who bombard universal humanity, men who plead for the outrage of slavery, men who grope to find under crowns and sceptres the infamous doctrines of servitude, — I do not wonder that they are pestered with the idea of man's infidelity. Why, that minister who preaches slavery out of the Bible is the father of infidelity! Sometimes men become infidel to the Church for the sake of fidelity to religion. The Bible may be so interpreted by a besotted priesthood, that plain men may be driven from the Book for their very faith in its essential contents. Every abomination on earth has been at one time or another justified from the Bible!

Thus men learn to hate the Bible, not for what it is in reality, but because it is made the bulwark of oppression; and they spurn it that they may answer the call of God in their own nature,—for to be free is a part of the sovereign call and election that God has given to every man who has a sense of his birthright and immortality. And in a community where the minister finds reason in the Bible for slavery, you may depend upon it that one of two things will take place: either there will be an inquisition to redeem the Bible from such abominable prostitution, or else the Bible will be spurned and trodden under the feet of men.

"I came to open the prison to them that are bound," said Christ; and that is the text on which men justify shutting them and locking them. "To proclaim liberty to the captives"; and that is the text out of which men spin cords to bind men, women, and children. "To set at liberty them that are bruised"; and that is the Book from out of which they argue, with amazing ingenuity, all the infernal meshes and snares by which to keep men in bondage. It is pitiful.

Now what has been the history of the Book but this: that wherever you have had an untrammelled Bible, you have had an untrammelled people; and that wherever you have had a Bible shut up, you have had a shut-up people? Where you have had a Bible that the priests interpreted, you have had a king. Where you have had a Bible that the common people interpreted; where the family has been the church; where father and mother have been God's ordained priests; where they have read its pages freely from beginning to end without gloss or commentary, without the church to tell them how, but with the illumination of God's Spirit in their hearts;— there you have had an indomitable yeomanry, a state that would not have a tyrant on the throne, a government that would not have a slave or a serf in the field. Wherever the Bible has been allowed to be free, wherever it has been knocked out of the king's hand, and out of the priest's hand, it has carried light like the morning sun, rising over hill and vale, round and round the world; and it will do it again! And yet there come up in our midst men that say that the Bible is in favor of slavery. And as men that are about to make a desperate jump go back and run before they jump, so these men have to go back to the twilight of creation and take a long run; and when they come to their jump, their strength is spent, and they but stumble!

It is in consideration of this wanton change which has taken place (and which ought never to have been permitted to take place, in view of the instruments that God put into our hands, and in view of the solemn responsibility that he has put upon us), — it is in consideration of this change which has taken place in the moral condition of the country, and in the opinions of this people respecting the great doctrine of liberty, and the worse change which has in part corrupted the Church at its very core, that I argue to-day the necessity of humiliation and repentance before God.

I shall first confess my own sin. Sometimes men think I have been unduly active. I think I have been indolent. In regard to my duty in my personal and professional life, I chide myself for nothing more than because I have not been more alert, more instant in season and out of season. If sometimes in intemperate earnestness I have wounded the feelings of any, if I have seemed to judge men harshly, for that I am sorry. But for holding the slave as my brother; for feeling that the Spirit of God is the spirit of liberty; for loving my country so well that I cannot bear to see a stain or a blot upon her; for endeavoring to take the sands from the river of life wherewith to scour white as snow the morals of my times, and to cleanse them to the uttermost of all spot and aspersion, — for that I have no tears to shed. I only mourn that I have not been more active and zealous, and I do not wish to separate myself from my share of the responsibility. I am willing to take my part of the yoke and burden. I will weep my tears before God, and pray my prayers of sincere contrition and penitence, that I have not been more faithful to liberty and religion in the North and the whole land.

But be sure of one thing: He that would not come when the sisters sent, but tarried, has come, and the stone is rolled away, and he stands by the side of the sepulchre. He has called, "Liberty, come forth!" and, bound yet hand and foot, it has come forth; and that same sovereign voice is saying, "Loose him, and let him go!" and from out of the tomb, the dust, the night, and the degradation, the better spirit of this people is now emerging at the voice of God. We have heard his call, we know the bidding, and Death itself cannot hold us any longer; and there is before us, we may fain believe, a new lease of life, a more blessed national existence. That there will not be concussions, and perhaps garments rolled in blood, I will not undertake to say: there may be some such things as these; but, brethren, this nation is not going to perish. This Union is not going to be broken and shivered like a crystal vase that can never be put together again. We are to be tested and tried; but if we are in earnest, and if we stand, as martyrs and confessors before us have stood, bearing witness in this thing for Christ, know ye that erelong God will appear, and be the leader and captain of our salvation, and we shall have given back to us this whole land, healed, restored to its right mind, and sitting at the feet of Jesus.

Love God, love men, love your dear fatherland; to-day confess your sins toward God, toward men, toward your own fatherland; and may that God that loves to forgive and forget, hear our cries and our petitions which we make, pardon the past, inspire the future, and bring the latter-day glory through a regenerated zeal and truth, inspired by his Spirit, in this nation. Amen, and amen.

IV.

THE BATTLE SET IN ARRAY.*

"And the Lord said unto Moses, Wherefore criest thou unto me? speak unto the children of Israel, that they go forward." — Exod. xiv. 15.

OSES was raised up to be the emancipator of three millions of people. At the age of forty, having, through a singular providence, been reared in the midst of luxury, in the proudest, most intelligent, and most civilized court on the globe, with a heart uncorrupt, with a genuine love of his own race and people, he began to act as their emancipator. He boldly slew one of their oppressors. And, seeing dissension among his brethren, he sought to bring them to peace. He was rejected, reproved, and reproached; and finding himself discovered, he fled, and, for the sake of liberty, became a fugitive and a martyr. For forty years, uncomplaining, he dwelt apart with his father-in-law, Jethro, in the wilderness, in the peaceful pursuits of a herdsman. At eighty — the time when most men lay down the burden of life, or have long laid it down — he began his life-work. He was called back by the voice of God; and now, accompanied with compan-

* Preached April 14, 1861, during the siege of Fort Sumter.

ions, he returned, confronted the king, and, moved by Divine inspiration, demanded, repeatedly, the release of his people. The first demand was sanctioned by a terrific plague; the second, by a second terrible judgment; the third, by a third frightful devastation; the fourth, by a fourth dreadful blow; the fifth, by a fifth desolating, sweeping mischief. A sixth, a seventh, an eighth, and a ninth time, he demanded their release. And when was there ever, on the face of the earth, a man that, once having power, would let it go till life itself went with it? Pharaoh, who is the grand type of oppressors, held on in spite of the Divine command and of the Divine punishment. Then God let fly the last terrific judgment, and smote the first-born of Egypt; and there was wailing in every house of the midnight land. And then, in the midst of the first gush of grief and anguish, the tyrant said, "Let them go! let them go!" And he did let them go; he shoved them out; and they went pell-mell in great confusion on their way, taking up their line of march, and escaped from Egypt. But as soon as the first effects of the grief and anguish had passed away, Pharaoh came back to his old nature,—just as many men whose hearts are softened, and whose lives are made better by affliction, come back to the old way of feeling and living, as soon as they have ceased to experience the first effects of the affliction,—and he followed on after the people. As they lay encamped—these three millions of people, men, women, and children—just apart from the land of bondage, near the fork and head of the Red Sea, with great hills on either side of them, and the sea before them, some one brought panic into the camp, saying, "I see the signs of an advancing host! The air far on the horizon is filled with rising clouds!" Presently, through these clouds, began to be seen glancing spears, mounted horsemen, and a great swelling army. Such, to these lately enslaved, but just emancipated people, was the first token of the coming adversary. Surely, they were unable to cope with the disciplined cohorts of this Egyptian king. They, that were unused to war, that had never been allowed to hold weapons in their hands, that were a poor, despoiled people not only, but that had been subjected to the blighting touch of slavery, had lost courage. They did not dare to be free. And there is no wonder, therefore, that they reproached Moses, and said, "Because there were no graves in Egypt, hast thou taken us away to die in the wilderness?"

I have no doubt that, if Pharaoh's courtiers had heard that, they would have said, "Ah! they do not want to be free. They do not believe in freedom."

"Because there were no graves in Egypt, hast thou taken us away to die in the wilderness? Wherefore hast thou dealt thus with us, to carry us forth out of Egypt?"

Were these people miserable specimens of humanity? They were just what slavery makes everybody to be.

"Is not this the word that we did tell thee in Egypt, saying, Let us alone, that we may serve the Egyptians?"

They would rather have had peace with servitude, than liberty with the manly daring required to obtain it.

"For it had been better for us to serve the Egyptians, than that we should die in the wilderness."

That is just the difference between a man and a slave. They would rather have lived slaves, and eaten their pottage, than to suffer for the sake of liberty; a *man* would rather die in his tracks, than live in ease as a slave.

These, then, were the people that Moses undertook to emancipate, and this was the beginning of Moses's life-work.

"And Moses said unto the people, Fear ye not, stand still —"

That was wrong, but he did not know any better.

"Fear ye not, stand still, and see the salvation of the Lord, which he will show you to-day: for the Egyptians, whom ye have seen to-day, ye shall see them again no more forever. The Lord shall fight for you, and ye shall hold your peace."

He was a little too fast. He was right in respect to the result, but wrong in respect to the means.

"And the Lord said unto Moses, Wherefore criest thou unto me? Speak unto the children of Israel, that they go forward."

They were, after all, to do something and dare something for their liberty. No standing still, but going forward!

"Lift up thy rod, and stretch out thine hand over the sea, and divide it; and the children of Israel shall go on dry ground through the midst of the sea."

You recollect the rest. They walked through the sea that stood up as a wall on either side for them. They reached the other side. They were divided from the camp of the Egyptians by a fiery cloud, and the Egyptians could not touch them. And what was the fate of the Egyptians? They attempted to follow the children of Israel through the sea, when the waters closed together, and their host was destroyed.

God has raised up many men, at different periods of the world, to bring his cause forth from its various exigencies. Wherever a man is called to defend a truth or a principle, a church or a people, a nation or an age, he may be said to be, like Moses, the leader of God's people. And in every period of the world God has shut up his people, at one time or another, to himself. He has brought their enemies behind them, as he brought the Egyptians behind the children of Israel. He has hedged them in on either hand. He has spread out the unfordable sea before them. He has so beset them with difficulties, when they were attempting to live for right, for duty, and for liberty, that they have been like Israel.

When men stand for a moral principle, their troubles are not a presumption that they are in the wrong. Since the world began, men that have stood for the right have had to stand for it, as Christ stood for the world, suffering for victory.

In the history which belongs peculiarly to us, over and over again the same thing has occurred. In that grand beginning struggle in which Luther figured so prominently, he stood in a doubtful conflict. He was in the minority; he was vehemently pressed with enemies on every side; nine times out of ten during his whole life the odds were against him. And yet he died victorious, and we reap the fruit of his victory.

In one of the consequences of that noble struggle,

the assertion in the Netherlands of civil liberty and religious toleration, the same thing took place. Almost the entire globe was against this amphibious republic, until England cared for them; and England cared for them but very doubtfully and very imperfectly. All the reigning influences, all the noblest of the commanding men of the Continent, were against them. The conflict was a long and dubious one, in which they suffered extremely, and conquered through their suffering.

In the resulting struggle in England, which was borrowed largely from the Continent, — the Puritan uprising, the Puritan struggle, — the same thing occurred. The Puritans were enveloped in darkness. Their enemies were more than their friends. The issue was exceedingly doubtful. Their very victory began in apparent defeat. For when at last, wearied and discouraged, they could no longer abide the restriction of their liberty in England, they fled away to plant colonies upon these shores. On the sea did they venture, but the ocean, black and wild, before they left it was covered with winter.

In every one of these instances darkness and the flood lay before the champions of truth and rectitude. God in his providence said to them, though they were without apparent instrumentalities, "Go forward! Venture everything! Endure everything! Yield the precious truths never! Live forever by them! Die with *them*, if you die at all."

The whole lesson of the past, then, is that safety and honor come by holding fast to one's principles; by pressing them with courage; by going into darkness and defeat cheerfully for them.

And now our turn has come. Right before us lies the Red Sea of war. It is red indeed. There is blood in it. We have come to the very edge of it, and the Word of God to us to-day is, "Speak unto this people that they go forward!" It is not of our procuring. It is not of our wishing. It is not our hand that has stricken the first stroke, nor drawn the first blood. We have prayed against it. We have struggled against it. Ten thousand times we have said, "Let this cup pass from us." It has been overruled. We have yielded everything but manhood, and principle, and truth, and honor, and we have heard the voice of God saying, "Yield these never!" And these not being yielded, war has been let loose upon this land.

Now, let us look both ways into this matter, that we may decide what it is our duty to do.

1. There is no fact susceptible of proof in history, if it be not true that this Federal Government was created for the purposes of justice and liberty; and not liberty, either, with the construction that traitorous or befooled heads are attempting to give it, — liberty with a devil in it! We know very well what was the breadth and the clarity of the faith of those men who formed the early constitutions of this nation. If there was any peculiarity in their faith, it was that their notion of liberty was often extravagant. But there was no doubtfulness in their position. And the instruments which accompanied and preceded it, and the opinions of the men that framed it, put this fact beyond all controversy: that the Constitution of the United States was meant to be as we now hold it, as we now defend it, as we have held it, and as we have

been defending it. And at length even this is conceded, as I shall have occasion to say further on, by the enemies of liberty in this country. The Vice-President of the so-called Southern Confederacy has stated recently that there was a blunder made in the construction of our Constitution on this very truth of universal liberty, thus admitting the grand fact that that immortal instrument, as held by the North, embodies the views of those who framed it; and that those views are unmistakably in favor of liberty to all.

2. There can be no disputing the fact that, from commercial and political causes, an element of slavery which had a temporary refuge in the beginning in this land swelled to an unforeseen and unexpected power, and for fifty years has held the administrative power of the country in its hands. No man acquainted with our politics hesitates to say, that while the spirit of liberty first suggested our national ideas and fashioned our national institutions, after that work was done the government passed into the hands of the slave-power; and that that power has administered these institutions during the last fifty years for its own purposes, or in a manner that has been antagonistic to the interests of this country.

3. Against this growing usurpation for the last twenty-five years there has been rising up and organizing a proper legal constitutional opposition, wishing not the circumscription or injury of any section in this land, but endeavoring to keep our institutions out of the hands of despotism and on the side of liberty. For twenty-five years there has been a struggle to see to it that those immortal instruments of

liberty should not be wrested from their original intent, — that they should be maintained for the objects for which they were created.

4. What are the means that have been employed to maintain our institutions? Free discussion. That simply. We have gone before the people in every proper form. For twenty years of defeat, though of growing influence, we have argued the questions of human rights and human liberty, and the doctrines of the Constitution and of our fathers; and we have maintained that the children should stand where the fathers did. At last the continent has consented. We began as a handful, in the midst of mobs and derision and obloquy. We have gone through the experience of Gethsemane and Calvary. The cause of Christ among his poor has suffered as the Master suffered, again and again and again; and at last the public sentiment of the North has been revolutionized. What! revolutionized away from the doctrines of the fathers? No; back to the doctrines of the fathers. Revolutionized against our institutions? No; in favor of our institutions. We have taken simply the old American principles. That is the history very simply stated. The children have gone back to the old landmarks. We stand for the doctrines and instruments that the fathers gave us.

5. The vast majority of this nation are now on the side of our American institutions, according to their original intent. We ask only this: that our government may be what it was made to be, — an instrument of justice and liberty. We ask no advantages, no new prerogatives, no privileges whatsoever. We merely say, "Let there be no intestine revolution in our

institutions, and let them stand as they were made, and for the purposes for which they were created." Is there anything unreasonable, anything wrong in that? Is it wrong to reason? Is it wrong to discuss? Is it wrong to go before a free people with their own business, and, in the field, in the caucus, in the assembly, in all deliberative bodies, to argue fairly, and express the result by the American means, — the omnipotence of the vote? Is that wrong? It is what we have been doing for the last few years. By the prescribed methods of the Constitution, and in the spirit of liberty which it embodied and evoked, we have done our proper work. Before God we cleanse our hands of all imputation of designing injustice or of seeking wrong. We have not sought any one's damage. We have aimed at no invidious restrictions for any. We have simply said, "God, through our fathers, committed to us certain institutions, and we will maintain them to the end of our lives, and to the end of time."

6. Seven States, however, in a manner revolutionary not only of government, but in violation of the rights and customs of their own people, have disowned their country and made war upon it! There has been a spirit of patriotism in the North; but never, within my memory, in the South. I never heard a man from the South speak of himself as an American. Men from the South always speak of themselves as Southerners. When I was abroad, I never spoke of myself as a Northerner, but always as a citizen of the United States. I love our country; and it is a love of the country, and not a love of the North alone, that pervades the people of the North. There has never been

witnessed such patience, such self-denial, such magnanimity, such true patriotism, under such circumstances, as that which has been manifested in the North. And in the South the feeling has been sectional, local. The people there have been proud, not that they belong to the nation, but that they were born where the sun burns. They are hot, narrow, and boastful,—for out of China there is not so much conceit as exists among them. They have been devoid of that large spirit which takes in the race, and the nation, and its institutions, and its history, and that which its history prophesies,—the prerogative of carrying the banner of liberty to the Pacific from the Atlantic.

Now, these States, in a spirit entirely in agreement with their past developments, have revolutionized and disowned the United States of America, and set up a so-called government of their own. Shall we, now, go forward under these circumstances?

For the first time in the history of this nation there is a deliberate and extensive preparation for war, and this country has received the deadly thrust of bullet and bayonet from the hands of her own children. If we could have prevented it, this should not have taken place. But it is a fact! It hath happened! The question is no longer a question of choice. The war is brought to us. Shall we retreat, or shall we accept the hard conditions on which we are to maintain the grounds of our fathers? Hearing the voice of God in his providence saying, "Go forward!" shall we go?

I go with those that go furthest in describing the wretchedness and wickedness and monstrosity of war. The only point on which I should probably differ from any is this: that while war is an evil so presented to our senses that we measure and estimate it, there are other evils just as great, and much more terrible, whose deadly mischiefs have no power upon the senses. I hold that it is ten thousand times better to have war than to have slavery. I hold that to be corrupted silently by giving up manhood, by degenerating, by becoming cravens, by yielding one right after another, is infinitely worse than war. Why, war is resurrection in comparison with the state to which we should be brought by such a course. And although war is a terrible evil, there are other evils that are more terrible. In our own peculiar case, though I would say nothing to garnish it, nothing to palliate it, nothing to alleviate it, nothing to make you more willing to have it, nothing to remove the just abhorrence which every man and patriot should have for it, yet I would say that, in the particular condition into which we have been brought, it will not be an unmixed evil. Eighty years of unexampled prosperity have gone far toward making us a people that judge of moral questions by their relation to our convenience and ease. We are in great danger of becoming a people that shall measure by earthly rules, — by the lowest standard of a commercial expediency. We have never suffered for our own principles. And now if it please God to do that which daily we pray that he may avert, — if it please God to wrap this nation in war, — one result will follow: we shall be called to suffer for our faith. We shall be called to the heroism of doing and daring, and bearing and suffering, for the things which we believe to be vital to the salvation of this people.

On what conditions, then, may we retreat from this war, and on what conditions may we have peace?

1. We may do it on condition that two thirds of this nation shall implicitly yield up to the dictation of one third. You can have peace on that ground. Italy could have had peace at the hands of Francis II. They had nothing to do but to say to that tyrant, "Here is my neck, put your foot on it," to obtain peace. The people of Hungary may have peace, if they will only say to him of Vienna, "Reign over us as you please; our lives are in your hands." There is never any trouble in having peace, if men will yield themselves to the control of those that have no business to control them. Two thirds of this nation unquestionably stand on the side of the original articles of our Constitution, and in the service of liberty, and one third deny and reject them. Now if the two thirds will give up to the one third, we can have peace — a little while.

2. We can have peace if we will legalize and establish the right of any discontented community to rebel, and to set up intestine governments within the government of the United States. Yield that principle, demoralize government, and you can have peace — for a little while. You cannot yield that principle and not demoralize government. And if it is right for seven States on the Gulf to secede, it is the right of seven States on the Lakes. If it is the right of seven States on the Lakes, it is the right of five or three States on the Ohio River. If it is the right of a number of States, it is the right of one State. And if it is the right of any State, there is not a State, a half of a State, a county, or a town, that has not the

same right. It is the right of disintegration. It is a right that aims at the destruction of the attraction of governmental cohesion. It is a right that invalidates all power in government. And if you will grant this right; if you will consent to have this government broken up; if you are willing that our country should degenerate to the condition of wrangling and rival States, — you can have peace — for a little while.

3. We can have peace if we will agree fundamentally to change our Constitution, and, instead of maintaining a charter of universal freedom, to write it out as a deliberate charter of oppression.

Mr. Stephens, the Vice-President of the so-called Confederate States, declared, in a formal speech, that our Constitution was framed on a fundamental mistake, inasmuch as it took it for granted that men were born for freedom and equality. They have expunged the doctrine of universal liberty, and put in its place the doctrine of liberty to the strong and servitude to the weak. It is said that the African race, by reason of their nationality and savagism, are not fit for liberty, and that the white race, by reason of their nationality and civilization, are fit to govern them. It is merely a plea that weak persons are not fit to take care of themselves, and that strong persons are fit to take care of them; and it is a plea that is just as applicable to any other peoples as to the Anglo-Saxons and the Africans. It is simply a doctrine that might makes right. It may be stated in this form: "You are weak and I am strong, and I am therefore your lawful master." If it is good for the Africans and the Anglo-Saxons, it is good for all other races. And if it is good in reference to races, it is good in reference to individuals. Therefore there is not a workman, there is not a poor man, there is not a man that is low in station, at the North, who is not interested in this matter, who is not touched in his rights, and who is not insulted by the spirit that is latent in the new Constitution of the so-called Confederate States. It holds that there is appointed of God a governing class and a class to be governed, — a class that are born governors because they are strong and smart and well-to-do, and a class that are born servants because they are poor and weak and unable to take care of themselves. Now take that glorious, flaming sentence in the Declaration of Independence, which asserts the right of every man to life, liberty, and the pursuit of happiness, and which pronounces that right to be alike inalienable to all, — take that and strike it out, and put in its place this infernal article of the new Constitution of the Southern States, and you can have peace — for a little while. There is no trouble about having peace. What an unreasonable people we are! If we will only pay enough for peace we can have it.

This diabolical principle is also deliberately held and advocated by the churches of the South. The Southern churches are all sound on the question of the Bible, and infidel on the question of its contents! They believe that this is God's Book; they believe that this Book is the world's charter; and they believe that it teaches the religion of servitude. Every sermon that I have received within the last year from the South has been a various echo of this one atrocious idea, held in common with all the despotic preachers of Europe. Any man that has read old South's sermons, has read over and over again all the arguments contained in the raw, jejune productions of Southern clerical advocates for oppression. In all the discussions between Milton and Salmasius, and in all the writings of Roman priests that have sought to bolster up sacerdotal rule, these arguments have been put forth far more ably than our unscholarly Southerners have put them forth. But this is the ground which has been taken by the Christian Church of the South: that in Christ Jesus all men are not created equal,—that white masters are, but that black servants are not!

And that is not all. Not only is this new government framed on this ground, and not only have all the churches of the South taken this ground, so that it may be said of the Southern Confederacy as it was said of one of the old revolted tribes, "They have a priest to their house," but there has just now been raised up in the North a club of the same kind,—a society for the promotion of *national unity*, on the basis of a change of our national instruments of government. This society proposes to restore peace to this country. And how? Exactly as you restore uniformity of color in a room where some things are red, some blue, and some yellow,—by blowing the light out so that in darkness all things will be of the same color! We are very much divided in this land, one part believing in liberty, and the other believing in servitude; and it is proposed to bring these two parts together in unity, by destroying the distinction between them. What is this society's own statement, as contained in the letter which they have put forth with their articles? They make this formal assertion: that that portion of our original Declaration of Independence which makes all men free and equal has been misinterpreted, or is false. They endeavor to say it softly, but it is a thing that cannot be said softly. To breathe it, to whisper it, makes it louder than thunder!

Indeed, it is true that men are not physiologically equal. No man ever believed that they were. They do not weigh alike. They differ in respect to bone and tissue. They are not the same as regards mental calibre. Their dynamic forces are different. They are not capable of exerting the same amount of political influence. In the nations of Europe it was held that the royal head, *jure Divino*, had privileges which the nobles had not; that there belonged to the nobles prerogatives which did not belong to the commonalty; and that the political rights of the great common people were to be graduated according to their status in society. But our fathers said, God gives the same political rights to all alike. The people are king, and the people are nobles. They are equal in this: that they all stand before the same law of justice, and that justice is to be the same to one as to another. The richest and the poorest, the wisest and the most ignorant, the highest and the lowest, are on an equality before the law. The Declaration of Independence taught simply, that every man born into life was born with such dignities, with such a nature conferred upon him, that, as a child of God, he has a right to confront government and legislature and laws, and say, "I demand, in common with every other man, equal justice, equal protection, to life, liberty, and in the pursuit of happiness." And this is what our society in the North for the promotion of national unity undertake, in their first article, to say is a lie!

Now, you can have your American eagle as you want it. If, with the South, you will strike out his eyes, then you shall stand well with Mr. Davis and Mr. Stephens of the Confederate States; if, with the Christians of the South, you will pluck off his wings, you shall stand well with the Southern churches; and if, with the new peace-makers that have risen up in the North, you will pull out his tail-feathers, you shall stand well with the society for the promotion of national unity! But when you have stricken out his eyes so that he can no longer see, when you have plucked off his wings so that he can no longer fly, and when you have pulled out his guiding tail-feathers so that he can no longer steer himself, but rolls in the dirt a mere buzzard, then will he be worth preserving? Such an eagle it is that they mean to depict upon the banner of America!

Now if any man is fierce for peace, and is willing to pay the price demanded for it, he can have it. On those conditions you can have peace as long as the Jews did. For three guilty days they were rid of the Saviour, and then he rose from the grave, with eternal power on his head, and beyond all touch of weakness or death, then ascended on high to the Source of eternal power, there to live, and to live forever!

4. We must accordingly, if we go on to purchase peace on these terms, become partners in slavery, and consent, for the sake of peace, to ratify this gigantic evil. We cannot wink at it. We are called to bear

overt witness either for or against it. Every State in this Union, according to the new Constitution, must be open to slavery. It is the design of not a few men at the North to make this the issue at the next election: whether we shall not reconstruct this government according to the Constitution of the Confederate States, one feature of which is that slavery shall have liberty to go wherever it pleases, — that slavery shall have the right of incursion to any part of this country. If you consent to such a reconstruction as is proposed, you must open every one of your States to the incoming of slavery. Not only that, but every territory on this continent is to be opened to slavery. We are called to take the executive lancet, and the virus of slavery, and lift up the arm of this virgin continent and inoculate it with this terrific poison. If you will do these things, you are to be permitted to escape war.

5. Next in order must of course be silence. When we have gone so far, we shall no longer have any right of discussion, of debate, of criticism, — we shall no longer have any right of *agitation*, as it is called.

On these conditions we may have peace. If we reject these conditions we are to have separation, demoralization of government, and war.

Now are you prepared to take peace on these conditions? You will not get it on any other conditions. If you have peace, you are to stigmatize the whole history of the past; you are to yield your religious convictions; you are to give over the government into the hands of factious revolutionists; you are to suppress every manly sentiment, and every sympathy for the oppressed. Will you take peace on such a ground as that? So far as I myself am concerned, I utterly abhor peace on any such grounds. Give me war redder than blood, and fiercer than fire, if this terrific infliction is necessary that I may maintain my faith of God in human liberty, my faith of the fathers in the instruments of liberty, my faith in this land as the appointed abode and chosen refuge of liberty for all the earth! War is terrible, but that abyss of ignominy is yet more terrible!

What, then, if we will go forward in the providence of God, and maintain our integrity, are the steps that are before us?

1. Instead of yielding our convictions, it is time to cleanse them, to deepen them, to give them more power, to make them more earnest and more religious. There is no reason, now, why we should compromise. There is nothing to be gained by compromising. And it is time that parents should talk on the great doctrine of human rights in the family, and indoctrinate their children with an abhorrence for slavery, and a love for liberty. It is time for schools to have their scholars instructed in these matters. It is time for every church to make its pews flame and glow with enthusiasm for freedom, and with hatred for oppression. While the air of the South is full of pestilent doctrines of slavery, accursed be our communities if we will not be as zealous and enthusiastic for liberty as they are against it! If their air is filled with the storm and madness of oppression, let ours be full of the sweet peace and love of liberty!

2. We must draw the lines. A great many men have been on both sides. A great many men have been thrown backward and forward, like a shuttle,

from one side to the other. It is now time for every man to choose one side or the other. We want no shufflers; we want no craven cowards; we want *men;* we want every man to stand forth, and say, "I am for liberty, and the Constitution, and the country, as our fathers gave them to us," or else, "I am against them."

Thousands, thank God, of great men have spoken to us; but I think that the war-voice of Sumter has done more to bring men together, and to produce unity of feeling among them on this subject, than the most eloquent-tongued orator.

We must say in this matter, my friends, as Christ said, "He that is not for us is against us." I will have no commerce, I will not cross palms with a man that disowns liberty in such a struggle as is before us! I will not give him shelter or house-room — except as a convicted sinner; then I will take him, as the prodigal was taken, in his rags and nakedness! But so long as he stands up with impudent face against the things that are dearest to God's heart, and dearest to the instincts of this people, I shall treat him as what he is, — a *traitor!* There ought to be but one feeling in the North, and that ought to be a feeling for liberty, which should sweep through the land like a mighty wind.

3. We must not stop to measure costs, — especially the costs of going forward, — on any basis so mean and narrow as that of pecuniary prosperity. We must put our honor and religion into this struggle. God is helping you; for, no matter how much you deplore the state of things, you cannot help yourselves. You may take counsel with your Till and Safe and Bank,

you may look at your accounts on both sides, but your talking and looking will make no difference with your affairs. The time is past in which these things could be of any avail. This matter must now be settled. You must have a part in settling it. The question is whether that shall be a manly or an ignoble part!

There are many reasons which make a good and thorough battle necessary. The Southern men are infatuated. They will not have peace. They are in arms. They have fired upon the American flag! That glorious banner has been borne through every climate, all over the globe, and for fifty years not a land or people has been found to scorn it, or dishonor it. At home, among the degenerate people of our own land, among Southern citizens, for the first time, has this glorious national flag been abased, and trampled to the ground! It is for our sons reverently to lift it, and to bear it full high again, to victory and national supremacy! Our arms, in this peculiar exigency, can lay the foundation of future union, in mutual respect. The South firmly believes that *cowardice* is the universal attribute of Northern men! Until they are most thoroughly convinced to the contrary, they will never cease arrogancy and aggression. But if now it please God to crown our arms with victory, we shall have gone far toward impressing Southern men with salutary respect. Good soldiers, brave men, hard fighting, will do more toward quiet than all the compromises and empty, wagging tongues in the world. Our reluctance to break peace, our unwillingness to shed blood, our patience, have all been misinterpreted. The more we have been generous and forbearing, the more thoroughly were they sure that it was because we dared not fight!

With the North is the strength, the population, the courage. There is not elsewhere on this continent that breadth of courage — the courage of a man in distinction from the courage of a brute beast — which there is in the free States of the North. It was General Scott who said that the New-Englanders were the hardest to get into a fight, and the most terrible to meet in a conflict, of any men on the globe.

We have no braggart courage; we have no courage that rushes into an affray for the love of fighting. We have that courage which comes from calm intelligence. We have that courage which comes from broad moral sentiment. We have no anger, but we have indignation. We have no irritable passion, but we have fixed will. We regard war and contest as terrible evils; but when, detesting them as we do, we are roused to enter into them, our courage will be of the measure of our detestation. You may be sure that the cause which can stir up the feelings of the North sufficiently to bring them into such a conflict, will develop in them a courage that will be terrific to the men who have to meet it. I could wish no worse punishment to those that decry the courage of the North, than that they shall have to meet her when she is once brought out and fairly in the field.

4. We must aim at a peace built on foundations so solid, of God's immutable truth, that nothing can reach to unsettle it. Let this conflict between liberty and slavery never come up again. Better have it thoroughly settled, though it take a score of years

to settle it, than to have an intermittent fever for the next century, breaking out at every five or ten years. It is bad, you say. That has nothing to do with the point. Your house is on fire, and the question is, What will you do? You are in the struggle, and the question is, Will you go through it in the spirit of your ancestors, in the spirit of Christians and patriots, in the spirit that belongs to the age of the world in which you live, and settle it so that it shall not be in the power of mischief to unsettle it? Or will you dally? Will you delay? I know which you will do. This question is now going forward to a settlement.

5. Let not our feelings be vengeful nor savage. We can go into this conflict with a spirit just as truly Christian as any that ever inspired us in the performance of a Christian duty. Indignation is very different from anger. Conscience is very different from revenge. The spirit of fury, — let it be far from us; but a spirit of earnestness, of willingness to do, to suffer, and to die, if need be, for our land and our principles, — that may be a religious spirit. We may consecrate it with prayer.

All through the struggle of the Revolution, men there were that preached on the Sabbath, and when not preaching went from tent to tent and performed kind offices to those that were sick or wounded, cheered those that were in despondency, encouraged those whose trials were severe, and led or accompanied their brethren to those conflicts which achieved liberty.

I believe that the old spirit will be found yet in the Church; and that in that patriotism which dares to do as well as teach, laymen and officers and pastors will be found no whit behind, in our day, what they were in the Revolutionary day.

Let me say two things more.

It is trying to live in suspense, to be in the tormenting whirl of rumor, now to see the banner up, and now to see it trailing in the dust. Early yesterday things seemed inauspicious. Toward evening all appeared calm and fair. To-day disastrous and depressing rumors were current. This evening I came hither sad from the tidings that that stronghold which seemed to guard the precious name and lasting fame of the noble and gallant ANDERSON had been given up; but since I came into this desk I have received a despatch from one of our most illustrious citizens, saying that Sumter is reinforced, and that Moultrie is the fort that has been destroyed. [*Tremendous and prolonged applause, expressed by enthusiastic cheers, clapping of hands, and waving of handkerchiefs.*] But what if the rising sun to-morrow should reverse the message? What if the tidings that greet you in the morning should be but the echo of the old tidings of disaster? You live in hours in which you are to suffer suspense. Now lifted up, you will be prematurely cheering, and now cast down, you will be prematurely desponding. Look forward, then, past the individual steps, the various vicissitudes of experience, to the glorious end that is coming! Look beyond the present to that assured victory which awaits us in the future.

Young men, you will live to see more auspicious days. Later sent, delayed in your voyage into life, you will see the bright consummation, in part at least, of that victory of this land, by which, with mortal throes, it shall cast out from itself all morbific influences, and cleanse itself from slavery. And you that are in middle life shall see the ultimate triumph advancing beyond anything that you have yet known. The sceptre shall not depart. The government shall not be shaken from its foundations.

Let no man, then, in this time of peril, fail to associate himself with that cause which is to be so entirely glorious. Let not your children, as they carry you to your burial, be ashamed to write upon your tombstone the truth of your history. Let every man that lives and owns himself an American, take the side of true American principles; — liberty for one, and liberty for all; liberty now, and liberty forever; liberty as the foundation of government, and liberty as the basis of union; liberty as against revolution, liberty, against anarchy, and liberty, against slavery; liberty here, and liberty everywhere, the world through!

When the trumpet of God has sounded, and that grand procession is forming; as Italy has risen, and is wheeling into the ranks; as Hungary, though mute, is beginning to beat time, and make ready for the march; as Poland, having long slept, has dreamt of liberty again, and is waking; as the thirty million serfs are hearing the roll of the drum, and are going forward toward citizenship, — let it not be your miserable fate, nor mine, to live in a nation that shall be seen reeling and staggering and wallowing in the orgies of despotism! We, too, have a right to march in this grand procession of liberty. By the memory of the fathers; by the sufferings of the Puritan ancestry; by the teaching of our national history; by our faith and hope of religion; by every line of the Declaration of Independence, and every article of our Constitution; by what we are and what our progenitors were, — we have a right to walk foremost in this procession of nations toward the bright millennial future!

V.

THE NATIONAL FLAG.*

"Thou hast given a banner to them that fear thee, that it may be displayed because of the truth." — Psalms lx. 4.

ROM the earliest periods nations seem to have gone forth to war under some banner. Sometimes it has been merely the pennon of a leader, and was only a rallying signal. So, doubtless, the habit began of carrying banners, to direct men in the confusion of conflict, that the leader might gather his followers around him when he himself was liable to be lost out of their sight.

Later in the history of nations the banner acquired other uses and peculiar significance from the parties, the orders, the houses, or governments, that adopted it. At length, as consolidated governments drank up into themselves all these lesser independent authorities, banners became significant chiefly of national authority. And thus in our day every people has its peculiar flag. There is no civilized nation without its banner.

A thoughtful mind, when it sees a nation's flag,

* Delivered to two companies of the "Brooklyn Fourteenth," many of them members of Plymouth Church. The Church on that day contributed $ 3,000 to aid in the equipment of this Regiment.

sees not the flag, but the nation itself. And whatever may be its symbols, its insignia, he reads chiefly in the flag, the government, the principles, the truths, the history that belong to the nation that sets it forth. When the French tricolor rolls out to the wind, we see France. When the new-found Italian flag is unfurled, we see resurrected Italy. When the other three-colored Hungarian flag shall be lifted to the wind, we shall see in it the long buried, but never dead, principles of Hungarian liberty. When the united crosses of St. Andrew and St. George, on a fiery ground, set forth the banner of Old England, we see not the cloth merely: there rises up before the mind the idea of that great monarchy.

This nation has a banner, too; and until recently wherever it streamed abroad men saw day-break bursting on their eyes. For until lately the American flag has been a symbol of Liberty, and men rejoiced in it. Not another flag on the globe had such an errand, or went forth upon the sea carrying everywhere, the world around, such hope to the captive, and such glorious tidings. The stars upon it were to the pining nations like the bright morning stars of God, and the stripes upon it were beams of morning light. As at early dawn the stars shine forth even while it grows light, and then as the sun advances that light breaks into banks and streaming lines of color, the glowing red and intense white striving together, and ribbing the horizon with bars effulgent, so, on the American flag, stars and beams of many-colored light shine out together. And wherever this flag comes, and men behold it, they see in its sacred emblazonry no ramping lion, and no fierce eagle; no embattled castles, or insignia of imperial authority: they see the symbols of light. It is the banner of Dawn. It means *Liberty;* and the galley-slave, the poor, oppressed conscript, the trodden-down creature of foreign despotism, sees in the American flag that very promise and prediction of God, — "The people which sat in darkness saw a great light; and to them which sat in the region and shadow of death light is sprung up."

Is this a mere fancy? On the 4th of July, 1776, the Declaration of American Independence was confirmed and promulgated. Already for more than a year the Colonies had been at war with the mother country. But until this time there had been no American flag. The flag of the mother country covered us as during all our colonial period; and each State that chose had a separate and significant State banner.

In 1777, within a few days of one year after the Declaration of Independence, and two years and more after the war began, upon the 14th of June, the Congress of the Colonies, or the Confederated States, assembled, and ordained this glorious National Flag which now we hold and defend, and advanced it full high before God and all men, as the Flag of Liberty. It was no holiday flag, gorgeously emblazoned for gayety or vanity. It was a solemn national signal. When that banner first unrolled to the sun, it was the symbol of all those holy truths and purposes which brought together the Colonial American Congress!

Consider the men who devised and set forth this banner. The Rutledges, the Pinckneys, the Jays, the Franklins, the Hamiltons, the Jeffersons, the Adamses, — these men were all either officially connected with it, or consulted concerning it. They were men that had taken their lives in their hands, and consecrated all their worldly possessions — for what? For the doctrines, and for the personal fact, of liberty, — for the right of *all* men to liberty. They had just given forth to the world a Declaration of Facts and Faiths out of which sprung the Constitution, and on which they now planted this new-devised flag of our Union.

If one, then, asks me the meaning of our flag, I say to him, It means just what Concord and Lexington meant, what Bunker Hill meant; it means the whole glorious Revolutionary War, which was, in short, the rising up of a valiant young people against an old tyranny, to establish the most momentous doctrine that the world had ever known, or has since known, — the right of men to their own selves and to their liberties.

In solemn conclave our fathers had issued to the world that glorious manifesto, the Declaration of Independence. A little later, that the fundamental principles of liberty might have the best organization, they gave to this land our imperishable Constitution. Our flag means, then, all that our fathers meant in the Revolutionary War; it means all that the Declaration of Independence meant; it means all that the Constitution of our people, organizing for justice, for liberty, and for happiness, meant. Our flag carries American ideas, American history and American feelings. Beginning with the Colonies, and coming down to our time, in its sacred heraldry, in its glorious insignia, it has gathered and stored chiefly this supreme idea: *Divine right of liberty in man.* Every color means liberty; every thread means liberty; every form of star and beam or stripe of light means liberty: not lawlessness, not license; but organized, institutional liberty, — liberty through law, and laws for liberty!

This American flag was the safeguard of liberty. Not an atom of crown was allowed to go into its insignia. Not a symbol of authority in the ruler was permitted to go into it. It was an ordinance of liberty by the people for the people. *That* it meant, *that* it means, and, by the blessing of God, *that* it shall mean to the end of time!

For God Almighty be thanked! that, when base and degenerate Southern men desired to set up a nefarious oppression, at war with every legend and every instinct of old American history, they could not do it under our bright flag! Its stars smote them with light like arrows shot from the bow of God. They must have another flag for such work; and they forged an infamous flag to do an infamous work, and, God be blessed! left our bright and starry banner untainted and untouched by disfigurement and disgrace! I thank them that they took another flag to do the Devil's work, and left our flag to do the work of God! [Applause.] So may it ever be, that men that would forge oppression shall be obliged to do it under some other banner than the Stars and the Stripes.

If ever the sentiment of our text, then, was fulfilled, it has been in our glorious American banner:

"Thou hast given a banner *to them that fear thee.*"

Our fathers were God-fearing men. Into their hands God committed this banner, and they have handed it down to us. And I thank God that it is still in the hands of men that fear him and love righteousness.

"Thou hast given a banner to them that fear thee, *that it may be displayed.*"

And displayed it shall be. Advanced full against the morning light, and borne with the growing and the glowing day, it shall take the last ruddy beams of the night, and from the Atlantic wave, clear across with eagle flight to the Pacific, that banner shall float, meaning all the liberty which it has ever meant! From the North, where snows and mountain ice stand solitary, clear to the glowing tropics and the Gulf, that banner that has hitherto waved shall wave and wave forever, — every star, every band, every thread and fold significant of Liberty! [Great applause.]

[*The speaker paused to check the too demonstrative enthusiasm of the audience, and continued:*] I do not doubt your patriotism. I know it is hard for men that are full of feeling not to give expression to it; yet excuse me if I request you to refrain from demonstrations of applause while I am speaking. It is not because I think Sunday too good a day, nor the church too holy a place for patriotic Christian men to express their feelings at such a time as this, and in behalf of such sentiments, but because by too frequent repetition applause becomes stale and common, that I make this request. Besides, outward expression is not our way. We are rather of a silent stock. We let our feelings work inwardly, so that they may have deeper channels and fuller floods.

"Thou hast given a banner to them that fear thee, that it may be displayed *because of the truth.*"

Because of that very truth we will display it! Not in mere national pride, not in any wantonness of vanity, not merely because we have been reared to honor it, not because we have an hereditary reverence for it, but with a full intelligence of what it is and what it means, and because we love the truth that is written in lines of living light all over it, we will advance it and maintain it against all comers from earth and hell.

The history of this banner is all on the side of rational liberty. Under it rode Washington and his armies,—Washington, much beloved and much abused by those that are his eulogists, who have described all that he was except his love of liberty, which has been forgotten. But Washington would be like a man without a heart, if you left out of him that high, almost imperial chivalric love of liberty for every human being. Under this banner rode he and his armies. Before it Burgoyne laid down his arms. It waved on the highlands at West Point. It floated over old Fort Montgomery, as over another Montgomery* it shall float! When Arnold would have surrendered these valuable fortresses and precious legacies, his night was turned into day, and his treachery was driven away, by the beams of light from this starry banner. It cheered our army, driven out from around New York, and in their painful pilgrimages through New Jersey. Sacred State of New Jersey! small, but comely and rich and imperishable in the drops of precious blood that have redeemed her sainted soil from barrenness. In New

* At that time Montgomery, Alabama, was the capital of the Southern Confederacy, afterwards removed to Richmond, Virginia.

Jersey more than in almost every other State grows the *trailing-arbutus*. Methinks it is sacred drops of Pilgrim blood that come forth in beauteous flowers on this sandiest of soils, for this sweet blossom that lays its cheek on the very snow is the true Pilgrim's *May-flower!* This banner streamed in light over the soldiers' heads at Valley Forge and at Morristown. It crossed the waters rolling with ice at Trenton, and when its stars gleamed in the cold morning with victory, a new day of hope dawned on the despondency of this nation. When South Carolina, in the Revolutionary struggle, utterly forgot what she never well remembered, courage and personal liberty, and yielded herself, — the only one, ignominious and infamous, of all the Revolutionary band of States, that gave in an adhesion again to the British government, — when she forgot courage and personal liberty, and yielded herself up, and made her peace, solitary and alone, with British generals, then it was this banner that led on the Virginia forces who conquered both the British and Carolinian armies, and brought the State again into our confederacy. Alas that the head should become the tail! Alas that old Virginia, that brought back the recreant South Carolina, should be tied to, and be dragged about the rebel camp at the tail of that same South Carolina!

And when at length the long years of war were drawing to a close, underneath the folds of this immortal banner sat Washington, while Yorktown surrendered its hosts, and our Revolutionary struggle ended with victory.

It waved thus over that whole historic period of struggle, and over that period in which sat that immortal Convention that framed our Constitution. It cheered the hardy pioneers that then began to go forth and explore the Western wilds, in all their desperate strifes with savage Indians. It was to them a memorial and symbol of comfort. Our States grew up under it. And when our ships began to swarm upon the ocean, to carry forth our commerce, and, inspired by the genial flame of liberty, to carry forth our ideas, and Great Britain arrogantly demanded the right to intrude her search-warrants upon American decks, then up went the lightning flag, and every star meant liberty, and every stripe streamed defiance.

The gallant fleet of Lake Erie, — have you forgotten it? The thunders that echoed to either shore were overshadowed by this broad ensign of our American liberty. Those glorious men that went forth in the old ship Constitution carried this banner to battle and to victory. The old ship is alive yet. The new traitors of the South could not burn her, they did not sink her; and she has been hauled out of the reach of hostile hands and traitorous bands. Bless the name, bless the ship, bless her historic memory, and bless the old flag that waves over her yet!

The Perrys, the Lawrences, the Biddles, the McDonoughs, the Porters, and a host of others whose names cannot die, — do you forget that they fought under this national banner, and fought for liberty?

How glorious, then, has been its origin! How glorious has been its history! How divine is its meaning! In all the world is there another banner that carries such hope, such grandeur of spirit, such soul-inspiring truth, as our dear old American flag? made by liberty, made for liberty, nourished in its spirit, carried in its service, and never, not once in all the earth, made to stoop to despotism! Never,— did I say? Alas! Only to that worst despotism, Southern slavery, has it bowed. Remember, every one of you, that the slaveholders of the South, alone of all the world, have put their feet upon the American flag!

And now this banner has been put on trial! It has been condemned. For what? Has it failed of duty? Has liberty lost color by it? Have moths of oppression eaten its folds? Has it refused to shine on freemen and given its light to despots? No. It has been true, brave, loyal. It has become too much a banner of liberty for men who mean and plot despotism. Remember, citizen! remember, Christian soldier! the American flag has been fired upon by Americans, and trodden down because it stood in the way of slavery! This is all that you have reaped for your long patience, for your many compromises, for your generous trust and your Christian forbearance! You may now see through all the South just what kind of patriotism slavery breeds! East of the mountains, I suppose you might travel through all Washington's State and not see one star nor one stripe. Thank God, Washington is dead, and has not lived to see the infamy and the disgrace that have fallen upon that recreant State! In all North Carolina I fear you shall find not one American flag. In Florida you shall not find one. In Georgia, I know not, except in the mountain fastnesses, if there be one. With a like exception, there is not one in Alabama. Neither is there one in repudiating Mississippi, nor in Louisiana, nor in Texas, ungrateful, nor in Arkansas. In all this waste and wilderness of States this banner has gone down, and a miserable counterfeit, a poor forgery, has been run up upon the recreant pole, to stand in the stead of the glorious old Revolutionary, historic American flag! And how is it in the great middle brood of States? As a star is obscured for an instant by a passing cloud, and then shines forth again, so in Maryland the flag and its stars were hid for a day, but they now flame out again. Maryland is safe. All honor to Delaware; she has never flinched. In Kentucky and Tennessee and Missouri the banner is at half-mast, uncertain whether it will go up or down. And of all these States I can say, with all my heart and soul, in the language of the Apocalypse: "I would thou wert cold or hot. So then because thou art lukewarm, and neither cold nor hot, I will spew thee out of my mouth." God hates lukewarm patriotism, as much as lukewarm religion; and we hate it too. We do not believe in hermaphrodite patriots. We want men to be men from the crown of their head to the sole of their foot, and to say *no* to oppression, and *yes* to liberty, and to say both as if thunder spoke!

But this is not the worst, — that this banner should have been lowered by the hands of recreants. It was upon these streaming bars and upon these bright stars that every one of that immense concentric range of guns was aimed, when Sumter was lifted up in the midst, almost like another witnessing Calvary; and that flag which Russia could not daunt, nor France intimidate, nor England conquer, has gone down beneath the fire of treacherous States within our own Union! And do you know that when it was fallen, in the streets of a Southern city, it was trailed, hooted at, pierced with swords? Men that have sat in the Senate of the United States ran out to trample upon it; it was fired on and slashed by the mob; it was dragged through the mud; it was hissed at and spit upon; and so it was carried through Southern cities! That our flag, which has found on the ocean, in the Indian Islands, in Sumatra, in Japan, in China, and in all the world, no enemies, either barbarian or civilized, that dared to touch it with foul aspersion,—that this flag should, in our own nation, and by our own people, be spit upon, and trampled under foot, is more than the heart of man can bear!

And what is its crime? If it had forgotten its origin, if it had gone over to oppression, if it had set these stars like so many blazing jewels in the tiara of imperial despotism, I should not have wondered at its going down. If it had been recreant to its trust of ideas of liberty, I should have expected to see it go down. But it has not failed to defend liberty. Have there been quartered on its armorial bearings any bastard symbols significant of oppression? None. It is guilty of nothing but of too much liberty. Its stars have too much promise in them for those that are born slaves; and its stripes stream too bright a light to those that sit in darkness. That is the crime of our national banner.

And now God speaks by the voice of his providence, saying, "Lift again that banner! Advance it full and high!" To your hand, and to yours, God and your country commit that imperishable trust. You go forth self-called, or rather called by the trust of your countrymen and by the Spirit of your God, to take that trailing banner out of the dust and out of the mire, and lift it again where God's rains can cleanse it, and where God's free air can cause it to unfold and stream as it has always floated before the wind. God bless the men that go forth to save from disgrace the American flag!

Accept it, then, in all its fulness of meaning. It is not a painted rag. It is a whole national history. It is the Constitution. It is the government. It is the free people that stand in the government on the Constitution. Forget not what it means; and for the sake of its ideas, rather than its mere emblazonry, be true to your country's flag. By your hands lift it; but let your lifting it be no holiday display. It must be advanced "*because of the truth.*"

That flag must go to the capital of this nation; and it must go not hidden, not secreted, not in a case or covering, but advanced full high, displayed, bright as the sun, clear as the moon, terrible as an army with banners! For a single week that disgraceful crook,* that shameful circuit, may be needful; but the way from New England, the way from New York, the way from New Jersey and Pennsylvania to Washington, *lies right through Baltimore;* and that is the way the flag must and shall go! [*Enthusiastic cheers.*] But that flag, borne by ten thousand and thrice ten thousand hands, from Connecticut, from Massachusetts, (God bless the State and all her men!) from shipbuilding Maine, from old Granite New Hampshire, from the Vermont of Bennington and Green-Mountain-Boy patriotism, from Rhode Island, not behind any in zeal and patriotism, from New York,

* The route through Baltimore was closed, and for weeks Washington was reached through Annapolis.

from Ohio, from Pennsylvania and New Jersey and Delaware, and the other loyal States, — that flag must be carried, bearing every one of its insignia, to the sound of the drum and the fife, into our national capital, until Washington shall seem to be a forest, in which every tree supports the American banner!

And it must not stop there. The country does not belong to us from the Lakes only to Washington, but from the Lakes to the Gulf of Mexico. The flag must go on. The land of Washington shall see Washington's flag again. The land that sits in darkness, and in which the people see no light, shall yet see light dawn, and liberty flash from the old American banner! It must see Charleston again, and float again over every fort in Charleston harbor. It must go further, to the Alligator State, and stand there again. And, sweeping up through all plantations, and over all fields of sugar and rice and tobacco, and every other thing, it must be found in every State till you touch the Mississippi. And, bathing in its waters, it must go across and fill Texas with its sacred light. Nor must it stop when it floats over every one of the States. That flag must stand, bearing its whole historic spirit and original meaning, in every Territory of this nation!

Have you not had enough mischief of slavery? Do you not see what men it breeds? It hatches cockatrice's eggs. Slavery breeds traitors in the masters and miserable slaves in the subjects. Slavery is the abominable poison that has circulated in the body politic, and corrupted this whole nation almost past healing. Blessed be God there is a medicine found.

Now, having had experience, and having seen what slavery does to the slave (and what it does to the slave is the least part of the evil. The slave is to be envied in the comparison. I would to God that the white man were half as little hurt by slavery); seeing how it blights the heart's core; how it corrupts the most sacred sentiments; how it brings down natures born for better things to the degradation of despotism, — having seen these things, can you, — I ask every man that has conscience, or reason, or hope, or fear, or love in his soul, — can you meet God Almighty's judgment, or the inquiring eye of God, if while you live you permit that evil to roll unchecked three thousand miles to the Pacific Ocean? Let, then, this banner go again into every recreant State, and float over every inch of territory, saying, "Defiance to slavery; all hail to liberty!"

Nor is it enough that that banner shall stand and merely reassert its authority. It is time now that that banner shall do as much for each man in our own country as it will in every other land on the globe. If I go to Constantinople, and a mob threatens me, that banner shines like lightning out of heaven, and I am safe. If I go to Jerusalem, or among the Bedouin Arabs, I have but to show that symbol, and I am safe. If I go to Africa, and skirt its coasts among the natives, and exhibit the colors of my country, I am safe. I can go around the globe under the protection of this flag. But it is denied me to go to Washington. I cannot go from my door to the capital of this nation, because the *American flag does not defend Americans on their own soil.* I cannot go to Virginia, nor North Carolina, nor South Carolina, nor Florida, nor Georgia, nor Alabama, nor Mississippi, nor Louisiana, nor Texas, nor Arkansas, nor to most of Kentucky and of Tennessee. We have not had a government for fifty years that dared to do a thing that slavery did not wish to have done. I suppose that within the last twenty years uncounted multitudes of men have been mulcted in property, mobbed, hung, murdered, for whose wrongs and blood no government has ever made any inquisition. It is permitted, to this hour, to one man to maltreat, to murder, to rob, to strip, to destroy another man, in Nashville, in Memphis, in New Orleans, in Mobile, in Charleston, and even in Richmond, close up under the eye of government. There has never been an hour for the last twenty-five years when government would lift a voice or stretch out a hand to protect Northern men against the outrages committed upon them by men at the South. Now I demand that, when the American flag is next unfurled in South Carolina, it shall protect *me* there, as it protects a South Carolinian in New York. I demand that it shall protect me in Mobile, as it protects a Mobilian here. I demand that this shall be a common country, and that all men shall enjoy the imperishable rights which the Constitution guarantees to every American citizen. I demand that there shall be such a victory of this flag as shall make the whole and undivided land the common possession of all and every one of its citizens!

If any man asks me whether I will consent to a compromise, I reply, Yes. I love compromises; they are dear to me — if I may make them. Give me a compromise that shall bring peace. Let me say, "Hang the ringleading traitors; suppress their armies; give peace to their fields; lift up the banner, and make a highway in which every true American citizen, minding his own business, can walk unmolested; free the Territories, and keep them free," — that is our compromise. Give to us the doctrine of the fathers, renew the Declaration of Independence, refill the Constitution with the original blood of liberty, destroy traitors and treason, make the doctrine of secession a byword and a hissing; make laws equal; let that justice for which they were ordained be the same in Maine or Carolina, to the rich and to the poor, the bond and the free, and thus we will *compromise.*

But as long as compromise means yokes on us and license to them, silence for liberty and open-mouthed freedom to despotism, so long compromise is a Devil's juggle; no man that is a freeman and a Christian should be caught in any such snare as that. I ask for nothing except that which the fathers meant. I ask for the fulfilment of Washington's prayer. I ask for the carrying out of the designs of those sacred men that sat in conclave at Independence Hall in Philadelphia, and framed our immortal Constitution. I ask for liberty in New York, in Carolina, in Alabama, in every State and in every Territory. I ask for it throughout the whole land. I ask no Northern advantage. It is a mere geographical accident that liberty is in the North. It is not because it is the North, but because the North is free, that I ask for the ascendency of Northern principles.

Ah! that Daniel Webster had lived to see what we do, — that strong man whose faith failed him in a fatal hour of ambition! I will read from a speech of his better days one of the noblest passages that ever issued from the uninspired pen of man. It is appropriate for this hour: —

> "When my eyes shall be turned to behold, for the last time, the sun in heaven, may I not see him shining on the broken and dishonored fragments of a once glorious Union; on States dissevered, discordant, belligerent; on a land rent with civil feuds, or drenched, it may be, in fraternal blood! Let their last feeble and lingering glance, rather, behold the gorgeous ensign of the Republic, now known and honored throughout the earth, still full high advanced, its arms and trophies streaming in their original lustre, not a stripe erased or polluted, nor a single star obscured, — bearing for its motto no such miserable interrogatory as *What is all this worth?* nor those other words of delusion and folly, *Liberty first, and Union afterwards,* — but everywhere, spread all over in characters of living light, blazing on all its ample folds, as they float over the sea and over the land, and in every wind under the whole heavens, that other sentiment, dear to every true American heart, — Liberty *and* Union, now and forever, one and inseparable."

God grant it, — *God grant it!*

You live in a civilized age. You go on a sacred mission. The prayers and sympathies of Christendom are with you. You go to open again the shut-up fountains of liberty, and to restore this disgraced banner to its honor. You go to serve your country in the cause of liberty; and if God brings you into conflict erelong with those misguided men of the South, when you see their miserable, new-vamped banner, remember what that flag means, — Treason, Slavery, Despotism; then look up and see the bright stars and the glorious stripes over your own head, and read in them Liberty, *Liberty*, LIBERTY!

And if you fall in that struggle, may some kind hand wrap around about you the flag of your country, and may you die with its sacred touch upon you. It shall be sweet to go to rest lying in the folds of your country's banner, meaning, as it shall mean, "Liberty *and* Union, now and forever."

We will not forget you. You go forth from us not to be easily and lightly passed over. The waves shall not close over the places which you have held; but when you return, not as you go, many of you inexperienced, and many of you unknown, you shall return from the conquests of liberty with a reputation and a character established forever to your children and your children's children. It shall be an honor, it shall be a legend, it shall be a historic truth; and your posterity shall say: "Our fathers stood up in the day of peril, and laid again the foundations of liberty that were shaken; and in their hands the banner of our country streamed forth like the morning star upon the night."

God bless you!

VI.

THE CAMP, ITS DANGERS AND DUTIES.*

"For the Lord thy God walketh in the midst of thy camp, to deliver thee, and to give up thine enemies before thee; therefore shall thy camp be holy; that he see no unclean thing in thee, and turn away from thee." — Deut. xxiii. 14.

THAT Christian people should learn to dread the camp is not strange. The evils which have gone along with armies, the dangers of moral infection in military camps, are not imaginary, and are perhaps not less than our greatest fears would lead us to believe them to be. And yet it ought not to be forgotten that these evils are vincible, and that, though real, they may be overcome. There are no circumstances where Christian courage may not gain a victory over the sharpest temptations. It should not be forgotten that the world is indebted to camp life for institutions which have done more to infuse order and civilization among men than any legislation. God's people lived in military camps for full half a century. In camps Moses promulgated the Hebrew code. In the camp they began to practise the matchless elements of the Hebrew Commonwealth. In the camp the slavish

* Preached during May, 1861.

habits which they had contracted were gradually worn off, their idolatrous tendencies were at last repressed, and their national education began. Perhaps the purest, most orderly and well-regulated period of the Hebrew history was that of their early camp life. More brilliant periods there were, under David and Solomon; but I doubt if ever there was, on the whole, a more moral period. Nor will a study of the rules and regulations of that life be unprofitable even now. For while Moses has nothing to teach us in strictly military matters, he has anticipated almost every effort of science for health, cleanliness, order, and good civic economy, striving, with imperfect means, to be sure, to do that which, with more perfect instrumentalities, science is now accomplishing.

Our text shows the influences upon which this effort was based. Religion was brought to bear, with its appropriate influences, upon camp life.

There can be no doubt that camp morals, subsequently to this epoch, and in other nations, have deserved all the ill repute which they have acquired. Nor can we suppose camp life ever, under the most favorable circumstances, to be as conducive to virtue as is the family state in civic communities.

But we must not look upon it as always and necessarily so great an evil as it was in the past ages of European military history. Camps do not need to continue to be what they have hitherto been. For the world has advanced. Every method of living has advanced. We know better what to do, we know how to do better, and we are doing better, in every element of life, than did ages past. The morals of the common people, and of soldiers, who spring from them, are eminently better than they used to be. The circumstances under which war is conducted are much changed, and changed much for the better. Experience, and the facilities for organizing and supplying armies, have removed many of the temptations to evil. At least, they have made it unnecessary for men to be wicked.

It has been the policy of this nation to discourage standing armies. It is a wise policy, and it never appeared so wise as now. Standing armies are always dangerous; and I can hardly doubt that, had there been a hundred thousand men subject to the control of those wicked men just ejected from this government, our liberties would have been in peril. They would have been suppressed, to be acquired again only by crossing a Red Sea of blood. We owe much of our salvation to the fact that there was not a military power in the hands of an Administration imbecile in all but corruption. Everything else had been got ready to overthrow the government but this infernal enginery of a standing army.

The theory of our people has been, that, as the common people framed their government, administer their government, and are the sources of power and of political influence in that government, so and in like manner the common people shall be their own soldiers, and do their own fighting, when it is necessary. War will not be unnecessarily provoked when the men that provoke the war are obliged themselves to wage it.

But with great wisdom two provisions have been made. First, the common people have been enrolled as a militia, and made to have some little idea of combination and drill. It has not been much, it has been just enough to subject them to the ridicule of professional blatterers; nevertheless, it has been sufficient. And whenever the common people of this land have been called upon for the defence of things that were worth fighting for, they have brought the conflict to a successful issue.

Next, public military academies have given the most rigid and thorough education to men selected from every State. And thus we have an intelligent and hardy common people, somewhat acquainted with the rudiments of army formations, and of the duties of soldiers, for a foundation; and for leaders, men of scientific military education.

And now, when war breaks out with us, the camp is both better and worse than European camps and camps of other countries. It is better, or may be, because it is made up, not of professional soldiers without civil sympathies, cut off from pursuits of ordinary life, but of citizens, pervaded with the sympathies of citizens; of men who go to war as one of life's duties, alternative duties, and not as their vocation. And such men ought to make better soldiers than others, more moral and more manly.

It is worse, because in regular armies, and among soldiers trained for years, there is an education toward neatness and order and economy of living which a body of volunteers suddenly gathered together are not likely to have. In the Mexican war, if I remember correctly, the deaths by sickness in the volunteer regiments were more than one hundred per cent greater than in the regular army; showing the difference between practised skill in living and the inexperience of the volunteers.

Such, with its faults, and with possible excellences, is the American military system. It is not our business now so much to subject it to criticism, as to accept it with its duties and responsibilities. For, in the providence of God, war is upon us. It is quite immaterial whether we wish it or not, whether we think it might have been avoided, or whether every step on either side has been the wisest. The past is past. Let the dead bury their dead. War, I repeat, is upon us. The army is collecting. Various camps are forming. The question for the whole Christian community is this: What is the duty of this country toward its camps?

It is not enough, then, that we should simply encourage men to volunteer in their country's cause, clothe them, equip them, get them off, and then consider them as no longer on our hands. It is a part of our duty to equip them, and see that they are well fitted out, and to send them off under good auspices; but we must also consider ourselves responsible for the continued well-being of that army which we send forth to do, not *their* work, but *our* work. It is not enough for us to do some things. That great army that is gathering around the government of this nation, to maintain its sacred laws and principles, must be adopted by all Christian men at home, and must be provided for, not simply in clothes and food, but in education and in morals. We must see to it that physically they are well equipped, and we must see to it that that moral care which comes from material sources (and there is a good deal of it) is provided;

but when we have provisioned and clothed and equipped the men, and put them beyond the reach of physical want, we have but just begun to discharge our duties toward them.

The army must feel that it is not a thing separated from society, and different from it. It is only the arm of society stretched out, not cut off, but joined to the body, receiving circulation from it yet, and in vital sympathy with it. That we may better understand our duties, I will point out some of the dangers to which our men are liable, and some of the measures by which these dangers may be averted.

1. As armies are formed, it must necessarily be the case that they shall come together in an ill-assorted and socially unfit manner. But a young man ought to learn how to live with men differing in every respect from himself. A young man must learn to live with men; with men mixed and various, good and bad, of all dispositions and habits; and surely, if a man does not learn it in the army, it is because he is not apt to learn. One can scarcely conceive of men brought together with less principle of assortment than in volunteer regiments. Many are ruined in learning this lesson; and many are ruined that need not have been, had some one taught them, warned them, and encouraged them to maintain their own individuality. Old and young are huddled together. Some of strong will and others of an impressible disposition are brought in contact with each other, and you know which will receive the dent. The hard and the soft are side by side. Among them are the proud man, that receives no impressions from others, and the approbative man, that stands on his own root by a slen-

der stem, and nods and bobs in the wind like a rush or daisy. It is a good school, if it did not spoil so many for the sake of making a few. But so it is. The army is so formed that the first lesson, and the first danger, is that of living with men who are entirely unlike themselves.

2. There is a sudden change of all the habits of life. Men become their own cooks, their own chambermaids, their own seamstresses, and their own washerwomen. Tables, linen, china cups, and delf plates disappear. Men go down to camp life to become almost savage in the simplicity of domestic economies. No beds receive them such as they have been accustomed to. No such relations of table and social intercourse as they have previously enjoyed are enjoyed by them now. They seem to have been stripped bare of the refinements of civilized society. All influences calculated to promote the exterior and physical proprieties of life seem to be removed from them. These things are apt to beget great carelessness and rudeness, and even a positive barbarism, unless they are resisted and counteracted.

It seems as though there were very little religious influence in a clean face, a clean skin, and a comely garb; but there is a good deal of simple moral influence in these things. When a man does not care for the neatness of his person, nor for the ordinary proprieties and economies of life, he is verging toward the barbarous state. It is so even with men of moral stamina and settled characters; but how much more, if character is unfashioned and habits unformed!

3. The restraints, the affections, the softening influences of the household, are taken away from the

soldier in the camp. No man can imagine the difference which this makes till he has seen it and felt it. Men that at home are not only moral and decorous, but who are without temptation or desire to be anything else, when away from home do things so utterly out of character that they seem not to be the same persons. There is, it may be said, a sort of mania or insanity that falls on men away from home. Men that at home not only do not drink, but do not want to, when they go away from home and the restraints of the family to reside for weeks, do drink and become intoxicated. Men that at home are never subject to vagrant thoughts, almost lose the power of regulated thought away from home. No one imagines how much he is upheld by the moral influences of those about him, and how little by his own will and character, till he goes abroad alone. When a man goes alone to England, he says, "There is not a man in this whole kingdom who will know what I do," and he has a morbid curiosity to know how he will feel under such and such circumstances, and he does things that he never did before, to satisfy that curiosity. A man in Paris who knows there is not a man in Paris that knows him, is not the same man that he was in New York. That is to say, he is subject to temptations and influences that he never would have been subject to at home. When men that are patterns of morality in the village come to New York, in spring and fall, to do business, they are not always patterns of morality. They seem to slough moral habits for the time being. Those that deal with them know it. It would not do for them to treat this or that man at home as they treated him the last time they were in New York. It would produce an uproar in the church, or an explosion in the family! It is not because they are hypocrites that they deport themselves in one way at home and in another way abroad; it is not because they are insincere; it is because men *are* stronger at home surrounded with friends, responsible to a public sentiment, sustained by example and social sympathies, than when they are left standing alone. It is so good to the soul and to the morals to be surrounded by those who bear sweet affinities and relationships, that when a man has them he is well, and when he has not he is sick or feeble. It is not surprising that young men should feel as older men have felt, since the world began, when removed from social restraints and domestic influences.

To this must be added the almost necessary rudeness of a womanless state. If God were to take the sun and moon and stars out of the heavens, the chances for husbandry would be what, if God were to take woman out of life, would be the chances for refinement and civilization. Woman carries civilization in her heart. It springs from her. Her power and influence mark the civilization of any country. A man that lives in a community where he has the privileges of woman's society, and is subject to woman's influence, is almost of necessity refined, more than he is aware of; and when men are removed from the genial influence of virtuous womanhood, the very best degenerate, or feel the deprivation.

There is something wanting in the air when you get west of the Alleghany Mountains on a sultry day of summer. The air east of the mountain is supplied with a sort of pabulum from the salt water of the ocean, by which one is sustained in the sultriest days of midsummer. Now what this salt is to the air, that is woman's influence to the virtue of a community. You breathe it without knowing it. All you know is that you are made stronger and better. And a man is not half a man unless a woman helps him to be!

One of the mischiefs of camp life is that women are removed from it. The men may not know what it is that lets them down to a lower state of feeling, or what that subtle influence was that kept them up to a higher state of refinement, but it is the absence of woman in the one case, as it was the presence of woman in the other. Woman is a light which God has set before man to show him which way to go, and blessed is he who has sense enough to follow it!

4. To this must be added the evils which are liable to spring out of the interplay and alternation of idleness and excessive exertion in camp life. Men whose habits are regular are half saved to begin with. A man who has an order of business which brings something to be done every hour, which fills every hour with occupation, is a match for the Devil. Satan finds plenty of mischief for idle hands to do, and very little for busy hands. But men whose calling is spasmodic, who use up their strength in a few hours, and then fall back upon indolence and self-indulgence, are peculiarly in danger. You shall find that those workmen who are excessively taxed, — glass-blowers, foundrymen, the boat hands on our Western rivers, expressmen, and the like, — who have, during one or two hours, to do work enough for eight or ten men to each man, and who are obliged to concentrate the whole energy of their life and power for this brief

period, and then fall back upon five or six indolent hours, are the men that are most in danger, and that are most apt to be reckless, wild, daring, and physically self-indulgent. Experience will show that while regular and successive industries, which furnish employment for every hour, conduce to morals, excessive labor for a few hours, followed by long intervals of indolence, is demoralizing. No man can go through the experience of such labor and alternate indolence and come out sound and well.

Now this is peculiarly the experience of the camp. The drill goes for nothing: that is mere play. But with camp life comes the long march to-day, and the lying still for three or four days; the desperate conflict, with all its excitement for a few hours, and the rest for the ensuing week; long periods of inactivity, interspersed with occasional intensifications of activity. These things shake the habits of the whole moral fabric of a man. Morbid appetites spring up from such irregularities. The body ceases to perform its normal functions, the tendencies of life are different, and the whole character is changed.

5. We must remember that the aim and end of war is physical violence. Now men cannot be associated with objects of violence and not receive collateral moral impressions from them. If men are educated, and if they bear with them a stern will, and look upon war as a terrible but necessary evil, they may go through it and escape unharmed. Such a man as Anderson can go through the most dreadful experiences of war and come out a Christian, a humane, a gentle man. Where a man brings a heart and a faith into experiences like these he may avoid harm, as

they did who went through the fire without even the smell of fire upon their garments; but raw, unenlightened, untrained natures cannot but be hardened and depraved by them. A man, however, cannot tell what effect they will have upon him till he is brought into the midst of them. Some are cured of cruelty by the sight of blood. They revolt from it with the whole force of their being. Some have a natural tendency to it; and when they come into the exercise of it they speedily sink into degeneracy, and drag others down with them. At any rate, this living for an end of violence must affect the whole moral nature. A life supremely devoted to resistance, to contention, to destruction, must be full of dangers.

6. We must consider the peculiar danger of camps in producing intemperance. So great is this danger that we might almost compromise, and say, "Give us release from that, and we will run the risk of every other one." The desire of excitement, for various reasons, is nowhere else, perhaps, so great as in the camp. Where, for instance, men are to prepare themselves for hard and successive work, it is not unnatural that they should seek to rouse up their energies with strong drink. And where men have gone through severe and long-continued labor, where they have been deprived of their appropriate food, where they have been exposed to extremes of heat or cold, where they have been taxed with a harassing watch or a desperate fight, where all their habits have been irregular, then nothing is more natural than that they should seek to repair their wasted strength by intoxicating drinks. But the indulgence in the use of ardent spirits for such purposes is a fatal indul-

gence. I think the distinction between the right and wrong use of alcoholic stimulants lies simply in this: The man that uses them for producing digestion, or so as to promote prompt and efficient action of the natural functions of the system, is using them medicinally; but the man that uses them either for the purpose of unnaturally exciting the physical energies, or for the purpose of repairing the waste of those energies by excessive exertion, is using them fatally. If you use them for the sake of fitting yourself to make a brilliant speech, you use them fatally. If you use them in order that you may supply the strength you want for an emergency, you use them fatally. And if you use them for the purpose of making up for the strength that you have lost in any severe undertaking, you use them fatally. If you use them either to create power, or to compensate for the exhaustion of power, of mind or body, you violate the laws of nature, and so use them fatally. When Paul said to Timothy, "Use a little wine for thy stomach's sake and thine often infirmities," he doubtless referred to the fact that Timothy had the dyspepsia, and that a little wine might help his digestion, and that it was through good digestion that he was to have good blood, good nerves, and good muscles! But if a man keeps a fiery stream of stimulus pouring upon his brain for the purpose of increasing its activity, he is a marked man, and his name is already written down in the book of death. When men are severely taxed, there is nothing more natural than that they should clutch at anything that will afford them momentary relief. And any indulgence in this practice is apt to be fatal, because when spirituous liquors have been taken for one thing, they will naturally be taken for others.

The dulness, the weariness, the *ennui* of camp life is greatly alleviated by the social festive glass.

The pernicious influence of example in the matter of drinking will also be felt in the camp. The young man who is not wont to drink may be led to do it because he has not the moral courage to resist the temptation under which he is brought. A young man in the ranks naturally wants to stand well with the officers, a young officer naturally wants to stand well with his superior officers, one that is weak naturally wants to stand well with those that are stronger than himself, and there is danger that many will fall into the habit of drinking for the sake of gaining favor. A man that is superior in any respect to his fellows has great power of persuasion over them, and can, if he be intemperate, do much toward drawing them into intemperance.

Could intoxicating drinks be kept away from camps, one half of their dangers would be obviated. And for any one that is going forth to meet the temptations of camp life, I had almost said I would sum up in one simple word of remembrance a talisman of safety,— *Temperance*, absolute temperance. There are other dangers of the camp, but there are so many connected with this that we almost forget the rest, and say that you will be safe if you are strictly temperate.

Why, I think war kills more after it is over than during its continuance. It is not the man who comes home limping on one usable leg that is most damaged: it is the man that comes home with two legs and two arms, and with no use for them. It is not the man who comes home pierced through so as to be all his life an invalid, that war most damages; it is the man that, pierced through with the liquid shot, comes reeling and staggering home to be all his life useless. And I say to every one that has anything to do with the camp, For the love of God, for the love of man, for the sake of patriotism, and for the salvation of those that are imperilled, take care of the young men, that they do not become drunkards!

7. There is an evil to be dreaded from the contagion of bad men in camp life. I am not referring to gross and shamelessly bad men. When a man becomes shamelessly bad, he becomes comparatively harmless. It is not the thing with poison scattered all over the outside that endangers anybody; it is the cake that is poison, but is sweetened and not seen to be poison; it is the liquor that is poisoned at the bottom, and is not suspected of being poisoned. I do not know, so far as my personal inspection is concerned, but certain companies that have been raised in New York are saints prepared for glory, but the papers do represent them as being made up of quite another class of men, and that they will leave New York wonderfully purified when they go forth to do a patriot's duty in a distant State! But if there should be found in the volunteer force a burglar, a thief, a scoundrel, a culprit, he is not the man to be very dangerous to young men. Do you suppose a virtuous young man is going to learn pocket picking in the camp? Do you suppose a young man is going to learn stealing there? These things do not come by contagion. They are the final

results of insidious causes. They are the desperate ends of fair beginnings. They are the holes through which men go out of our sight into perdition. It is not the endings, but the beginnings, that are to be guarded against.

The men that are dangerous in camps are not bloated drunkards, shameless gamblers, and such as they. But an accomplished officer, a brilliant fellow, who knows the world, who is gentle in language, who understands all the etiquettes of society, who is fearless of God, who believes nothing in religion, who does not hesitate with wit and humor to jeer at sacred things, who takes an infernal pleasure in winding around his finger the young about him, who is polished and wicked, and walks as an angel of light to tempt his fellow-men, as Satan did to tempt our first parents, — if there be in the camp such a one, he is the dangerous man! And the camp is full of such ones. The worst of it is that the young do not suspect them till it is too late to avoid them. There is a sort of dynamic influence that superior natures exert upon inferior ones. It is said that a cat can fascinate a bird, and that a snake fascinates its own victims. There is no doubt that one human being can fascinate another. There is no doubt that one man built in a certain way has almost complete ascendency over another man built in a different way. This fact is fearfully illustrated in the camp by the contamination of the young and inexperienced under the influence of bad men with whom they come in contact.

I shall not mention the petty vices of lawlessness that grow up in war. When men are assaulting an enemy, and overrunning an enemy's territory, when a town having resisted them, they have, by the strength of their right hand, broken through all obstacles, and taken possession of it, they are not apt to be too respectful of the rights of those that are at their mercy. Rapine and thefts and various violence grow up under such circumstances.

I shall mention but one other danger, and that only indirectly has a moral bearing upon this subject, — I mean the danger of neglecting to observe the laws of health. I have been very much affected in seeing how men that are gathered into our regiments live. You and I that live in ceiled houses, and have changes of apparel for all the seasons, — spring, summer, autumn, and winter, — and many of them for each season, can scarcely form a conception of the poverty and destitution of many laboring men, but particularly foreigners, who enlist in the army. When their shoes give out, they have to make a special campaign to get another pair. When their hat gives out, they wear it still. When their coat gives out, they get another if they can. How little these men know of the laws of health! How little they know of the economies of life! Now hurry a thousand, or ten thousand of these men, by land and water away from home, oblige them to be irregular in their habits, give them poor food miserably cooked, let them after a long, fagging day's journey go to camp so tired that they can hardly see, and throw themselves down under the first bush or tree, no matter whether the ground is wet or dry, so that when they wake up they feel as though a ramrod had been run through their arms and their legs, — and is it to be wondered at that multitudes of them sicken and die? The hospitals that receive the sick from armies are a commentary on the knowledge that prevails among men respecting the laws of health. In ninety-nine cases out of a hundred the sickness of camp life is owing to the fact that men do not know how to take care of themselves. Were I a chaplain in the army, while I would preach and distribute books and tracts, and do special ministerial work, I would, in the main, see to it that the health of the soldiers was not neglected. I would explain to them health-laws, and urge them to observe them, and watch over them as tenderly as a mother watches over her child. And to any man that is going as chaplain I would say, Take care of your men's health. For although health is not religion, religion is very much dependent on health. A candle is not a candlestick, but a candle without a candlestick is of little account. If a man is going to keep his soul alight, he must have a good body to hold it in. And one important duty of the sanctuary is to teach the ignorant and unknowing of these matters which are so vital to their prosperity.

Thus much on that side. Allow me a few words now to those who go.

There are going out in all our companies not a few who, thank God, have been religiously trained, and are themselves professors of religion, and yet more who, though they may not be professors of religion, are really moral and virtuous men. I exhort all such that they should see eye to eye; that they should find each other out; that they should band together for the right. Where two men come together on the ground of moral principle, there is a church. Where two men associate themselves together for the purpose of promoting a moral cause, there is a church. An ocean is nothing but an aggregate of drops; and every drop is a factor of that ocean. And large churches are nothing but collections of multitudinous drops. But where there are two men united in a Christian work there is a church; and there ought to be in every regiment and company and platoon a little church. If in any regiment or company or platoon there are two men that are moral and good, they ought to stand out at once and take ground for goodness and morality. It is a shame to see how fearlessly bad men take ground for iniquity, and how shy good men are of avowing religion. There ought to be a bold stand taken in favor of virtue by the good in each one of the various companies. If there is not such a stand taken in Company C of the Fourteenth Regiment, I shall be ashamed of my preaching. We have sent out fifteen or twenty young men that are distributed through the companies of another regiment; but we have sent more in this particular regiment, because they have remained later upon our hands. And I expect that there will be a real moral influence exerted through the regiment by the young men that are in it who have gone out of this church.

There ought to be in the camp a provision made to supply the wants of the men in the intervals of drill and conflict. I have spoken of the temptations of indolence. We shall be utterly delinquent in duty if we make no provision of reading for them. They have nothing to do; their camp-fire is burning; the sun has just sunk below the horizon; they sit in groups here and there; the story-teller is in vogue;

the man that has the most fluent tongue, and that is the most amusing, is the man that is popular,— not the man that retires to his tent, or at a little distance, to commune with God; but the entertaining man, the man that knows how to lessen the tedium of the hour. This gives ascendency to dangerous men. But if every day there was something to read, this evil would be in a great measure overcome. A daily newspaper has become almost as necessary to us at home as our daily food! The want will be felt in camp. We cannot eat our breakfast without a morning paper, nor our supper without an evening paper; and I should not be surprised if before long we should think we could not get our dinner without a noon paper. Of course Bibles and Testaments will go with the men, but there ought to be other reading for them. We have at least two Tract Societies; and it seems to me that, while they send some tracts, and a few books, they could not put the greater proportion of their funds to so good a use as that of subscribing for good sound papers, to be read by the soldiers during leisure hours, or while sitting in the doors of their tents. There is a moral influence in such reading. Not only does it occupy their leisure hours, but it takes them out of the dangers of camp life, and carries them back to their homes, and leads them to think of father and mother, and sisters and brothers, and childhood. It abolishes distance. It annihilates separation. It quickens their memory and awakens their imagination. It prevents them from losing their identity. See that the men have books and papers enough. And if the great publishing houses feel as if it is not in their line to give secular reading-matter, there ought to be organizations formed by which the camp shall be filled with newspapers. The most efficacious secular book that ever was published in America is the newspaper!

In other ways there should be kept alive sympathy between the camp and the community; between the camp and home. Ah! the chaplain may go round and talk to the men as much as he pleases, but I tell you, the things that work most powerfully on them are the thoughts of home and friends that pass through their minds when they sit with their elbows on their knees, and with their eyes shut, and say to themselves, "My mother is singing," or, "My father is praying." Those golden threads that go forth out of the much-weaving mother's heart; those threads of love and domesticity that never break by long stretching, that go around and around the globe itself and yet keep fast hold, — these, after all, are the things that work most powerfully on men!

Now, let them be supplied with tokens, mementos, remembrancers, from those that are left behind. When the soldier looks upon the little things that have been sent him by dear ones at home, he cannot suppress his tears. But do you suppose it is because he has a few luxuries? It is not the things themselves that he cares for. As likely as not he gives these away to his comrades. But loving hearts were prompted to send them to him, and kind hands placed them in the box! They are evidences of affectionate regard cherished for him. All these things work wonders in the camp.

Let us take care of those that go out from among us. It would be a shame if this Christian community, having sent forth young men to fight the battles of the country, should forget them. You have but just begun your duty toward them. The most serious part of that duty is to take care of the camp!

My Christian friends, I have the utmost confidence, I need not tell you, in the American principle of self-government. Anything on God's earth can be done by an intelligent, virtuous, self-governing people; and though monarchies cannot have camps without mischief, the American people can civilize and Christianize the camp. I roll the responsibility of doing this upon our churches. I assume my part of the responsibility. It will be a shame to our civilization and Christianity if we are not able to take these camps in the arms of a sanctifying faith, and lift them above those corrupting tendencies which are inseparable from war. I hope to see those who go from this church come back, not only as good as they go, but better, more manly, more fearless for the right. I do not expect that there will be any castaways among them. I do not believe that one of them will be a deserter from the faith. I feel assured that they will all be more confirmed soldiers of the Lord Jesus Christ, — and they will be better soldiers of him by as much as they are good soldiers of their country.

Now let us acknowledge our obligations in this matter, and take hold of hands and discharge those obligations. While you thank God that he has raised up so many that are willing and eager to defend our country, and although you have contributed liberally of your means to prepare them to go, you must remember that your duty toward them has but just begun to be performed. You must follow them with your prayers, morning, noon, and night. Not only that, you must see that their wants are provided for, and, more than all other things, that their moral wants are provided for. The church and camp must work together in this great emergency.

May God speed them that go forth. Every morning, when I have arisen, for a week or ten days past, I have rushed down expecting to hear the tocsin of the battle. But as some lurid days that have thunders in them will not storm, but hold themselves aloof, and gather copper color in the sky, because the bolt is to fall with more terrific violence; so it seems to me that in the impressive silence which prevails the storm of battle is only collecting, and collecting, because the great conflict is coming erelong like God's thunder-crack! When it does come I have not the least doubt as to where victory will issue; I have not the least doubt as to which side will triumph. I foresee the victory. I rejoice in it, in anticipation; not because it is to be on our side, but because it has pleased God, in his infinite mercy, to make liberty our side; not because we are North and they are South, but because we have civilization and they have barbarism, because we stand on the principle of equity and liberty, and they stand on the principle of slavery and injustice. It will be a moral victory more than a military victory.

May God speed the day, give the victory, crown it with peace, restore unity, and make it more compact and enduring because freed from this contamination, this poison, in our system!

VII.

ENERGY OF ADMINISTRATION DEMANDED.*

"Now Elisha was fallen sick, of his sickness whereof he died. And Joash the king of Israel came down unto him, and wept over his face, and said, O my father, my father! the chariot of Israel, and the horsemen thereof! And Elisha said unto him, Take bow and arrows. And he took unto him bow and arrows. And he said to the king of Israel, Put thine hand upon the bow. And he put his hand upon it; and Elisha put his hands upon the king's hands. And he said, Open the window eastward. And he opened it. Then Elisha said, Shoot. And he shot. And he said, The arrow of the Lord's deliverance, and the arrow of deliverance from Syria: for thou shalt smite the Syrians in Aphek, till thou have consumed them. And he said, Take the arrows. And he took them. And he said unto the king of Israel, Smite upon the ground. And he smote thrice, and stayed. And the man of God was wroth with him, and said, Thou shouldest have smitten five or six times; then hadst thou smitten Syria till thou hadst consumed it: whereas now thou shalt smite Syria but thrice." — 2 Kings xiii. 14 – 19.

T is characteristic of the early and rude state of society, that military matters were conducted much more frequently under the suggestions of prophets and priests than of generals and kings. And in part this arose from the fact that the best heads were usually on the shoulders of prophets, and that they gave the best counsels that were to be had anywhere.

The king visited this dying prophet, and received

* Preached during June, 1861.

from him instruction in respect to the destruction of the Syrians. They were the life-long enemies of the Israelites. Putting his hand on the king's hand, and drawing the bow, and shooting forth the arrow, that the whole imagination and attention might be excited, he said to the king, "Now take the arrows, and smite on the ground." If the king had been enthusiastic in his proper work, if his soul had been in the business, he would have smitten the ground with a witness, and with oft-repeated strokes. And Elisha was wroth. He was a long way ahead of the king; and he said to him, "You are not thorough; your heart is not in this business; you ought to have smitten five or six times." Not that the smiting was anything; but the spirit that made him smite three times when he should have smitten five or six, was a good deal; and he rebuked him, saying, in substance, "Had you been zealous, you should have destroyed your enemies; whereas now you shall gain a short advantage, and they shall live to vex you and torment you."

I entirely understand the hesitation and reluctance which so many experience at the prospects before us. If I could, I certainly would change the condition of things. If it were in my power, I would make every State that is in rebellion return to its allegiance. If I could, I would cause the laws to be respected throughout the whole dominion of this government. If I could, I would settle this great controversy of the age without the shedding of a drop of blood. If I *could?* I cannot; you cannot; nobody can. Yet I quite understand, and in some sense respect, the scruple and the hesitation of many good men on the eve of forthcoming events.

I know how sad, to many persons, must be the foreshadowings of a civil war. If I thought of nothing else, it would be equally so to me. I understand the entire prostration of business, and the commercial distress which is prevalent in every part of our land, and which must continue for months, and perhaps for years. I do not attempt to undervalue the inconvenience, nor to ignore the portents, of the time in which we live. I know what sectional bitterness is liable to spring up as the fruit of civil war; and I quite understand their fears who dread the coming of such bitterness. I understand, too, a good man's love of quiet, the moral repulsiveness to him of violence, and the attractiveness of peace. I understand the weariness which men come at last to have of agitation, and of perpetual and reduplicated excitements.

I understand the ties which connect so many families North and South together, and which will make a rupture terrible. For there are multitudes reluctant from reasons of heart, quite independently of reasonings of intellect. I rejoice at the unanimity of public sentiment which makes the expression of such views rather dangerous. Yet I do not believe in any tyranny which makes free speech dangerous. At any rate, whether on one side or the other, whether for us or against us, it seems to me a great deal better to meet with thorough discussion and satisfying statements these silent scruples, these reluctances, these hesitations of good men, than to put them down by an enforced silence.

Therefore it is to the inward thoughts, to the undisclosed feelings, to that reluctance, moral and social, which men are feeling at the idea of war, that I shall speak to-night, rather than to their ordinary and disclosed speech.

I purpose considering, then, the duty of this land, unitedly, and with the utmost energy and decision, to maintain the government of these United States in its original form, over its whole territory, unchanged in its Constitution, and unimpaired in every respect. That is my position; and I purpose to discuss the reasons why that is the only ground of safety and of duty.

I. It is a duty to maintain the constituted government of these United States. It was organized with as much wisdom as has ever been brought to bear upon any set of civil institutions in the history of the world. Its wisdom has been proved by the results which it has wrought out. For three quarters of a century it has been in operation with a success which has made the world marvel. Under this government has grown up a prosperity, advancing throughout every part of this land, until this nation has become a first-class nation in wealth and civilization. There are men yet living who saw the period of the Revolutionary War, when we were a despised people, scattered in a savage territory, numbering three millions,—not three millions strong, but three millions weak. And yet, within the lifetime of a single man, this nation has, under the benign protection of this government, sprung to a position second to that of no nation on the globe. Nor was there ever a government that, for a period of seventy-five years, or thereabouts, was administered with as much wisdom, and with so many benefits, as that government which now it is sought to overthrow.

A good government is not an accident. It is a growth. It is the laborious result of painful experiences. And when a nation has attained to the blessing of a good government, it is a blessing not to be tampered with, nor lightly changed, nor rudely thrown away. And if there be one duty which God has made obligatory upon this people, and upon us in particular, it is to see to it that this government be not overthrown without cause, and that its career of unrivalled prosperity be not stopped at midway.

II. The maintenance of this government in its original jurisdiction is demanded, not alone because it is so good to us, but because it has such signal relations to the prosperity of the whole world. It was an experiment, — an experiment ridiculed at first, then feared, and now detested, by absolute monarchs. This government was an experiment that caused the first dawn of hope upon the minds of nations struggling in fetters and in bondage; and it has inspired the hope that there was coming a period when the common people, the world around, should be redeemed from thraldom, and when human rights should be respected by governments. Strong governments — that is, governments which are not of the people — have been put on trial for thousands of years, and condemned. If there be anything about which the minds of the common people are united, it is this: that governments which derive their powers, not from the governed, but from the ruling class, are inexpedient and mischievous. In my own opinion, those governments which have derived their powers, not from the governed, but from the governing class, have been ten thousand times more mischievous to the nations than anarchy itself could have been. We have been taught in the church and state to speak of anarchy as the worst of evils; but absolute monarchy may be worse than anarchy. Such governments have stood in the way of religion, of civilization, of industry, of popular development; they have heaped up the road along which men were walking with obstacles, and kept back the world thousands of years. And anarchy would have been a blessing compared with multitudes of them.

Now this government alone has had the opportunity of developing in a practical form that which has been theoretically developed by wise and good men, not a few, in every age. It has demonstrated the heresy of absolute governments, and the orthodoxy of popular governments. The period had come in which men ceased to say that free governments could not stand. Everybody pointed to these United States, and said, "Behold whether they can or cannot!" They waited for our stumbling and downfall for a long time; and now, in the prospect of the dismemberment of this nation, all nations are waiting to see whether that shall come to pass which has been predicted, — whether it is possible for this government to maintain itself. That it can against foreign aggression is conceded; but whether it can against intestine mischiefs is the question. I think it can. I have such faith in true Christian democracy, and in the governments that are derived immediately from the people, and that are kept strong and pure by the infusion of the popular element, that I regard this government not only as abundantly able to cope with foreign aggression, but as able also to take care of the worst mischiefs at home. And if, from a false sense of peace and immediate security, we yield to dismemberment, the whole world that is sitting in judgment upon us will at once say, "Popular governments may do to repel exterior aggression, but they are too weak to resist interior mischiefs, and their period is past."

I anticipate — and that, too, before five or three years have rolled away — that republican institutions will stand in more respect and awe throughout the civilized world than they have ever before done. We are on the eve of developing such victorious power, I believe, that the nations of the earth which now, on the one side, are beginning to fear, or, on the other, are beginning to rejoice over our downfall, are soon to see a spectacle of surprising triumph.

III. The maintenance of this government over all its original territory is demanded, because the permission of a rebellion such as that now existing undermines not only this government, but all government. The rebellion which we are appointed to quell has disdained to take one step according to law and according to constitutional agreement. It is not revolution, even, in any proper and dignified sense of the term. Had the measure of territorial division been ever so wise, the method by which it has been sought is anarchical, and will put back our government a hundred years if it be permitted. We, above all people on earth, are so free that we cannot afford to have laws and institutions trodden under foot. Nowhere else is disrespect of constituted forms so dangerous as among a people that are so high-spirited, so potent, and so full of resources as this people are. In monarchies, if anywhere, neglect of laws and constitutions can be afforded. If anywhere, in republican governments must a mark be made, and a signal example be set, upon all attempts to do things otherwise than according to law and according to constitution.

The treading under foot of every decency and of all popular rights has been consistent throughout on the part of those that are in armed rebellion against this government. Free speech has been permitted nowhere, freedom of the vote has been overruled everywhere, political management, eventuating in military despotism, has been carried from bad to worse, in all the steps taken for the overthrow of this government. Rebel politicians have despised not the National Government alone, but State governments as well. They have set aside not alone the General Government, but all government, of every kind. And we are called upon to maintain, not only the sacredness of this government, but the sacredness of the principle of governing.

IV. The maintenance of this government, in its entire jurisdiction, and in its original form, is necessary for the final settlement of the authority, dignity, and power of the nation over the separate and constituent elements of it. This Nation is greater than the States that compose it. Republicanism is not on trial. It is the principle of federation. It is the grand and final conflict of jurisdiction, State and National. It is a strife between local and general sovereignty. By our Constitution, States are shorn of absolute sovereignty, and are limited in jurisdiction to their own local interests. Beyond that, in the sphere of interests common to all, the authority of All, represented by the Federal Government, takes precedence, and is sovereign, and forms the only absolute sovereignty known to our system of government.

There is at present, in nearly one half of this nation, an almost entire want of national feeling. There is State feeling, and there is sectional feeling, but no national feeling, in the Southern portion of this country; nor has there been. And it is one of the objects to be secured by the present great uprising of the public mind, to set up and to maintain the dignity of national government, in distinction from local government. This land is but just beginning to be settled. Our nation is yet in the gristle. This people is scarcely more than the leaven of the people that is to fill this continent. The imagination fails in every endeavor to conceive of the grandeur of that national form which awaits us, if we resist steadfastly, year by year, every attempt at dismemberment. If we maintain, in the sphere in which our fathers placed it, the General Government, then the lower and the subordinate jurisdictions will themselves be empowered, and, from ocean to ocean, and from the Lakes to the Gulf, there will rise a fabric of wealth and greatness more noble and sublime than it hath entered the hearts of men to conceive.

V. This government should be maintained in its original territory and jurisdiction, as the only wise method of maintaining peace and prosperity among the people of this continent. It is often said by mild and good men, "Is not this territory large enough for two nations?" No, it is not. There is not room for two nations between the Lakes and the Gulf in this land. There is not room between the Atlantic and Pacific Oceans for two national governments. It is said, "Why not let the South go, if they do not wish to stay with us?" Is this nation a boarding-house, from which any dissatisfied boarder can go at his option? Is there no sanctity of the national government? Do the States owe no duties and obligations to the national government? Is there no national law? Is there no right in this matter?

But even considering it as a mere question of peace, — if you want to walk into the very red-hot gates of war, make peace by dismemberment! If you want to make war chronic and eternal, if you want to make dividing lines blaze with perpetual conflicts, then make peace now by dismemberment! And if you want peace permanent and perpetual, see to it that you fight this battle out thoroughly! The road to peace will lead to war, and the road to war will bring peace!

This plea for peace addresses always a thousand better feelings in the breasts of tens of thousands of good men. It is very insidious. It is in accordance with all our religious teachings and with all our more amiable feelings. It is so sweet to say, "Why should we go to war with our brethren? Why should we not have peace? How much better it is to have prosperity in the shop, prosperity in the ship, prosperity in the field, and prosperity all through the land! O, why should we not get back to the good old days of peace and prosperity?" If you could get back to the good old days of peace and prosperity, it would be all very well; but you cannot get back. There is a stream of nations that is deeper and stronger than the Gulf Stream of the Atlantic Ocean. There is a providence of God that is being wrought out in the events of the present. And I defy you to get back to peace and prosperity except in the line of that providence. If you take that which you think will bring peace, you will find it, instead of being an instrument of peace, to be an egg of war; and it will hatch cockatrices in your hand and in your nest!

There cannot be erected one nation on the North, and another on the South, and have the trouble stop with their establishment. Remember that the men whose passions and whose interests make all the disturbance of the present among us would not be got rid of by a division of this land into two governments. They would still live who have turmoiled us and vexed us. Not only would their ambition be as fierce as now, but success would make it still more imperious. If peace meant the obscuration of bad men in the South, there would be some reason for aspiring to it; but peace will not rid us of them. If we compromise this matter, and let them go, while we remain north of Mason and Dixon's line, the very men who have fomented trouble for fifteen or twenty years in this land would live with more power and more audacity; and they would be more capable of evil than ever before, because they would be organized, and would do under form of legitimate law and government what now they are obliged to do in rebellion.

Nor is that all. Those very elements of discord which have embroiled this nation would exist just as much if there were two, as they would if there was only one government; and they would act with double force. Slavery would still impoverish the South, and the prosperity of free industry would present a baleful contrast to the results of servile institutions. Slavery would still breed men imperious, domineering, and aggressive, who would demand of a neighboring nation more than is now demanded by the South of neighboring States. By dividing the country you would take away that comity and interchange of rights which exists between States under one Constitution. That which makes the South restless and discontented is, that it has disease in its bowels. And that disease will not be cured by separation. It will still be there. The pains of the Southern people, their pangs, their cravings, their wants, are constitutional and organic; and if you separate yourselves from them, you will grow rich and they poor. Will they like poverty any better because they are a separate nation? If you do their trading, they will still say that you get rich by cheating them.

Their slaves will not be any more contented or industrious or profitable. Riches are said to make to themselves wings and fly away; and, changing the figure, such riches as these make to themselves feet and run away! They will be as peripatetic then as now. And you will be less inclined to return them, while their owners will be more angry if you do not. The causes of jangling will be greatly increased. The edges of the two nations will be like the edges of two saws, and there will be a perpetual tearing and gashing of each other. Do you not know what frets there always are on the borders of two nations that are at variance with each other? Do you not know how many living lines of painful light shoot back into the body politic under such circumstances? And if you bring together the edges of two governments made from this nation, do you suppose the seam will be a seam of peace? It will be like the coming together of two opposing rivers, that chafe and cast up their foamy waves upon each other. You will not get peace by separation.

Nor is that all. Separation would not stop with the North and South. There would be in the end, under the precedent established by the division of this country into two governments, other divisions. Ambitious men would seek perpetually to institute new governments; for every new government involves the necessity of more offices, and gives a chance for more ambitious men; and if you should consent to separation, you would put a premium upon baleful ambition. The result would be the Pacific government, the Atlantic government, one or more grand Middle governments, and the Southern government. You would bring Central Europe into the midst of this nation.

Now consider whether a Northern, a Southern, a Middle, and a Western government would make for peace,—for this is the question that I am arguing; whether the recognition or permission of this rebellion, and the allowing it to solidify into a separate government, would bring you peace. It would result in the institution of many governments. What has been the effect of dividing Europe into ten or fifteen governments? Every single nation is obliged to watch and be watched. Every frontier of each one is lined with fortified cities and forts. Every nation is obliged to support a standing army. Look at France, with her half a million of paid men; look at Prussia, with her hundreds of thousands of paid men;

look at Austria, broken down by the waste of the ulcer of an army; look at Italy, that is obliged to expend her nascent energy in the maintenance of a gigantic standing army. Were this nation to be divided, the South would support its hundred and fifty thousand men, the North would support its two hundred and fifty thousand men, and the great Middle government would support its three hundred thousand men, as standing armies. If this country should be divided into five separate national governments, they would require a million men for their standing armies, in order to maintain their respective rights.

What has been the history of armies in this country? Twenty-five thousand troops — ridiculous handful! — have answered, for the last fifty years, the national exigencies of these United States of America. Split this continent into different nations, and a million men would not be enough to protect them in their rights.

Many men say, "O this war, this fighting of brethren, is terrible! Why not let the South go, and bring peace?" As if that would bring peace! As if that were not the way to touch the earth and bring armed men from every league of the soil! I tell you, separation is preparation for endless standing armies and future wars; and if you want peace, you must fight!

There is one other consideration in respect to this question of peace. If we were to recognize the Confederate States as a separate nation, we should speedily bring upon ourselves that evil which, from the earliest days of this government, our wisest men have feared, — the intrusion of European politics. The design of the South is no longer disguised. They mean, as soon as they shall have established themselves as a separate nation, to thrust out their hands westward, and clutch more territory, and erect in Central America a vast slaveholding empire. Now the Spanish, the French, and the English governments have interests involved in such movements, and in the event of the success of the South they would have a right, as they would have a purpose, to interfere. And as soon as they had a right to put their foot on this continent, and to make our interior affairs a part of their affairs, they would never lack an excuse for maintaining this right. Thus far, what has been called "the Monroe Doctrine" has been maintained in this land; but separate the North and the South, and let the South carry out its schemes of aggression, and the right of intrusion by European monarchies is established beyond peradventure. And with so fair a field as this continent partly within their grasp, they will not easily abandon their advantages.

VI. This government should be maintained in this whole land in its original integrity, because, in God's providence, it seems destined to have a great influence upon that greatest national calamity and sin, slavery. This government has no right directly to interfere with the institution of slavery; nor do I know of any man, called to exercise the functions of the government, who believes it expedient to do so. For myself, I have not hesitated to avow that we have no right politically, or by the hand of government, in time of peace, to interfere with the institution of slavery in any State where it exists by the laws of that State. We not only have no right, but we have no disposition to do it. But that is not saying that we have no right morally to influence the minds of men. It is not tantamount to saying that a government based on a free constitution will not have an indirect tendency to liberty, and gradually modify, and finally destroy slavery. For a government administered in the spirit of a free constitution is like a law of nature that acts silently through long periods, and that, though not decisive at any single period, is in the end very effective. This is the secret reason now avowed of the rebellion that exists in this land. It is said by the South that slavery cannot flourish in these United States as they at present exist. But for that very reason let us hold to the Constitution most rigidly. While in its infancy this nation has been unable to resist the institution of slavery, it has done much to influence it. And the time has come when it will exert, not only a legitimate, but a designed influence upon it. The Constitution, when our fathers formed it, was not meant to be an instrument for the perpetuation of slavery. What are called the compromises of it were never intended to ratify slavery. They were merely expedients to maintain unity and peace until other elements of popular sentiment and laws and institutions should work a legitimate and gradual end of slavery. It was then understood that our Constitution was to be single in object; not with a hidden danger, a contrariety of institution, within it. At last we have come to that period when the original intent of that instrument will be carried out, and when it is felt against slavery and for freedom. And that is the secret reason of the rebellion of the South. Politicians saw that under the Constitution slavery must decrease, and liberty must increase. We see it, too; and therefore we say that we have a right, according to the original compact, according to the spirit of the Constitution, in the most legal and equitable manner, to abate now, and finally to do away, that curse and pest, slavery.

While speaking of slavery, let me interject a remark or two. I cannot but think that the progress of this war is to have, in the providence of God, a most remarkable influence upon the existence of this institution. The subject is so vast, it is so intricate, and there are so many contingencies connected with it, that it is hazardous to make prophecies respecting it; but one thing is apparent: that you cannot march columns of freemen straight through these rebellious States on a mission of liberty, and for the maintenance of a free Constitution, and leave no trace behind. I do not believe in marching an army through the South to set the slaves free, unless it is required as a war measure. I do not believe in the doctrine of insurrections, either for the whites or the blacks. I do not believe we are called to any such work as that of inciting insurrections among the slaves. It would ruin the cause of the slave. Not until we are prepared to defend him by the whole power of the government should he be encouraged to free himself. But, on the other hand, Southern men, having the institution of slavery in their midst, have been foolish enough to provoke a conflict in which we are bound, by justice, by law, by oath, by everything that we hold sacred, to maintain the government of this land; and it is impossible for us to do that without producing, whether we mean it or not, a prodigious influence upon the tenure of property in man. When this war ceases, the foundations of slavery will be much weakened, if not undermined. Not because we go to work on purpose to destroy it, but because we cannot maintain the Constitution and the government, and not weaken or undermine it.

Suppose slavery should come peremptorily to an end, do you suppose murder and riot and bloodshed would take place in the South? What! do you say that men who do not murder now that they are in bondage and oppression, would murder if they were set free and had their rights given to them? Is it sound reasoning to say that men who, when you goad them with aggravating injuries, do not murder, would become angry when the wrongs are righted, and revenge themselves upon their benefactors? Will kindness and justice make men do worse things than cruelty and injustice? Freedom is safer, ten thousand times, for white and black, than oppression.

But it is supposed that, if the slaves were to be suddenly emancipated, a black deluge would pour into our Free States, and come in competition with our laborers. No. The climate is against it. Besides, once let there be emancipation and free labor at the South, and there would not be laborers enough for the quickened industry that would follow. The Southern States would demand all the free colored men at the North. Nothing would empty Canada, New England, and the Middle States of colored people so quick as having free colored labor normal and universal in the South. The warm latitudes are the natural home of the Africans. They flourish there, and nowhere else. In cold latitudes consumption and other diseases carry them off. Natural laws are against them here. But in the South they thrive wonderfully. Let labor be free on the plantation, and the proprietor would derive more advantage from his workmen. If emancipation should take place, instead of the North being overwhelmed by hordes of colored people, the North would have fewer; and the South would require more, because a system of free labor requires more hands than servile labor.

I need not protract these remarks to a greater length. Whatever view you please to take, our duty and our interest are the same. Since, in the providence of God, without fault of our own, and without our wish, the wrath of man has been permitted to bring to pass this issue and this war, our duty is, first, to meet manfully the issue, and, second, to strike, not *three* times, but *seven.* Cut short this work in righteousness. There can be no policy so disastrous, it seems to me, as one of temporizing, tantalizing warfare. The hearts of the people are united. The prostration of industry has given the masses nothing to do. We have the men, the means, and the disposition. We have the right hand of empire on our side. The power of God rests upon the feelings of our people. There is a sacred enthusiasm pervading the whole North. And now, when the fire of patriotism is burning at its full height, is the time to manifest the might of this government, and crush out the rebellion that threatens our very existence as a free people.

My friends, we stand just on the edge of a conflict. It is a new thing for us; but I know not why we should not have an occasional experience of this kind.

What nation on the globe has been as exempt as we from civil war? Since England had a history, how many, many times has she been deluged, in all her fields, with civil war. And is there a nation known that is more harmonious within than England? England and Ireland are not very consonant, but they never had very much fighting together. There is too much water between them. But England and Scotland were always fighting each other; and they are now joined firmer than two hands clasped. You cannot make civil war between them. And do you say that, if there is war in this country, there must be everlasting dissensions between the North and the South? How many times has France been against France; and when was France more united than now? How many hundreds of times has Italy been against Italy? How many times have misguided, ambitious men risen up to subvert her interests? How many times have her separate States been arrayed against each other in war? And now Italy has asserted her power, and there is but one glorious opinion, and her people love as if the sword of brother had never struck brother within her borders. It is a sad thing to have civil war; but let no man say that there can be no peace nor harmony between the two sections of this country after they have been engaged in bloody conflict. Every nation in the world gives the lie to the assertion. There is not a people on the earth that has not had internal conflicts, and that has not been as harmonious after them as though they had never taken place.

And when these evils which are the cause of the mischiefs which we are experiencing, when this poison of death which exists in our national system shall have been done away, I think there will be nothing more to breed civil wars among us; and this great nation will move forward in an era of peace.

Let us do the work of to-day, and leave the morrow to God. Let us do that which ought to be done, and God will take care of the consequences.

VIII.

MODES AND DUTIES OF EMANCIPATION.*

"And after a time he returned to take her, and he turned aside to see the carcass of the lion; and, behold, there was a swarm of bees and honey in the carcass of the lion." — Judges xiv. 8.

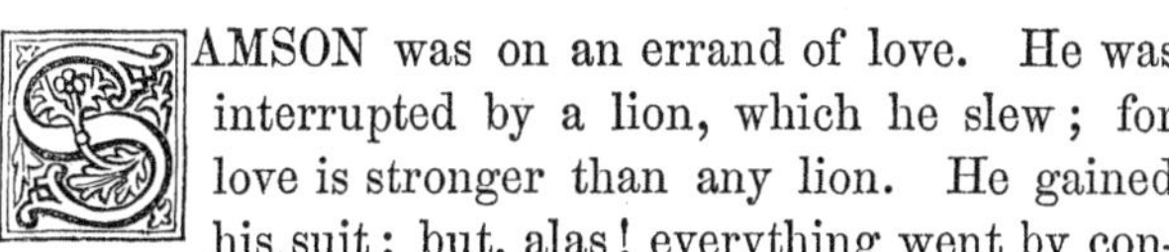

SAMSON was on an errand of love. He was interrupted by a lion, which he slew; for love is stronger than any lion. He gained his suit; but, alas! everything went by contraries thereafter. The woman whose love was at first sweeter to him than honey, betrayed him. She was his lion. Whereas, on his way to her he found that bees had possession of the real lion's carcass, and had filled it with honey. And so, in the end, the lion was better to him than his wife.

But how full of suggestions is this incident. Who would have looked for honey behind a lion's paws? While he was yet roaring and striking at Samson, there seemed very little likelihood of his finding a honeyed meal in him. But if lions bravely slain yield such food, let them become emblems! The bee signifies industry, among all nations; and honey is the very ideal of sweetness.

* Thanksgiving Day, November 26, 1861.

To-day war is upon us. A lion is on our path. But, being bravely met, in its track shall industry settle, and we shall yet fetch honey from the carcass of war. You will not object, then, if, to-day, I bring you honey from this lion's body.

At first, and to unhopeful souls, it would seem as if no day of Thanksgiving ever were so sadly planted. Nor will I undertake to persuade you that there are no evils to bemoan: there are many. But the evils are transient, superficial, and vincible; the benefits are permanent, radical, and multiplying.

Not long ago we were a united nation. Our industry was bringing in riches as the tides of the ocean; and no man could imagine the manhood of a continent whose youth was so august.

Now, a line of fire runs through from east to west, and more than half a million men confront each other with hostile arms. Villages are burned; farms are deserted; neighbors are at bloody variance; industry stands still through fifteen States, or only forges implements of war. The sky at night is red with camp-fires; by day the ground trembles with the tramp of armies. Yet, amid many great and undeniable evils, which every Christian patriot must bitterly lament, there are eminent reasons for thankfulness, several of which I shall point out to you.

I. Since we must accept this war, with all its undeniable evils, it is a matter for thanksgiving that the citizens and their lawful government of these United States can appeal to the Judge of the universe and to all right-minded men, to bear witness that it is not a war waged in the interest of any base passion, but, truly and religiously, in the defence of the highest interests ever committed to national keeping. It is not, on our side, a war of passion; nor of avarice; nor of anger; nor of revenge; nor of fear and jealousy.

We hold that the territory of these United States is common to all its inhabitants; and is, not simply a possession, but a trust. Unless by the deliberate decision of the lawfully assembled people of these United States, constitutionally expressed, that territory may neither be abandoned, alienated, nor partitioned. We hold it in trust for the Future. Is it the duty of New York to defend its territory against foes without, and evil men within, from the Lake to Montauk Point? Is it the duty of each New England State to defend every foot within its jurisdiction? In like manner, and for the same reasons, but in greater force, it is the duty of all the States collectively to maintain the integrity of the national domain. It is not a question of whether we will or will not. By the appointed and appropriate methods of the Constitution that question has been taken from our hands. It is not subject to our volition. But we are bound, by that silent oath which every man assumes who comes to years of maturity as a citizen, to maintain inviolate the territory of these United States.

It is the duty of the citizens, also, to stand up for their government; to protect its just authority; to maintain all its attributes; and to see to it that its jurisdiction is not restricted except by those methods which have been predetermined and agreed upon in that Constitution on which it stands.

But in our particular case, the reasons for maintaining the government in all its ample jurisdiction are intensified beyond all measuring by the fact that the dangers which are threatening it arise, confessedly and undeniably, *not* from a perversion of the principles of our Constitution in our hands, nor from an oppressive administration of our government under these principles, but because a large body of men, gradually infected with new political doctrines, in their nature irreconcilable with the *root principle* of our government, have determined to overthrow it, that they may change its fundamental principles. We are not left to infer this. There is this merit in Southern politicians, that they are frank and open in the declaration of their political doctrines. The best head among them is that of Mr. Stephens; and he declares in the most unequivocal manner that the object of this rebellion is to introduce new principles in government. I shall read from him.

"The new Constitution has put at rest *forever* all the agitating questions relating to our peculiar institutions, — African slavery as it exists among us, — the proper status of the negro in our form of civilization."

We shall see whether it has put them at rest "forever" or not.

"*This was the immediate cause of the late rupture and present revolution.* JEFFERSON, in his forecast, had anticipated this, as the 'rock upon which the old Union would split.' He was right. What was conjecture with him, is now a realized fact. But whether he fully comprehended the great truth upon which that rock *stood* and *stands*, may be doubted. *The prevailing ideas entertained by him, and most of the leading statesmen at the time of the formation of the old Constitution, were, that the enslavement of the African was in violation of the laws of nature; that it was wrong in principle, socially, morally, and politically.*"

I thank him for that testimony.

"It was an evil they knew not well how to deal with; but the general opinion of the men of that day was, that, somehow or other, in the order of Providence, the institution would be evanescent and pass away. This idea, though not incorporated in the Constitution, was the prevailing idea at the time."

This, you understand, is from the Vice-President of the Southern Confederacy, Alexander H. Stephens.

"The Constitution, it is true, secured every essential guaranty to the institution while it should last, and hence no argument can be justly used against the constitutional guaranties thus secured, because of the common sentiment of the day. *Those ideas, however, were fundamentally wrong. They rested upon the assumption of the equality of races. This was an error.* It was a sandy foundation, and the idea of a government built upon it, — when the 'storm came and the wind blew, it fell.' *Our new government is founded upon exactly the opposite ideas.*"

I thank him for his candor.

"*Its foundations are laid, its corner-stone rests, upon the great truth that the negro is not equal to the white man; that slavery, subordination to the superior race, is his natural and normal condition.*"

What a corner-stone that is for a government!

"*This, our new government, is the first in the history of the world based upon this great physical, philosophical, and moral truth.*"

And I will take the leave so far to interpolate his speech as to say that it will be the last! Further on he says (it is such excellent reading that I cannot deny myself the pleasure of edifying you): —

"May we not therefore look with confidence to the ultimate universal acknowledgment of the truths upon which our system rests? It is the first government ever instituted upon principles in strict conformity to nature, and the ordination of Providence, in furnishing the materials of human society. Many governments have been founded upon the principles of certain classes; but the classes thus enslaved were of the same race, and in violation of the laws of nature. Our system commits no such violation of nature's laws. The negro by nature, or by the curse against Canaan, is fitted for that condition which he occupies in our system. The architect, in the construction of buildings, lays the foundation with the proper material, — the granite, — then comes the brick or the marble. The substratum of our society is made of the material fitted by nature for it, and by experience we know that it is the best, not only for the superior, but for the inferior race, that it should be so. It is, indeed, in conformity with the Creator. *It is not for us to inquire into the wisdom of his ordinances, or to question them.* For his own purposes he has made one race to differ from another, as he has made 'one star to differ from another in glory.' The great objects of humanity are best attained when conformed to his laws and decrees, in the formation of governments as well as in all things else. Our Confederacy is founded upon principles in strict conformity with these laws. This stone which was rejected by the first builders '*is become the chief stone of the corner*' in our new edifice."

These words, you will remember, were spoken of the Lord Jesus Christ, when he was set at naught and rejected by the Jews, his countrymen; and this Vice-President of the so-called Confederate States of America does not hesitate to declare that slavery stands, in their new system, in the place that the Lord Jesus Christ holds in the Christian system! It is the soul and centre of it. It is the foundation and corner-stone.

Dr. Smyth of South Carolina says: —

"What is the difficulty, and what the remedy? Not in the election of Republican Presidents. No. Not in the non-execution of the Fugitive Bill. No. But it lies back of all these. It is found in that *Atheistic Red Republican doctrine of the Declaration of Independence! Until that is trampled under foot, there can be no peace.*"

Until either that or its antagonist is trampled under foot, truly there can be no peace! Which is to go under time will show.

This is, then, mark you, a rebellion, not against an oppressive administration, but against the fundamental right of liberty in every man who has not forfeited it by crime. And it is declared, without equivocation or disguise, that the rebellion and the war are brought upon us because our Constitution contains and our government will enforce great principles of equity. The people of this nation are aroused to defend their Constitution and their government, not simply because they are assailed; but — as if Providence meant to make this conflict illustrious in the annals of the world — because they are assailed in those very respects in which they embody the latest fruits of Christianity and the latest attainments of modern civilization. The very things that belong to our age, in distinction from every age before it, are the things that are singled out and made the objects of attack. We would defend our Constitution at any rate; but when it is charged with the noblest principles as if they were crimes, it appeals for its defence to every conscience and to every heart in this land with a solemnity as of the day of judgment.

We are contending, not for that part of the Constitution which came in any way from Roman law, and expressed justice as it had been developed in the iron-hearted realm; but for that part which Christianity gave us, and which has been working forth into laws and customs for eighteen hundred years. The principle now in conflict is that very one which gives unity to history: it is that golden thread that leads us through the dark maze of nearly two thousand years, and connects us with the immortal Head of the Church, — the principle of man's rights based upon the divinity of his origin. Man from God, God a Father, and the race brothers, all alike standing on one great platform of justice and love, — the principle herein expressed has been the foundation of the struggle of eighteen hundred years; and it has been embodied (thanks to Puritan influence) in our Constitution. And this the exponent of Southern views plainly declares to be the point of offence in our government. He says, in unmeasured terms, and with impious boldness, that it is to put down that principle that the South are up in arms to-day.

Is it no cause for thanksgiving, then, that since we must war, God has called us to battle on ground so high, for ends so noble, in a cause so pure, and for results so universal? For this is not a battle for ourselves alone. Every great deed nobly done is done for all mankind. A battle on the Potomac for our Constitution, as a document of liberty, is the world's battle. We are fighting, not merely for our liberty, but for those ideas that are the seeds and strength of liberty throughout the earth. There is not a man that feels the chain, there is not a man whose neck is stiff under the yoke, whether that man be serf, yeoman, or slave, who has not an interest in the conflict that we are set, in the providence of God, to wage against this monstrous doctrine of iniquity. There is honey in that lion!

II. It is matter of thanksgiving that we have not sought this war, but, by a long and magnanimous course, have endured shame, and political loss, and disturbance the most serious, rather than peril the Union. Indeed, I am bound to say, that so strong was the national feeling with us, and so weak with

Southern men, that we made an idol of that which they trod under foot with contempt; and like idolaters we threw ourselves down at the expense of our very self-respect before our idol of the Union. I do not mean that it would have been wrong to have taken the initiative in a cause so sacred as that which impels this conflict; but if, where the end is right and the cause is sacred, it can also be shown that there has been patience, honest and long-continued effort to preserve the right by peaceful methods, — by reasoning and by moral appeal, — and that that most desperate of all remedies, war, has been forced upon us (not sought, nor wished, but accepted reluctantly) by the overt act of the rebellious States, then this patience and forbearance will give an added lustre to our cause.

I make these remarks out of respect to the Christian Public Sentiment of Nations. Contiguity is raising up a new element of power on the globe; and we do not hesitate to pay a just respect to the opinions and expectations which Christian men and philanthropists of other lands have entertained. We stand up boldly before the earnest peace men, the kind advisers, the yearning mediators, yea, and before the body of Christ, — his Church on earth, — and declare that this war, which we could not avert without giving up all that Christian civilization has set us to guard and transmit, cannot be abandoned without betraying every principle of justice, rectitude, and liberty. We do not fear search and trial before the tribunal of the Christian world! In the end, those who should have given sympathy, but have given, instead, chilling advice and ignorant rebuke, shall confess their mistake, and own our fealty to God, to government, and to mankind. When it would have swelled our sails, there was no breath of applause or sympathy. When the gale is no longer needed, and our victorious voyage is ended, we shall have incense and admiration enough! But, meanwhile, God has called us to war upon a plane higher than feet ever trod before. Though we did not seek it, but prayed against it, and with long endurance sought to avoid and avert it, and reluctantly accepted it; now that it has come, it is infinite satisfaction to know that we can stand acquitted before the Christianity of the globe in such a conflict as this. There is honey in that lion!

III. It is a matter of thanksgiving that this war promises to solve those difficult problems which have baffled the wisdom of our wisest counsellors.

There stands in the Vatican at Rome a marble prophecy of America, — a noble and heroic man, on either side a lovely son, but all, father and sons, grasped in the coils of a many-times-enfolding serpent, whose tightening hold not their utmost strength can resist; and, with agonizing face, Laocoön looks up, as if his anguish said, "Only the gods can save, whose hate we have offended!"

So sat America. Around this government, and around the clustered States, twined the gigantic serpent of slavery. But here let the emblem stop. Let us hope another history than that of the fabled Greek.

Secret and open reasons many have made slavery a matter most unmanageable in our national councils. Had it been desired to test to the uttermost the power of republican institutions to sustain good government, no other conceivable trial can be imagined that would do it as this has done, and as it will do it. It gathered up into its coils almost every one of those unmanageable elements, each one of which, alone, in other lands is counted a match for human wisdom. An inferior race, separated from us by physiological badges the most marked, and upon whom rested the added stigma of servitude; a people who coming from a tropical land brought in the element of climate; whose existence, in the relations of society and government, fed every one of the fiercer passions, touched but few of the moral sentiments, and these feebly, and educated men to idleness, avarice, lust, and pride of dominion, — these poor African bondmen, in all their helplessness and weakness, were yet able to plunge this nation into troubles and difficulties, of caste, of race, of condition, of climate, and of ambitious wealth, which the strongest and the wisest knew not how to heal or to endure. War seems likely to clear up the questions that Politics could not manage.

By our organic law we were forbidden to meddle with local institutions, though they were injecting the national veins with poison. Though we saw that from these local institutions general and national influences were going forth, yet our organic principle of government would not permit us to lay our hand upon them. Neither could we bring to bear, for their suppression, in any ample degree, the moral forces by which other evils were met. No public sentiment in the North could make itself felt upon slavery: partly because no public sentiment can ever be transported from one section to another, — for ideas may travel, but influences must be developed among the people on whom they are to act, — and partly because of the ignorance that prevailed, and must always prevail, among the common people where slave institutions exist. There was also a sectional pride, a sensitive jealousy, that must have prevented access to the South of any moral influence, unless it had been high, pure, and commanding. But the North had no such moral sentiment. The antislavery feeling of the North has always lacked unity. The whole North, by the insidious influences of commerce, of politics, and of sectarian religion, has been divided into three principal sections: the lowest, composed of those that were either indifferent to slavery or who favored it; the next, and most numerous, composed of those who, believing it to be an evil, deemed themselves bound by political considerations, and by commercial interests, to forbear meddling with it; and the last, composed of the antislavery men of the North. These have been so divided among themselves, and so intolerant of each other's doctrines, that they may be said to have expended as much strength against each other as they have unitedly exerted against slavery itself. What public sentiment could be hoped from such a condition of the community, that would have authority, or even influence, in the South?

And so we were drifting every year; the North, partly from the force of moral considerations, but even more from the amazing folly and arrogance of Southern political management, growing more and more consolidated for liberty; and the South, changing all its original political doctrines, and carrying down, with fatal gravitation, the conscience of the

Church and the convictions of a feeble ministry, was becoming every year more determined for slavery. Thus each was having less and less influence with the other.

It has pleased God, by the very infatuation of this gigantic evil, rudely to dash these two sections together. That out of this conflict liberty will come triumphant we do not for one moment doubt. That we see the beginning of national emancipation we firmly believe. And we would have you firmly to believe it, lest, fearing the loss of such an opportunity, you should over-eagerly grasp at accidental advantages, and seek to press forward the consummation by methods and measures which, freeing you from one evil, shall open the door for innumerable others, and fill our future with conflicts and immedicable trouble.

Good men in Great Britain expect us to make a Decree of Universal Emancipation. Had England, either by her government, or by the unmistakable language of the Christian public, given the South to understand that there could be no possible sympathy or help for them from slave-hating England in their nefarious rebellion, we do not believe that this conspiracy against human rights would ever have taken its present terrible proportions. Whether England meant it or not, she has influenced the South powerfully in its attack against the Federal Government, and in its determination to establish republican institutions upon the principle of slavery. And this misfortune is not remedied by the condition upon which good men in England have been pleased to promise their sympathy, — namely, that our government, assuming and usurping the proper power of the States, should pronounce a decree of universal emancipation, and convert this struggle into a war only for liberty to the African. It was not by England's sympathy that we became independent; it was not by her advice that we have grown to be her equal among the nations of the world; and we shall be able to settle our present troubles without her sympathy or succor. I am not so ungenerous as to cherish unkind feelings against the stock from which I am proud to have come. I am not surprised that the English nation, seldom able to understand foreign ideas and institutions, should be ignorant of the structure and nature of our government. We have been prepared, unfortunately, for such a course by her past conduct. The *literature* of England has been a fountain of liberty to Europe and the world; but the *government* of England, more than any other on the globe, has frowned upon nations struggling for liberty, and subsidized the despots that were seeking to crush them. It is a matter of thanksgiving to God, that we are not placed in a condition where our success depends upon her succor. Let England abide at home and twirl her million spindles, and web the globe with her fabrics. She will not be a helper, but she *shall* be a spectator. In the quick-coming end, when all our troubles are settled, she will not then ungenerously withhold from us her admiration. When by actions and results we have proved ourselves worthy of those doctrines of human rights which God has intrusted to our advocacy and defence, in common with her, she shall give us, not, as now, ignorant advice, but, though late, a full measure of praise. Meanwhile, we shall trust in God and do without England.

It cannot be denied that this recommendation of immediate universal emancipation falls in with the Northern popular impulse. The evils of slavery have augmented to such a degree, the perils which it brings around our government have been now so strikingly revealed, that it is not surprising that men should desire at one blow to end the matter. If the Constitution of these United States, fairly interpreted, gives us the power to bring slavery to an end, God forbid that we should neglect such an opportunity for its exercise. But if that power is withheld, or can be exercised only with the most doubtful construction, — by a construction which shall not only weaken that instrument, but essentially change its nature, withdrawing from the States local sovereignty, and conferring upon Congress those rights of government which have thus been withdrawn from States, — then will not only slavery be destroyed, but with it our very government. How far our government, by a just use of its legitimate powers under the Constitution, can avail itself of this war to limit or even to bring slavery to an end, is matter for the wisest deliberation of the wisest men. If there be in the hand of the war-power, as John Quincy Adams thought there was, a right of emancipation, then let that be shown, and, in God's name, be employed. But if there be given to us no right by our Constitution to enter upon the States with a legislation subversive of their whole interior economy, not all the mischiefs of slavery, and certainly not our own impatience under its burdens and vexations, should tempt us to usurp it. This conflict must be carried on *through* our institutions, not over them. Revolution is not the remedy for rebellion. The exercise on the part of our government of unlawful powers cannot be justified, except to save the nation from absolute destruction.

The South, like an immense field of nettles, has been overrun with the pestilent heresies of State rights. Because our hands are stinging with these poisonous weeds, we shall be tempted inconsiderately to go to the opposite extreme, and to gather up the diffused powers of the State and consolidate and centralize them in the National Government. We must not forget that, while a government of confederated States sprang up, as it were, accidentally, it was yet one of those divine accidents which revealed the strongest form of government yet known to the world. No central government can ever take the place of State governments. No central heart could ever drive life-blood to the extremities of this vast empire. If all the myriad necessities and ever-growing interests of this continent are to be cared for; if the extremest State along the Russian frontier of the Northwest, or the southernmost one that neighbors Mexico, or the lacustrine States of the North, are all equally and alike to experience the benefits of good government, it must be by maintaining unimpaired in all its beneficence the American doctrine of the sovereignty of local government, except in those elements which have been clearly and undeniably transferred to the Federal Government.

Slavery is our present evil and danger, but it is not the only danger; and we firmly believe that it has passed its crisis, and is running to its end. We are not to forget that Future which rises before the prophetic vision, with promises of millennial glory.

And yet every promise has its shadow. With every benefit there is a corresponding danger. When slavery shall have wasted away, we shall not then be a nation without dangers. Foes lie concealed from us, but ready to spring from unsuspected ambush. The human heart is the great human enemy. Lawless passions are the State's perpetual danger. Destroy slavery, and you have not destroyed depravity. What is slavery but one way in which lust and avarice and ambition and indolence have sought to enthrone themselves? Destroy this throne, and will you have destroyed the occupants? In the vast increase of States along the Pacific bounds, in the numerous brood of States born in that continental intervale which the Mississippi drains, in the older States along the Atlantic coast, are there to be no more gigantic strides of ambition, no factions, no infuriated military struggles, no overgrown people drunk with prosperity? The ocean will sooner cease to be swept by storms, than this nation to be agitated by the passions of men. And while we array against these, in private, the influences of religion, the forces of education, and all the ameliorating influences of civilization, the nation itself will still need some armor of defence. That armor is the Constitution. Take that away, and this nation goes down into the field of its conflicts like a warrior without armor.

This is not a plea against immediate emancipation; it is but a solemn caution, lest, smarting from wrong, we seize the opportunity inconsiderately to destroy one evil by a process that shall leave us at the mercy of all others that time may bring.

Does any one ask me whether a law or a constitution is superior to the original principle of justice and of liberty? No; when law and constitution necessarily violate them, let them be changed; but when morality and justice and liberty may be wrought out by the constitution, be that method chosen. Besides, plighted faith is itself in the nature of a sacred moral principle. The Constitution of these United States stands upon the plighted faith of all the several States over which it has authority. When we cannot abide by our promises, then in methods expressly provided we must withdraw the pledge and agreements, and stand apart, not only as separate peoples, but under new governments.

These reasonings are all the more imperative because we are not shut up to doubtful constructions or violent methods for the suppression of slavery. We have seen its worst periods. The strength of its evil manhood is gone. Henceforth it is a decrepit giant, growing daily more infirm. That it has been stricken with infatuation is shown by that war which it has provoked, and which will carry emancipation where slavery meant to secure new strength. What the pen of the legislator could not do, that the sword shall do. The South have brought upon themselves what we never could have thrust upon them. There never was a more memorable instance of condign punishment following at the heels of transgression. The torch which they kindled for our destruction shall light the slaves to liberty. The true policy for slavery was to have retired their system from public view; but they have obtruded it, rather, with singular impertinence. They should have hidden it; but they have cast it before them as a very bulwark. They should have shielded it; but they have made it, rather, a shield for themselves, and compelled the armies of the United States, in striking at rebellion, to strike through the shield of slavery. Less than any other system would it bear disturbance; and yet they have brought an earthquake upon it. We have not destroyed the government that we might strike slavery; they have sought to destroy the government that they might establish slavery; and if in re-establishing again the government, the sword shall strike off the shackle, it will be but one more illustration of that overruling Providence by which the wrath of man is made to praise God. Once more the stars on our immortal flag are stars of liberty. Wherever our armies go, emancipation goes. Confiscation is the punishment of rebellion, and when applied to men, confiscation means liberty.

What do we behold? Men, not in scores, but in hundreds and thousands, set free by no act of their masters, and by no rescript of mere political authority, are held by our government. Only six months ago these men, women, and children were under the local law in the South; but now they have gone out of the hands of their local masters, and our government holds them. And how does it hold them? Are they men or chattels? Where will you find a law or a constitutional clause that gives the United States a right to look upon its subjects — human beings, endowed with intelligence, and with immortality behind that intelligence — as anything else than men? You may call them "contraband," — you may with dexterity call them ingenious or evasive names, but the Southern law that said Slave! is broken! Slaves in the possession of the government of these United States can be nothing else than men. They are emancipated. There are to-day thousands and thousands of emancipated men in the possession of this government, and it is bound to treat them in some sort, if not as citizens, yet as men.

And consider what will be the effect of the disturbance as our armies advance; — what swarms will rise up so soon as liberty is given them. In so vast a system as that of slavery, so loosely compacted, and so subject to fevers and inflammations, the reasons of the very disturbances of it, of the interruption of the occupations of the slaves, must break into their own darkened minds. The drilling of them for service, the putting them to the erection of fortifications, the inuring them to work for purposes of manhood, — all these things are preparing them for freedom.

But that is not all: the South has consented to pay a premium of about two hundred millions of dollars for the encouragement of free-labor cotton! Never was there such liberality since the world began! They have said to the world, "If you will only outbid us in the market, we will give you the opportunity. We have made our profits out of cotton, but we will agree to tie up our hands for two years, and let others take the two hundred millions of dollars, and raise the cotton." So the West Indies have planted cotton; India is raising it; China is raising it; they are planting cotton on the shores of Africa; and all the world has become a cotton-field, because there is a premium offered upon cotton that industry cannot but be interested in. And the thunder that rocks us is the calm that raises cotton in other lands. There seems a peculiar beauty in that justice by which since cotton on these shores invoked the African from Africa, cotton on the African shores shall reach out its soft white hand and strike off the shackle on these shores. As cotton has made slavery, so cotton shall cure it.

Let me, then, present, as another cause for the most profound thanksgiving, the fact that, although all the steps and details of the process by which emancipation is to be accomplished are not yet apparent, we see the direction in which it is coming, and towards which it is travelling. War will do what peace could not; and what war leaves unaccomplished must soon come to pass from commercial reasons. For the first time since our Revolution, good men see the end of slavery near at hand!

Once more. When this great struggle is passed, it will lay the foundations of a peace firmer than we have ever had before. First, because it must extinguish that pestilent heresy of the absolute sovereignty of individual States. We are not thirty crowned sovereigns sitting in council together; we are thirty united States whose general union and whose local independence are both and alike distinct and immutable. The government cannot take away the local authority of the States, and the States may not usurp or resist the Federal Government in its proper sphere. Slavery is the burglar, but absolute State sovereignty is the crevice into which the powder was sifted that was expected to explode this government. The government must be made burglar-proof by stopping up all such seams.

In the next place, this conflict, when ended, will bring the North and the South into a better mutual knowledge and respect. They have hitherto met chiefly in two places; at the watering-place, and in Congress. The South have come hither to such places as Saratoga and Newport. The people who congregate at our fashionable watering-places are not always the best exponents of Northern society. The other place where the North and the South met was in the halls of Congress; and Heaven forbid that it should be thought that the men hitherto there have fairly represented Northern virtue or courage! But now we have sent a representative body that we are quite willing should march through the South to tell them what Northern men are, and what Northern men can do. By the time our army has gone through the Southern States, there will be a change in public opinion there, with respect to the manhood, the courage, the power, and the resources of the North. They have not respected us. They have not understood our civilization. Such is the inevitable condition of the men that slavery breeds, that they cannot understand the patience and forbearance of Christian civilization; and the thing that will best inoculate them with a proper appreciation of these matters is the armed hand. And when they find that we are courageous, a match, and more than a match, for them in arms, from that moment they will respect us. And when there is more respect in the South for the North, there will be a better chance for peace.

There are likewise causes of rejoicing for the providential events that have accompanied this struggle thus far. There have been years when, if this war had broken out, I know not how we should have maintained it. I shudder when I look back upon the condition in which the North has been. If ten years ago this struggle had been forced upon us, our foes would have been of our own household. But what a journey have we made in ten years! Not the distance from the Red Sea to the promised land was half so long as that over which we have passed. A great change has within that period taken place in the public sentiment of the North, and in the unity of good men. Since 1850 we have been going through a wonderful transformation. And not until we were in some sense prepared for it did God permit the evolution of the causes that brought to pass this crisis. And now it is a matter of thanksgiving that we are an undivided North. I do not mean that there are no reptiles that lurk and hiss; but I mean that they no sooner put their head above the earth than they are scotched! The North stands like the old Apostle who, when he threw fuel on the fire, found a viper fastened on his hand. When the spectators saw it, they thought that he was only an escaped criminal, and that he would die; but when he shook the serpent off, and suffered no harm, they thought he was a god. And so the North, standing by its fiery war, and casting on fuel, finds upon its hand vipers; but it shakes them off and suffers no harm. We are a united, infrangible, indivisible North; and just as sure as the sun rises and sets, we shall be victorious.

Nor are we to forget that as the stars in their courses fought against Sisera, as it were prefiguring the working of natural laws for God's purposes among men, so great agencies of nature have been, in this conflict, co-operating with us. Who of us that mourned and shuddered in the crisis of '57 knew that God was saying to us, "Take in your sails; put your ship in order: a great hurricane is about to fall upon you?" Nevertheless, we did put the ship in good condition; and now that the storm has fallen we understand the warning. And never was the North so well able to bear the pressure of war as now. Although individual men are failing, yet never was the North so rich, and so competent to carry on this conflict as now.

Nor was that all: it pleased God to say to the winds, that did not know the reason; and to the rains, that knew not why; and to the sun, that, travelling far and near, fulfils God's purposes unknowingly, "Make the earth teem! breed corn in every clod!" And he that made the seven years of plenty to stand against the seven years of famine in Egypt, made two years of superabundance in our land, — for what? To take the crown from the head of cotton, and put it on the head of corn. And why? Because this has been the peculiar boast of the South: "Cotton is king, and by its power we will bring France, with her haughty Emperor, and England, with her needy mechanics, to our terms; and then we will crush the North." We do not know what God is saying to us. I went through the corn-field, — ignorant soul that I was, — and heard the rustling of the leaves. I thought it was only the wind blowing through the corn, and I did not hear the messages. It was God speaking in a literature that was uninterpreted to me then, but which now I understand. Every field in the North lifted up its long sword-blades and prefigured victorious arms; and every wind that came said, "Liberty is coming; emancipation is coming; corn shall dethrone cotton!" For now, just when manufacturing England would have required our ports to be opened, she happens to need our corn more than the cotton of the Southern States. She must feed her men before she gives their hands anything to do. We come nearer to keeping them from starving than the South does to clothing them. And what do we see in France? The Emperor sits on his precarious seat, and finds it at present expedient to lay aside his prerogative of opening fresh budgets of expenses; and offers to restrict himself, and to economize and to save money in various ways; while, if France had been in a condition of boundless prosperity, she might have wished to have a finger in matters here. Thus France is obliged to cut down her army. So we have guaranties for peace there, and guaranties for peace in England; and they will not stir to interfere with our affairs. This fight is to be fought out by ourselves. While preparations for this conflict have been going on, God has poured money into our coffers, and taken it away from those that might use it to our harm. He is holding back France and England, and saying to all men and nations, "Appoint the bounds! Let none enter the lists to interfere, while those gigantic warriors battle for victory! Liberty and God, and slavery and the Devil, stand over against each other, and let no man put hand or foot into the ring till they have done battle unto death!" Amen. Even so, Lord God Almighty. It is thy decree! And it shall stand! And when the victory shall come, not unto us, not unto us, but — in the voice of thrice ten thousand, and thousands of thousands of ransomed ones, mingling with thine earthly children's gladness — unto thee shall be the praise and the glory, for ever and ever. Amen.

IX.

THE CHURCH'S DUTY TO SLAVERY.*

"But Jesus called them unto him, and said, Ye know that the princes of the Gentiles exercise dominion over them, and they that are great exercise authority upon them. But it shall not be so among you: but whosoever will be great among you, let him be your minister; and whosoever will be chief among you, let him be your servant: even as the Son of man came not to be ministered unto, but to minister, and to give his life a ransom for many." — Matt. xx. 25-28.

HEN Paul was sent by James, Peter, and John to the Gentiles, their only charge to him was that he should "remember the poor"; and his only remark upon the charge was, that it was the very thing that he was always anxious to do.

I have already spoken to you from this fact, basing upon it two statements: that the state of mind which is most completely filled with a disposition to take care of the weak and the poor, and to employ one's gifts and strength in serving them, is the one best fitted to make known the real truth of the power of Christ and of the Gospel; and that any system of polity which shall contain a sufficient provision for the weak and poor, will contain the very best provision,

* January 12, 1862.

also, for the wise and the strong. We come, from a different side, and with different language, which I have to-night read in your hearing, to precisely the same practical results.

This statement does not mean that society should be divided, and that there should be two classes: the educated, the intelligent, and the virtuous, on the one side, and the ignorant, the vicious, and the rude, on the other; and that a preference should be given to the bottom over the top. It does not mean that being prosperous and wise and good is a fault, or that being poor and ignorant is a virtue. It does not mean that we should neglect men who are wise and strong, or that we should not be in sympathy with them. It does not mean that we should not do what we can to help them. It does not mean that we should not preach to them, and minister to them all elements of civil culture. It does not, on the other hand, mean that we are to have a moral preference for men simply because they are poor, as if that gave them special rights. In other words, we are not to reverse the old state of things, and crown the bottom at the expense of the top, just as all through the world, from the beginning to this time, the top has been crowned at the expense of the bottom. That would only be turning the old mistake bottom-side up.

It means only that as the spirit of Christianity is essentially the spirit of equitable love, and as it is not the love of attractiveness but of benevolence, and therefore augments and abounds in the ratio of the necessity of the object of it, rather than of his lovableness, so it should be strongest toward the neediest. We are always more tender of the sick than of the well: not because we hate the well, or are indifferent to them; but simply because the sick need most. And where benevolence is so developed as fully to be in sympathy with the lowest men, it is by that very fact so ample as to include all others. The best way to take care of the higher, is to take care of the lower. If you put yourself into such a Christian frame that you know how to endure the unlovely, how much more will you be in a condition to endure the lovely! If you receive the grace of Christ into the soul with a potency that is adequate to the wants of the most undeserving, how much more will it be adequate to the wants of the deserving!

And, in like manner, in respect to all institutions, and all means of propagating Christian influences, we do not mean to teach that they are to be constructed exclusively for the poor; or that all churches, or religious societies, should specially or exclusively address themselves to the poor as a class; but that all Christian institutions should, in their nature and tendency, conduce to the benefit of the lowest as well as of the highest. They should not be established for the benefit of any class, top or bottom. They should be as universal as the spirit whose name they take.

And especially, in gauging their use of means, all Christian institutions should, in spirit and in power, be competent to the wants of the lowest and of the neediest in society.

Christians are called to love and to serve all men. Christian churches are not to pick the few and the fair, and serve them; but every Christian church is to be in spirit competent to the wants of the highest and of the lowest alike. No Christian church is wisely and well constituted that has not provision for every condition of men, from the top of society to the bottom. The Christian Church is to be universal: not by geographical extent, but by moral adaptation to the wants of universal human nature. It is, then, to make distinctions in favor of no class. It is simply to have an average and universal moral power, that, being sufficient for the lowest, is, of necessity, sufficient for the highest. If these institutions are gauged to be sufficient for the wants of the higher natures only, they may be insufficient to reach down to the lowest; while if they are gauged to the necessity of the least developed and the most necessitous, they will, in the nature of things, have all the more power upon the higher. Summer must have heat for the things that are most torpid. Of course, then, the easily excitable things will grow. The chickweed will sprout and grow with the thermometer at 45°. The cypress-vine and the tuberose require it to be at 70° or 80°. Now, a summer fitted for the early plants, would leave the year half unblossomed; but a summer that carries in its heart a warmth strong enough to call up the reluctant plants, will on its way to them of course wake up also the plants that begin to dream of waking even while the snow is on their eyelids. And so it must be with the heat of the Church.

So much for the general statement. Let us make it more apparent by special applications.

I. Churches that rule their pulpits to a preaching exclusively for the cultivated and refined, are out of harmony with the New Testament, and out of the legitimate sphere of Christianity. A church is not necessarily a Christian church because it preaches Christianity; for it is not the dogma or the doctrine that you preach, but the spirit in which you preach it, that constitutes Christianity in a church. A church that preaches sound doctrine all through, but that preaches it so that it is meat only for the few, and is not universal food, has gone aside from the Master. Preaching may be universal and yet refined. There is no necessary connection between rudeness and the wants of rude people. The heart is the universal medium. A man that is to the last degree cultured in thought and in language, a man that is polished to the last degree in manly excellence, may be acceptable to all men, so that he presents the universal letter of introduction, — the feeling that brings heart to heart, high and low; for it is that that makes all men kindred. But, often, pulpits are made partial by a way of treating subjects that is partial and excluding. Ministers are wrongly taught: not on purpose, not willingly; but from a wrong conception. The young preacher has inculcated upon him by those from whom he receives his instruction, a range of topics interesting to higher natures, but to no others. It is easy to select out of the Word of God themes which may be discussed with great profit to men who are accustomed to think, and to dwell much on such themes, but the discussion of which is almost profitless to others. A historic, a philosophic, a scholastic conception, even of a common theme, may put it out of the reach of the more uninstructed classes. Let a man discuss the love of Christ, not as a living, flaming fact made clear to the comprehension of every child, but as an abstract thing; let him consider the mode of loving, the potency of divine affections, and the relations of the emotions of love in man to the divine feeling and the divine government; let him lift the subject up above the heart into the mind, and he will remove it beyond the range in which the common mind walks. As far as the benefit of the average classes of society is concerned, you might just as well preach in Greek as in abstract language. One is just as foreign to men's ordinary comprehension as the other.

Language, too, may be employed for the sake of scholastic and literary finish, so as almost, if not quite to deaden the effect of what a man preaches. The use of latinized words and periphrases in what is called elegant speaking and fine writing, is a common vice. There is a great tendency on the part of writers and speakers to avoid domestic words and colloquialisms, as they are called.

Now, all words are pegs to hang ideas on; and as a wooden peg in the hall, on which the father and the grandfather were accustomed to hang the coat and hat, is to the child's eye more beautiful than the most exquisite picture that could be hung on the wall, so the most common and familiar words are more powerful than any abstract and arbitrary ones.

What does *home* mean? When you speak that word it is as if you struck a bee-hive, and a thousand bees begin to buzz and hum music in your mind. *Father* and *mother* are words that children learn on the hearth and in the nursery. They are nursery and childhood companions; and they do not cease to be companions in after life. They are always linked with our early associations. And when you attempt to express the thought which belongs to *father* or *mother*, by saying "parent," you kill it. When you say "woman" you mean what the world has taught of woman; but when you say "female," you mean what a fool might mean that does not know how to use language.

The difference between one man and another in the use of words is, that one uses familiar words, and uses them in their ordinary sense, and the other uses words that are not familiar, and uses them in a sense that is unusual. Some ministers use words in such a way that they flash, as it were, and wake men up, and give them feelings which they cannot account for. They pick out words that are adapted to the comprehension of their people, and employ them so that they shall have a meaning over and above the philosophical meaning. But there are thousands of ministers that charm men when they talk in private conversation, because they are sensible then, who are fools when they come to preach, — and not according to the Apostle's idea of the "foolishness of preaching," either. They say, "We are bound to bring our people up to us, and not to go down to them." I beg your pardon, you will honor yourselves by going down to them. No man need be ashamed to use the language of common life, for that is the language of power and eloquence. The man that knows how, like old Bunyan, like Baxter, and like South (scholarly as he was), to take the Saxon colloquial terms of the household, of the kitchen, of the parlor, of the nursery, of the field, where men live, and employ them in his preaching, is a powerful and eloquent preacher. These old, brawny, large-meaning words, heavily laden with precious associations, are words of might. But how many of our preachers, for the sake of being literary, for the sake of being polished, step aside from the great highway of power in language, into the little lanes of exclusiveness, where there is no power!

And so of discussing questions foreign to men's lives and interests; or, of discussing those that belong to their interests in a philosophical vein, in order to lift them up to the plane of the highest natures, thus lifting them up so high that the greatest number cannot see them. When men discuss questions foreign to the wants of the community, or discuss questions in such a way as to make them foreign to the wants of the community, the few, the very few, can go with them, but all the rest are unfed. How many congregations say, "Our minister is a dear man; we love to have him come and see us; his conversation in the family seems profitable; the children all like him; but somehow (and I suppose it is my fault) I cannot keep awake when he preaches." It is not your fault. And I do not make myself an exception. If you come here and go to sleep under my preaching when the air is good, it is my fault, and not yours, that you do not keep awake. If, after people have listened to a minister, they say, "His preaching does not do me any good," do not let him excuse himself by saying that they are inattentive. I hold that the Gospel abounds in elements the most universally interesting of any that can be conceived of; and if a man stands in the sacred desk with all the resources of the Gospel, and speaks without interesting his hearers, it is because he does not know how to handle his tools.

And all this exclusiveness that I have pointed out is the fault of the modern pulpit, and is especially the fault of the city pulpit. It is a world too genteel; it is a world too refined; it is a world too learned; it has got up on stilts; it thinks and talks in such philosophical and scholarly language that the masses of the common people do not get anything from it. It does not come to the poor. The Gospel that it dispenses is a Gospel kept for the dainty, for connoisseurs in Gospel matters. The modern pulpit is strong in learning, and in a noble devotion to higher natures; but it is weak in that it clothes itself in such forms as to make it, by elective affinity, the organ of only the higher natures. The Apostles were selected just because they could not do that. One is surprised when he examines the materials out of which the Apostles were made. I have wondered that the stuff for the Apostles was not imported from Athens. There were better men there. Those that were chosen were the poorest materials that were ever hewn out into apostleship, or anything else official. If you take James, John, and Peter out of the Apostles, you have taken out all that left any record. Paul was added; he was an educated man, and he did more than all the others put together; but of the original Apostles, with the exception of those three, it seems to me that the eight others (Judas being left uncounted) were material than which you can scarcely imagine any with less natural fitness and adaptation. Why did Christ select these men? For the very reason that from their calling and position they did not know anything else, and could not learn anything else in their lifetime, than the simple things taught them in the simplest language; and, that, therefore, when they should speak, their words would go right home to their fellows, the poor and common people. Christ came to preach the Gospel to the mass of humanity, and they were poor. Christ came to lift up the world; and it had all sunk down to the bottom of society. There were ten million men below the medium line where there was one above it. And to preach the Gospel, it was necessary to have men that were free from any temptation, in their teaching, to rise above the comprehension of the lower classes; and the Apostles were selected accordingly; and it was wise. And in later periods, those ministries that have been the most like them in their method of working, whether from necessity or choice, have been the most successful. There is no ministry that have been more successful, or that have raised up a better monument as the result of their labors, than the Methodist clergy. Why? Not alone because they have had a consummate system of organization, though that has helped a great deal; not because they have had a certain lithe, elastic method of procedure, in not being limited and fixed, but kept roving from one place to another, which had some advantages to the early settlements, but disadvantages to the permanent churches: but because men of all pursuits and callings were appointed to preach. And as long as the Methodist Church felt willing to preach among the poor and common people, so long they triumphed gloriously; but in proportion as they get the spirit of preaching to the upper classes, and of building churches for them, their success diminishes. I think the Methodist churches are getting to be the most splendid churches. We have got to take their places, and go down and take care of the poor. Somebody must do it. And I give warning to our Methodist brethren that if they are going to abandon that field there are enough to occupy it; but that if they want to keep their glory, and transmit it to other generations, they must remember the poor. Be proud of that field. Take care of those that nobody else takes care of. Take heed to the bottom, and God will see that your love and fidelity shall work all the way up to the top. I do not object to the Methodists' preaching to the most cultivated audiences: all I object to is, that they should lose a conception of the sacredness of human nature clear down to the bottom.

The fault of the churches is not that they provide for the wants of the higher, but that they do not provide in such a way as shall also meet the necessities of the lower. We are providing for special class-wants, and leaving out the lower classes. A bucket whose bottom has dropped out will not hold water; and a church whose poor have dropped out will not hold grace.

II. Christian institutions must be gauged to the same dominant spirit. All Christian societies for spreading knowledge, all Christian societies for sustaining ministers and missionaries, all Christian institutions which are in the nature of propagating institutions, if they are in accordance with their Master, must go to the bottom, and, taking sides with the lowest, make everything consistent with that initial element. And if there is anything to be sacrificed anywhere, it must be among the strong and the high, and never among the low and the weak.

And this has been the battle of the day in which we live. In general assemblies, synods, and presbyteries; in associations and local churches; in tract societies and missionary societies, — in them all men have refused, for a quarter of a century, to go down to the low, to stand by them, and to declare a Gospel that was in sympathy with them, and would protect them, whatever came to anybody else. They have refused to bring the whole divine power of the Gospel to the rescue of the poorest and the lowest.

The slave, in our time, has been God's touchstone of the nation, of its religion, and of its religious institutions; and these have been found grievously wanting. They are coming right now, and coming right fast, but for the last twenty-five years they have been grievously wrong. The question has been of the confidence of "great and good men in the church, in the society, in the institution"; of the opinions of "the most influential men." Prudential questions have been put before moral ones. Questions of the necessity of holding things together, of receipts and means, have too often ruled moral questions out.

Ever since about the time when I entered public life, the question of religion for the African slave in our nation has been agitated. The substantial conflict of the times has been whether there was in the Church and Christian institutions (we knew there was in the Bible) a Christianity that dared to stand by the side of the slave, and say, "In the name of Jesus, that made us all of one blood, we demand justice, and education, and humanity, for the low, and for the lowest." And the churches have refused to demand it. The assemblies, and synods, and presbyteries, and associations, and tract societies, and missionary societies, have refused to do it. The Christianity of the age, for twenty-five years, has not had the strength to do it. These institutions were in connection with the educated, with the judicious, with the prudent, with the wealthy; they belonged to the higher classes, and represented the average conscience and the average feeling of the higher classes; and they were not willing to humble themselves, and go down to the bottom, and say, "God sent us first to the poor, and we must take care of them, whatever becomes of the others." If there had been a spirit large enough to take in the poor, there would have been a spirit large enough to evangelize this nation years and years ago. And war; the rebellion which is the cause of the war; the ruthless destruction which it occasions; the terrible garment of blood that is threatened to be wrapped round and round the corse of this nation, — these things have come upon us because there was not salt enough to save us in the embodied religious institutions of our time. Now, shall we take no heed? Shall these facts stare us in the face, and no man note for the future?

III. That which is true of churches, and of Christian institutions, is in like manner true of Christian public sentiment in this nation, in relation to the questions of our times.

The American mind has hitherto sustained the relation of the most absolute selfishness in respect to the African, practically. We had a general sympathy for the poor and the oppressed up to about fifteen years ago; and we talked of them on the Fourth of July, and prayed for them a good deal, up to about ten years ago. About ten years ago it came to be a little critical to pray that way. Men feared that it might be supposed that they meant to pray for the overturning of oppression on the plantation, when they meant to pray for its overturning two or three thousand miles off. Men, when they talked of opening the prison doors, meant the prison doors in Hindostan, in Japan, in Madagascar, in New Holland, in South America, perhaps in Central America, but not on the North American continent. Ministers did not wish it to be understood at all that they meant to pray for the downtrodden in this land. They prayed for the poor everywhere but at home. They prayed for the oppressed everywhere but in America. They prayed for the righting of the wronged and the punishment of the wronger all the world over except in certain latitudes and longitudes on this Western shore. Men were faithful in the denunciation of all sins except those that lay near their ship, their store, and their pocket.

But although there has been this selfishness of the American mind, yet as the tide, coming steadily from the ocean, works in, and encroaches, and rises, and deepens the shallow places, and covers sticks and stones, and all the landmarks, till the whole bay is full, and the very heart of the ocean pulsates against the shore, and the indentations of it; so God has been filling steadily the mind of this great nation by the tide setting from the eternal fulness of his own heart; and the day of this delinquency has passed away, and we are going to see better times.

Hitherto the history of this nation has been one of selfishness, in enslaving the African at the South; in indifference, substantially, to his enslavement at the North; and in the avoidance of the vexed question of slavery by the Church. Do you not know that this has been the stone of stumbling and rock of offence everywhere? It is so now in many places. It is so in this city to a great extent. I suspect that the pastors of half the churches in this city, if you should go to them and urge them to preach right out the duty of the Church in this matter, would tell you that they were in full sympathy with the cause of justice and liberty as applied to the slave, and would say, "My heart is willing, but I am so situated that I cannot. The most influential men in my church would not tolerate it; and I do not think I am bound to do it." I do not believe that half the churches of Brooklyn are in such a state that their ministers would dare to preach the full Gospel on the subject of the slave. And yet I take it that Brooklyn is far in advance of many other places in this respect.

But everywhere this has been the vexed question, to be avoided in prayer-meetings, in conference-meetings, in monthly concerts, in religious assemblies of every description. And now, many ministers, if they were to offer up a petition for the slave by name, would have a visit from a committee the next day, with good advice. And the American Church, taken comprehensively, for a long period of years, has avoided this question. You must, however, exempt the churches in many parts of our country for the last ten or fifteen years. I think that the churches in New England, for the last fifteen years, have done much to redeem themselves from this delinquency, as have also the Western and the Northwestern churches. But the

Southern Church is an apostate church. There is no church in the South. That which is called the Church there is the Devil's den, and not Christ's home nor house. But in the Middle States, and in our great commercial cities, the churches have been, and are now, with reference to slavery, much like a doctor in a plague, who should think that his first duty was to see that he did not get infected himself, and that he did not waste his medicines. What would you think of a doctor whose idea of practice was that he should take care not to get sick? He was made a doctor to cure the sick, to go where they are, to think of them, and not to think about himself. And what is medicine for, but to give to sick men? And yet our dainty doctors in the Church take out their white powders of truth, and when a poor diseased man comes to be cured, they say, "Why, that man's mouth is impure, and for him to take these beautiful powders would be to waste them!" Their Gospel is so respectable, their Christian institutions are so nice, there are such good and influential men in them, their doctrines are so fine, and their Christianity is so clothed in white raiment, that they do not want to soil them by handling this vulgar question of slavery, *slavery*, SLAVERY, nothing but slavery, — this everlasting ism, negrophilism. *Negrophilism!* I thank you for that word. It takes me back to the days when the Jews reproached Christ because he would go with sinners, and eat with them, and preach to them. Christ was charged with being a vulgar fellow because he would go with bad men, when he made this reply: "They that be whole need not a physician, but they that are sick." But our American Church has refused to follow the example of Christ, to go down to the poor and needy, and to hold and preach a Gospel that was for the poorest and the neediest. And God has seen, and history will record, that in the critical years of the American nation, the American Church has been faithless to the poor. God has begun to call her back. With stripes and chastisements is she coming back; and it is high time.

In all attempts to settle anything, thus far, the assumed basis is, and has been, that the peace and prosperity of this great white nation must be the gauge and rule. In and out of Congress, in the most respectable quarters, as the world goes, it is said, "We must not destroy this fair white nation for the sake of taking care of a few negroes." A white nation that is saved by the sacrifice of a few negroes, or a million negroes, is not worth saving. The essential moral qualities of a nation are all that make it worth saving; and if this nation turns aside from its manifest duty, and agrees merely to save itself, it is not worth saving. But I say that its salvation is through the dark gate. If we would save ourselves, we must be willing to imitate our Master, who came "not to be ministered unto, but to minister"; that is, not to be served, but to serve. He came not to be the chief, but to be the servant. This willingness to serve is the legacy which he has left to the Church; and a Christian nation, if it would endure, must have the attitude and spirit of the Master. If it wants to save the top, it must save the bottom. Our wisdom is like that of a man who, knowing that the sills of his dwelling are rotting out, goes and puts new shingles on the roof, and gilds the tip of the lightning-rod. The rotting continues, and a corner sags, and the rooms get out of shape, and the doors refuse to be shut, and the windows will not budge, and he keeps on rigging and tinkering at the top. Now the way to save the top is to save the bottom, and that is the only way. And there are four million foundation men in this nation. You cannot get them out from under you. They are more vital than you are. They are like purslain ; the more you cut it up the more it spreads. They are like thistles. Every stroke you give them, you sow seeds from which new ones spring up. It is the children of Israel over again. The Egyptians tried all sorts of ways to get rid of them ; but they increased upon them, and finally destroyed them. And yet the old Egyptians, with Pharaoh at their head, did not feel a whit more secure than we, nor a whit more vain of their superiority over the detested Hebrew, than we are of our superiority over the negro.

Our danger lies in moral delinquency. We are liable to have the foundations of our nation rot out from under us, because we will not, in the spirit of Christ, preach the Gospel, with all its justice and humanity, in behalf of the poor and the oppressed. If we had the courage to do that, we should be in no danger at all. Our danger will be gone the moment we are converted to Christianity in that simple thing.

In all attempts now making, as far as I can see, by this government, and the Christian public sentiment of this nation, to meet the present case of the nation, the implied and assumed basis of proceeding is not *what is right and just to the slave*, but *what will be best for the whites.* The vice of our times is unconscious selfishness.

I do not speak this to denounce or deride the Administration. You are well aware of the esteem in which I hold them, and how grateful I am that God has been pleased to give us such a chief magistrate as President Lincoln. It is a comfort and a consolation to have an unrotten man in that chair at Washington, and not a day goes over my head that I do not feel, unconsciously and involuntarily an emotion of gratitude to God that there is a man there who, whatever may be his mistakes, wants to do right, and means to do right. It is a great thing to have a President that the nation can trust; for trust has been a commodity the rarest and most exquisitely precious in Washington for the last fifty years. And yet while I have this high regard for, and this great trust in, the Administration at Washington, it seems to me that the basis of their action is no better than that which is implied or assumed by the churches or the Christian public sentiment of this nation. We are altogether webbed in a common selfishness, and our common thought is, "How shall we white folks get rid of this intolerable vexation? how shall we set ourselves free from these embarrassments?" It is self, *self*, SELF, all the way through. Nor do I anywhere hear men saying, "It is the voice of Christ, by the providence of God, calling us to labor for the poor. I am an ordained man, sent to preach the Gospel to the poor, as well as to the rich. My Gospel must be so full of justice and humanity that it shall take care of the bottom at all events, since that which takes care of the bottom will of necessity take care of the top."

The only Christian beginning, then, in this matter, is to ask simply: "What is best for both black and white?" A justice and benevolence that goes down to the slave, as Christ did to the publican and the sinner, and contemplates no measure less than such as shall meet the exigency of his case, is the only one adequate to our emergency. And this should be said more emphatically because there is in the American mind a tendency to settle moral questions as they build houses in new settlements, where they throw the hammer at the nail, and call that nailing; where they think nothing of commencing a house at sunrise and completing it at sunset; where they put up the plainest and most tumble-down structures, and call them substantial dwellings. The disposition to drive ahead, and throw everything out the way that hinders our progress, has led to a mode of patching and making use of expedients. We are like the doctor who, instead of making thorough work with his patient, gives him a little physic and puts him on his feet again as speedily as possible; or like the doctor who dries up the sores of his patient, instead of curing them. Quick! *quick!* QUICK! is our idea! Thorough! *thorough!* THOROUGH! is God's idea! And the peculiar temptation of our times will be the feeling, "Let us get this war off our hands; let us be done with it; let us tie up these things; let us heal over this rupture; because we want to build more ships; because we want to start more factories; because we want to hear the forge again; because we want to see everything buzzing and spinning once more." We shall be anxious to go back to materiality. We are materialists. We live by the senses, and for the senses. We live for business and for the world. We do not live for God, for spiritual things, nor for eternity. And this feeling pervades and vitiates our public policy. Somewhere there must a stand be made. There must be a point about which health can be organized. Is it not time that somebody should speak on this subject?

And now, with respect to the theories that are being advocated in reference to the disposition to be made of the Africans. President Lincoln advocates colonization. I see that a bill has been introduced providing for the purchase of territory for their occupation. It is asserted by published letters on this subject that President Lincoln is opposed to any settlement that does not carry with it the enforced colonization of the freedmen of this nation. Now if the Africans want to go to a tropical land; if they think it will be for their interest to try their hand in Central America, or in some part of Mexico, let them have the liberty of doing it; but, in the name of God and eternal justice, I protest against the spectacle, shameful to Christianity and to us, of this great and powerful nation taking the poor, wronged, stripped African, and carrying him an exile from the land which is his native land, and therefore the land of his preference. Compulsory colonization is a wanton violation of the spirit and letter of Christianity. The true and right spirit is, as fast as God in his providence proclaims liberty to the captive, to give him succor in every possible way. Wherever the American banner floats again, wherever its stars shine out again, wherever its stripes wave again, there every man should be a freeman; and the duty of the Government to every slave that is liberated is to give him books, to give him education, to give him wages, to give him land, and to give him a chance for Christian manhood.

What does the negro that stands knocking at our door demand? Does he demand equality? No. We do not give that to our own white citizens. An ignorant man is not equal to an educated one. A man of slender endowments is not equal to a man of brilliant genius. Equality, in the sense of social equality, is not known to nature, nor to grace, even. And we do not demand for the African equality. When Vice-President Stephens argues against the equality of the blacks and the whites, he sets up a man of straw that he may knock it down again. Does the African demand intermarriage or interfiliation? No such thing. He has more sense, and we have more sense than to do that. What does he demand? He stands up and says, "God made me, and gave me reason, and moral sense, and affections: I only claim the air, and the earth, and a place to use these things, and make as much of them as I can, unhindered. Take off from me the law that will not let me be my own, and that will not let me own my wife and children. Take off from me the law that makes it a crime for me or mine to have a book. Take off from me the law that will not let me expand and develop all that God put in me when he created me." Was there ever a petition more reasonable and right? And what shall the judgment-day do to you and me, if, being factors of the public sentiment of this nation, we fail to impress upon it that Christian equity and Christian humanity which give a chance to the African to be what he can be? That is all he asks. It seems to me there never was a day when it was so incumbent upon us to go into the control of public affairs in the spirit of the text of to-night, and carry the Gospel to the poor, as now. Whatever comes of anything else, see to it that your Gospel is of a temper of justice and of humanity, such that it will, like Christ, go down to the wants of the lowest and the least; and God will see to it, then, that there shall flame forth a divine influence that shall illumine and take care of all the rest in human society.

It will not be long before you and I lay off this habiliment of flesh. Our days and our hours are numbered, and we are quick passengers to that bar of impartial justice where God shall sit without prejudice to judge our prejudiced lives. Young man, dainty maiden, brother of middle life, venerable sir, when you are dying, and going up to that judgment, it will give you more joy to think that you have befriended a poor African slave, than to have taken the hand of Napoleon, or worn a crown of empire. In that day the things that you have done for those that were sick and imprisoned, the things that you have done for Christ in the form of his poor despised ones, will be like balm and frankincense to your spirit as it is going up before the Father of all. Remember that every living creature is God's child. If you had abused my child in the street, how would you dare meet me? and if you abuse one of God's children, how will you dare meet him? In respect to four million men, Christ stands in our midst to day, saying, "Inasmuch as you do it unto the least of these, ye do it unto me." If you buffet and spit upon them, Christ is buffetted and spit upon; but if you clothe them and feed them and lift them up, Christ is clothed and fed and lifted up.

X.

THE BEGINNING OF FREEDOM.*

"Go through, go through the gates; prepare ye the way of the people; cast up, cast up the highway; gather out the stones; lift up a standard for the people. Behold, the Lord hath proclaimed unto the end of the world, Say ye to the daughter of Zion, Behold, thy salvation cometh; behold, his reward is with him, and his work before him. And they shall call them, The holy people, the redeemed of the Lord: and thou shalt be called, Sought out, A city not forsaken." — Isaiah lxii. 10, 11, 12.

GREAT reformations in morals can never stop with individuals. As corruption of the citizen soon infects the institutions and the laws of the land, so the reformation of the citizen reforms laws and usages. It is such a reformation that the prophet celebrates. It is a proclamation, therefore, of blessings from God, founded upon the willingness of the people to follow the Divine rule. These blessings are to result from righteousness. And the prophet, instructed of God, calls upon the nation to look forward and expect the coming of God, and to make preparation for it; and that in no small measure.

We, too, have occasion for rejoicing as Christians, as churches, as philanthropists, and as a nation.

I hold in my hand the latest Proclamation of the

* Preached March 9, 1862, at the time of the compensated emancipation Message of President Lincoln.

President of these United States. A *Message*, we call it, and yet it is inevitably a Proclamation. I do not hesitate to say that it stands absolutely alone. Never before has there been in the history of this Government, such a message. If it be considered in its relations to our past history and to our future, it is not too much to say that there has never been such a state paper before in this nation. Dates will begin from it. In the year of this Message of President Lincoln will begin a new cycle of our national career. If it be considered in its relations to purity, to peace, to liberty, and to unity, it must also take rank as an eminent moral force. And I should deem myself delinquent if I did not pause, and call the attention of this Christian people to some considerations of duty, arising from the great deliverance which God is about to give us,—for there are grave duties devolving upon us. Our work is not to be done for us: our work is to be done *through* us, and *by* us. And God is saying to us, "Prepare the way of the people; cast up, cast up the highway; gather out the stones,"—take away the hinderances and the obstructions; "lift up a standard for the people,"—make ready to begin the work. With the ideas that you know that I hold, as to the duty of a preacher in this country, where all citizens are legislators and judges, where all power resides with the people, who are its administrators, I should be unfaithful if I did not advertise you of this emergency, and put you upon doing your duty.

Let me read some parts of this Message in your hearing.

"*Fellow Citizens of the Senate and House of Representatives:* I recommend the adoption of a joint resolution by your honorable bodies, which shall be substantially as follows: —

"*Resolved*, That the United States ought to co-operate with any State which may adopt a gradual abolishment of slavery, giving to such State pecuniary aid to be used by such State in its discretion to compensate for the inconveniences, public and private, produced by such change of system.

"If the proposition contained in the resolution does not meet the approval of Congress and the country, there is the end."

So far as he is concerned; but it is not the end: there is a President; and there is also a God above him.

"But if it does meet such approval, I deem it important that the States and people immediately interested should at once be distinctly notified of the fact, so that they may begin to consider whether to accept or reject it."

And now take notice that it has been openly declared by our Chief Magistrate that slavery is incompatible with good government. What a day we have reached! What a day has come to us! A sentiment, half of which, fifteen or twenty years ago, would have driven a man down the streets of New York before a mob, and rendered him liable to have his property sacked, is now uttered by the Chief Magistrate of this nation, and is about to be made the subject of legislation in our land. Mark the words: —

"The Federal Government would find its highest interest in such a measure as one of the most efficient means of self-preservation."

It is the abolishment of slavery which is thus spoken of.

"The leaders of the existing insurrection entertain the hope that the Government will ultimately be forced to acknowledge the independence of some part of the disaffected region, and that all the slave States north of such parts will then say, 'The Union for which we have struggled being already gone, we now choose to go with the Southern section.' To deprive them of this hope substantially ends the rebellion, and the initiation of emancipation completely deprives them of it. As to all the States initiating it, the point is not that all the States tolerating slavery would very soon, if at all, initiate emancipation, but that, while the offer is equally made to all, the more Northern shall, by such initiation, make it certain to the more Southern, that in no event will the former ever join the latter in their proposed Confederacy."

There is one other passage that I wish to read, and that is a significant intimation of a principle, the acknowledgment of which and its adoption in practice by the people and the national authorities, must bring the war to a speedy close.

"If, however, resistance continues, the war must also continue, and it is impossible to foresee all the incidents which may attend, and all the ruin which may follow it. Such as may seem indispensable, or may obviously promise great efficiency toward ending the struggle, must and will come."

So says President Lincoln, and generally what he says he means.

The fact of the existence of such a document at all is the most noticeable feature in it. How strange it is! You cannot appreciate the strangeness of it if you judge it by the events that have been occurring within the past few months. But go back a few years, and imagine such a document issuing from President Buchanan's administration. It makes one smile to mention it. Imagine the issue, by the President of the United States, of a document initiating emancipation, or the *abolishment* of slavery, as President Lincoln peculiarly styles it, in the time of Mr. Pierce's administration. Imagine such a document issuing from the administration of President Fillmore, or Polk, or Tyler, or Van Buren. To think of it takes a man's breath away! But we have come quietly down by steps of four years, until at last this glorious period is reached, in our own day, and while men are yet young who saw the beginning of the great antislavery struggle that seems likely to be soon ended. We have come quietly down to the period when a document is issued by the President of the United States inaugurating emancipation, and looking to the extinction of slavery in this nation, and pledging the power and resources of this great people to the work. There never was such a revolution since the world began, upon such a scale, involving such interests, and taking place within so short a time.

I propose, then, to make a few remarks upon this Message of the President. I wish to contribute my share, and to have you contribute your share of that approbation and sympathy which our rulers need in taking such a step as this. It is a sublime responsibility that is assumed. It required, to be sure, sagacity; but, more than that, it required courage, for the Chief Magistrate of this people to determine upon such a step, and issue such a paper; and that courage should be met with such instant sympathy and support from the whole people, as shall induce the President not only to maintain this stand, but efficiently to go forward from it.

I. This paper completes a circle, and brings the Government of these United States back to that point at which it stood upon the adoption of our present Constitution. When the fathers, finding the articles of confederation which were agreed upon during the revolutionary war to be insufficient, and the government to be weak in the performance of its unavoidable functions, convoked that convention out of which grew the Constitution of the United States, slavery was existing, but in a languishing and declining condition. It existed in most of the Northern States, but to a very limited extent. All the political ideas of the times were against it, and all the moral influences of the times were against it, and it was not uncommon to hear, not only men from Virginia, but the Gadsdens and Laurenses and Pinckneys of Carolina, as much as any others, admit the right of the African to liberty. Slavery was not attempted to be defended upon original grounds, political or moral. And when the Constitution was adopted there was one universal wish, and, I may say, one universal expectation, that slavery would cease. And the Constitution takes its form in consequence of that impression; for it was refused to dishonor that immortal document by the insertion into it of the word *slavery*. It was understood that when that vile system passed away, there should be no such trace of it left. Unexpectedly it received development. In God's mysterious providence slavery had a part to play in the history of the country. It was to be an educating force in this nation. Among those things which God was to employ in working out the sublime results that he had decreed, was slavery. As there was need for a Judas to a Christ, that the world's salvation might be wrought out; so there must be a slavery to liberty, to betray it, that it might suffer, and revive, and triumph. And we have seen, since the adoption of the Constitution, the inflation of the system of slavery, and its augmenting power and influence in politics. We have gone through a complete period. And now this document brings back the last link, which touches the first one. As represented by the President of the United States, this country stands where it did when the Constitution was adopted. Slavery existed, but with the desire and expectation and intention of its extinction. For ten years, for twenty years, for thirty years, for fifty years, slavery has intended to live, and its advocates have attempted to give it permanency; and the last form it assumed was to declare that liberty absolute was false, and that the only true foundation of society was slavery. And the Constitution of these United States has been set aside by the Southern Confederacy on the explicit ground that it was false, in that it asserted the right of all men equally to liberty. Slavery, going on and setting up these claims, has gone through one great period of trial, and we have come back, in this Message of the President, to the place where our fathers stood. Slavery exists as a fact, but the moral feelings of the people are against it; not against slaveholders personally, but against the accursed thing itself.

II. In that great cycle which now is completed, slavery has achieved a history. Certain unalterable results have been wrought out. It has been put upon trial before the land. And what it has been is not to be ascertained from the speculations of those that have defended it, but from the effects that have been wrought out by it in the national life. What are some of the results that have been produced under its influence? It has been tried in almost every great department of human industry, and if there be one thing susceptible of demonstration above another, it is that there is no industrial pursuit which is not blighted by slavery. The fire does not scorch the prairie in autumnal days more certainly than does the foot of slavery scorch and burn out the fertility of the soil. The slave system impoverishes the community in every State where it exists. It may enrich a class in the community, but it always impoverishes the community as a whole. It has therefore demonstrated itself to be unfit for universal husbandry. It has demonstrated itself to be malignant to the mechanic arts. It has demonstrated itself to be hateful to that last grand modern idea for the common people, *work*. It has demonstrated itself, also, to be utterly irreconcilable with general intelligence. Where slavery exists there must be ignorance. Ignorance is the swaddling-garment in which alone it can thrive. And where it is necessary for four millions of people to be ignorant, it is impossible that there should be an atmosphere of intelligence. If the slaves must be ignorant, so must their fellows, the white people. But for the prevalent ignorance of the South, we should have been spared this gigantic rebellion. They could not understand. They have received every possible misrepresentation into too credulous ears. It is because they have not intelligence to know the truth that they have been so grossly misled by their perverted teachers and leaders.

Slavery has revealed, also, what kind of citizens grow up under its influence, and what sort of patriotism it breeds. Liberty has been at work breeding citizens at the North. They are national. They love the whole country. And other citizens have been reared and educated at the South. On the first test of selfish interest it has cost them nothing to snap the sacred golden chain that bound these United States together. It cost them nothing to throw away all the history of the past, and all the venerable associations of the fathers. It cost them nothing to pull down that dear old flag that has been carried so many years with such glory around the world, to tread it under foot, and to substitute for it a bastard rag. And round about this false symbol, this new flag of dishonor, they have gathered together, not so much to lay the foundation of new institutions and new States, as to say to the world, "This rebellious rabble bears witness to the effect of slavery in educating citizens." That is the stuff that it makes of them. By nature they were as good as we were; but the Devil educated them, and the Lord educated us!

It has entered also the temple of God; and we have the record of the evil influences exerted by slavery upon the morals and the beliefs of the people. It has drugged the priests at the altar. It has put false fire thereon, and in the lurid light of that fire it has read God's word backward, making the charter of liberty for the world to be the charter of despotism. The apostasy of the Southern churches is one of the most extraordinary that ever took place. Never was the foul virus and bitterness of slavery shown before as it has been in the prostration of the churches of the

South, and the utter apostasy of the ministers of the Gospel belonging to them. They have forsworn the Lord that bought them, in trampling under foot his poor and abused ones. You may reason as you please; you may weave your political sophistries as you please, but these great facts stand out. Statistics reveal them. So manifest are they, that though all the statistics have been gathered by men appointed by pro-slavery administrations, and strained and doctored by them, it has not been possible for the utmost amount of perversion to present them so as not to have it stand out in living characters, that slavery degrades, demoralizes, and destroys; while on the other side it has been made to appear that liberty enriches, makes more intelligent, promotes good morals, and gives every element of prosperity. These results are not speculations; they are historic, tabulated facts.

Now that it has been done, I thank God that this gigantic mischief and evil has been wrought out. It has been a dreary history to go through, that of the last hundred years, while God has been developing these results; and yet, now that the work is done, I am glad of it. The arrest of Christ, the mockery of his trial, his crown of thorns, his buffetings, his crucifixion, and his burial, were awful things; but now that they are past, who would take one day from the dark days? Who would take one thorn from the crown? Who would take one pang from the suffering? For all of these are now the elements of a sublime triumph. And now that the days of slavery are drawing to a close, and the dawn is in the east, and God is giving to the world this last demonstration of the abominations of this monstrous iniquity, why should we not rejoice in the elements of triumph which its history has revealed?

III. There is a sublimity in this result, as being the practical and slowly formed conviction of a great people of the mischiefs of despotism. President Lincoln has not shot out this conviction merely by the force of his own reflection. He is not a voice crying in the wilderness. He has felt the dropping of the great heart of this people. He has heard the great voice that has gone up toward him. All the conventions that have met, all the meetings that have been held, all the speeches that have been made, and all the sermons that have been preached, have wafted their influence down to Washington, and President Lincoln understands distinctly that while he acts in his own right as a Magistrate, he yet is to speak the public sentiment of this nation in declaring that the time for emancipation has come. He is eminently a man of the people; and there never was a lip that spoke more absolutely for this people than he has now spoken, in declaring substantially that this government requires that slavery shall be done away, in order to preserve its own existence. The time has come, and the work must begin. You feel it; I feel it; the North feels it, and means it.

We believed in the benefits of liberty before this great experiment, theoretically and romantically. Ideas of liberty filled all the earliest and most generous impulses of the young heart. And we believed in liberty also as a fact for ourselves. We asserted it as a selfish instinct. We held the faith of liberty. Liberty never becomes a moral sentiment until it is universal. When you achieve it for yourselves, and demand it for those that cannot earn it for themselves, then it becomes a moral sentiment, and a religion. We valued liberty as a blessing for ourselves. Then came the fatal bribe. Slavery had it in its power, by impoverishing the South, to make the North temporarily rich. It said to the North, "I will not permit a various industry. Only two or three things will I permit to be raised at the South. Whatever else is required here your fields shall supply. I will not permit the loom here to go. I will not permit the anvil here to thrive. I will not permit the arts nor the elements of civilization here to flourish. To you I will give the monopoly of furnishing the South with most of the articles which they require for their physical life, and you shall grow rich, if you will let me alone." It was a dreadful bribe. It has had a wonderful effect upon our commercial towns and villages. It is the secret spring of the feeling yet existing in the North, which resists emancipation in the South. There are many who do not like the idea of the community there becoming able to supply its own necessities. Their desire is not so much that every State of this great country shall have the means of livelihood, as that one part shall be kept weak and dependent, that the other part, by supplying its wants, may become rich and strong. But it is not growth: it is bloat. All that the North gains at such a price is not strength nor riches. It is rather the bloat of vice and intemperance.

But in spite of all this prodigious bribe, that did work for a time, blinding the eye, hardening the heart, suppressing the conscience, perverting the faith, and turning back the courage of this people, the great industrial North, convinced by plain facts, has come to the full, irreversible conviction, that slavery is a nuisance, and that a republican government cannot exist in connection with national slavery. If there is one result which we have come to more thoroughly than to another, that is it. Our choice is between republican liberty and slavery. You must have one or the other. You cannot have both. And the North has made up its mind that it is going to have republican liberty. The gains of slavery are believed to be illusory. Its disturbances and corruptions are believed to endanger every household, every farm, every shop, every ship, every law, and every government on this whole continent. That is the popular feeling. It has become such in your day and mine. And it is not going to be unmade. It is the result of long discussion. It is the result of the most thorough writing and reading. It is the result of the deliberation of a great, intelligent common people, and of that of its moral and political leaders. They have considered for themselves. They have heard both sides. They have examined the facts. And, without being biassed by one side or the other, the loyal States have come to the irreversible conviction that slavery is a gigantic mischief and nuisance, incompatible with good government on this continent.

This conviction has been slowly wrought out. It is not a theorist's saying. It is not even a moral philosophy. It is hardly to be regarded as a doctrine of political economy or of politics. It is simply a practical judgment, a popular decision.

Loyal citizens differ exceedingly as to the character

of the African; as to the benefit of slavery or liberty to him; as to his rights; as to the best way of letting him go free; as to the disposal of him afterward; but I think it may be said that, while these discrepancies exist, there is a united and settled popular conviction that slavery is bad all round, — bad to the States that have it, and bad to the States that are united with them. And I think there is also a conviction that slavery must come to an end. I *know* it. There are as great discrepancies in the opinions of men as to many of the questions connected with slavery as ever, and we must expect that there will continue to be; but I think that on one point there is no discrepancy. I think it may be said that public opinion has doomed slavery. We look upon it as a great dismal swamp. We look upon its influence as upon poisonous malaria rising up. For many years its evils have swept over the whole land, and all the country has had chills and fever. And now the nation has said, "Let us take quinine, and besides, not only that we may cure these results, but prevent their recurrence hereafter, let us drain that swamp!" And it is going to be drained into the Gulf. *They* may do the work; but if they do not, we will do it for them. That dismal swamp, by them or by us, is going to be drained. This nation is not going to have the chills and fever for another hundred years.

IV. It is a memorable epoch that is marked by this state paper, as illustrating a complete trial and triumph of the power of free discussion and moral influences applied to the removal of national evils. The men are yet alive, and many of them are scarcely old yet, who saw the beginning of that agitation which, having gone through most remarkable phases, has resulted at last in this substantial change of the public mind and feeling. I remember the first outbreaks. I remember well when William Lloyd Garrison lay in a jail in the South on the charge of using inflammatory language. I remember the great stir that there was in the churches when he came North and began in unmeasured, and I cannot say justifiable language, to denounce the mischiefs of slavery. The men are yet alive who were mobbed for the assertion of those truths that are now uttered by the President of these United States, when he declares that slavery is inconsistent with the safety of this government. I must read that sentence again: —

> "The Federal Government would find its highest interest in such a measure as one of the most efficient means of self-preservation."

What measure? The abolishment of slavery. The President of these United States is not mobbed for that assertion. Mr. Lewis Tappan was, in his day; and Mr. Arthur Tappan; and Dr. Cox; and Mr. Garrison; and Mr. Phillips; and Mr. Alvan Stuart, of blessed memory. All these men, and many more, a large proportion of whom are yet at work with harness on, lost place, lost caste, lost preferment, lost influence with bad men, and only gained it with good, for the declaration of principles not so offensive as that which is made the very axis of the Message of the President of the United States, — that this government cannot exist without the abolishment of slavery.

The battles of the Presbyteries of the West were

under my notice. Every device was employed to prevent the going forth from those bodies of the declaration that slavery was sinful. In about every Presbytery and ecclesiastical convention or assembly in the North, the determination was that there should not be an utterance of the religious community against slavery. The first great controversy was as to whether they ought to call it an evil. They did not think they ought to call it anything. They thought they ought to let it alone. They deemed it to be none of their business. But when they were pressed to call it, not only an evil, but a sin to be repented of and renounced, they would call it an evil, but they would not call it a sin. When, further, they were pressed, not only to call it a sin, but to discipline and cut off from communion those that indulged in it, they would call it a sin, but they would not make it a matter of discipline. And so, step by step, the controversy went on till it divided those churches that would not let it come in. It has torn asunder church after church, and the rupture has not hurt them, either: it has been the best thing that could happen to them,—for to rend a church is like tearing a miser's treasures from him. He hoarded them, and made them instruments of his own selfishness; and when they are scattered and put into circulation, they subserve a far better purpose than they did while stowed away in coffers. How poor men laugh when a miser dies! His money is unlocked then. And when a church is sundered, and the fastenings of its temporal power are broken, the Gospel flows out, and gains circulation, and exerts an influence that it could not exert when it was simply ministering to those whose supreme desire was to take care of themselves.

Though men were despised for holding and advocating the doctrines of liberty, yet such as those whom I have named, and many more, gave themselves willingly to contempt for the sake of justice and truth. They were the instruments that God employed. And what had they? They had no power in the Church, and no power in the State. They had no power anywhere. They had nothing but the invincible power of weakness. They had nothing but the righteousness of their cause. They had their faith in God. They had their love of Christ. They had their unwavering conviction that the right was with them. And this inspired them with intense enthusiasm. And continuing on, they have wrought out results the importance of which cannot be estimated. They have been the pioneers in this great revolution. They are men whose shoes' latchets we are not worthy to unloose. I revere them as the prophets of the American people.

V. One great reason of the importance of this Message of the President of these United States, this turning-point in the present great crisis, this first pronunciation of the new dispensation, this first utterance from the lip of the Supreme Magistrate of this nation in favor of liberty to the captive, consists in the fact that it demonstrates the power of self-government among an intelligent and religious common people. Europe cannot, and does not, understand our order of nobility. We have an order of nobility in this country. We call it *the common people*. We believe it to be the most sublime order of nobility that the world has ever seen. We give all rights to it, and all prerogatives. Whatever there is that can be given to any order of nobility, we give to our order of the common people. We rest in it. We have faith in its integrity, in its power of government, and in its substantial justice. It takes more time for it to move, because it is so vast. An order of nobility that includes but about five hundred members can confer readily, and move with celerity; but for an order of nobility that includes twenty millions to confer and move, takes more time. What is the difference between choir singing and congregational singing? The choir is composed of but a few members, and they are more gifted, and can make themselves proficient sooner than the average of the many that compose the congregation; but when the congregation does become proficient, its singing is like the voice of mighty thunders and great waters. There is no choir like the choral thousands. And though the selected or hereditary nobility of the monarchies of Europe can move more quickly than our nobility of the common people, they cannot move with more power and efficiency. I say nothing to the discredit of the nobility of Europe; but I do not hesitate to say that everything that they can do, our order of the common people can do, and much more.

This republican government has made itself felt on the other side of the Atlantic. Sometimes storms that take place so far off that the wind does not touch these shores, and the clouds are not visible here, report themselves to us by the waves that they drive hither. I have heard my father tell how, on a tranquil evening like this, as he went out of the church at East Hampton, on the distant shore of Long Island, he heard the waves dashing against the beach, with a noise like thunder; and he ran down to see them roll, as they did in terrible majesty. There had been a storm afar off, and the waves which it created reached the shore, though the storm reported itself in no other way. And so the great popular wave, set in motion by this nation, surges and breaks on the shore of Europe. Though the Constitution, the laws, and the doctrines that prevail here are never carried over there, yet the popular impulse is; and thrones are unquiet, and dynasties are disturbed. Monarchs do not like the doctrines of the common people on this side of the water. And when it was supposed that this government was dissolved in its own weakness, when it was supposed that this government was unable to cope with the mischiefs that had grown up in its own midst, there can be no doubt that there were great rejoicings (blessed be God, premature rejoicings,) over us.

Now the power of this people to stand when betrayed by their Government; the power of this people to organize an army and navy for magnitude and efficiency second to none; the power of this people to hold all their passions in restraint, and to maintain unity and power under the most provoking and irritating circumstances; the power of this people to submit their pride and their very national name to the decree of their own chosen and trusted rulers; the power of this people to throw off a gigantic evil from their very vitals, and to compel and maintain national unity against the most enormous rebellion that was ever generated; the power of this common people, not only to do these things, but to do them justly, deliberately, temperately, magnanimously, as they will, is to read a lesson of self-government to Europe that has never been read before.

And in the midst of this conflict, one voice rises above the storm. It will be heard on every throne, and by every people of Europe. The dungeons will hear it. The serfs and slaves will hear it. It is the voice of the Chief Magistrate of this nation, saying, "We must emancipate!" We shall have made a greater stride in moral influence in this nation during the last year than we made in the fifty years previous. We have hitherto made great strides in material aggrandizement; but these have not, I think, given us moral power.

VI. God, by giving us such schooling, such discipline, and such a glorious issue, indicates to us that he means to employ this nation upon this whole continent, for a glorious purpose and destiny. The auspices of the future — what imagination can conceive of and follow them? God has given us a wonderful history, and I believe that he means by it that we shall be a right hand of power to accomplish his purposes on this whole continent.

I want to call your attention, before making the applications, to two or three great coincidences that are very noticeable at this time. One is that the Czar of Russia, representing the extreme of monarchy, and the President of the United States, representing the extreme of republicanism, are, by a Divine Providence sent at the same moment on the same errand. The Czar has issued a proclamation of emancipation to the serfs of Russia. On those plains where the plant of liberty has never grown before, and where the seeds of despotism have come up and flourished, the Czar has planted the seeds of liberty. God be thanked that he has raised up a Moses, not near the throne of Egypt, but on the throne of a prouder and vaster empire, and that while he has inspired him to issue a decree of emancipation to the serfs within his dominions, he has inspired this people to appoint a Chief Magistrate who has just issued a Message for the emancipation of the slaves in our land. The work is not accomplished, but it is *initiated*, as he says. It is initiated just as the spring is. The snow is not gone, but it is going; and it will not come back; or, if it does, it will not remain long. The season and the elements are against it.

And let me not omit to speak a word of gratitude to this imperial throne for the sympathy that has come thence to us in the hour of our trial. When those who should have first of all given sympathy neither knew us nor spoke an encouraging word, but juggled and colluded with rebels; when those who were blood of our blood and bone of our bone swarmed our shores with fleets and armies, seeking to destroy us; when selfish England forgot her child and kindred, then Russia opened her heart, — yet warm, though beating in the frozen North, and near Siberia, — and sent us words of cheer.

Another coincidence is this: that while the common people of this land are now engaged in a war for liberty, and while they are taking the first steps toward the extinction of slavery in one part of this continent, England and France and Spain are leagued together in another part, in Mexico, to destroy the liberty of the people of that country, to build up a throne, and to put upon it a member of the most infamous of all the reigning houses of Europe, the accursed house of Hapsburg.* There are the three crowns and the three flags attempting the work of subjugation and of despotism. Right alongside is the work of republican America, breaking the bond, sundering the chain, opening the prison-house, and giving wider swing and reach to the immortal doctrines of liberty. Let them build deep the foundations of that throne. Let them put good timber into it. There is a ground-swell beginning, that shall smite it, so that no man shall find one stick joined to another. Let Europe attempt to establish despotism on this continent! We have commenced the work of overthrowing oppression; and there shall be neither slavery nor despotism between the sounds of the waves on the shores of the Pacific and the Atlantic. This continent is for liberty.

One other coincidence is this: that during this dark period, when all business has been shocked; when all the ordinary courses of affairs have been blocked up; when almost every family has some representative on the field of battle; when mothers are solicitous, and fathers are watchful; when our brothers, our sons, and our friends are in peril of life; when every morning is a morning of intense anxiety to know the tidings of yesterday, — that during this period God has been pleased to reveal the hand of his power, and revivals of religion are breaking out in churches, and going all around the land. In the midst of all this gigantic agitation, blessings abound in the sanctuary. War and trouble in the State; peace and prosperity in the Church. What a strange

* Such was the original plan of the Mexican invasion.

coincidence! It is God's doing. God is in our midst.

And now, a word as to our duties. In the first place, it is the duty of the whole loyal North, and of the Middle States, to send up to the President of these United States, and to the Congress assembled, the most unmistakable tokens, not only of their thanks, but of their sympathy, and their earnest and energetic co-operation. I would to God that it might have been so that every church in our land could have spoken to-day upon this Message of the President. I would that in every town and village in the loyal States public meetings might be appointed to accord instant and hearty sympathy to the Chief Magistrate of this nation. As the tide rolls into the Bay of Fundy thirty feet perpendicular, and abreast, so let the tide of public sympathy roll to Washington, and carry on this great inspiring work in the hearts of our rulers. It is the duty of this people to say amen, as the voice of the ocean, to this Proclamation.

Then, secondly, it is the duty of all the loyal States to prepare themselves to take part in this great work. They should lay aside all causes of division and alienation among themselves, so that citizens may stand together on a ground common to them all. Let the old feuds die out. Put out the party watch-fires, and throw away the weapons of war. Let newspapers forget the animosities that have been fomented by ill-concealed selfishness and rivalry. Let the old and the new come together. Let the conservative and the progressive find something in common. For once, let there be a glorious fusion of all sides for the sake of liberty. We have a leader. No man can complain of this document of his on the score of moderation. It is among the marvels that all the papers that I have seen thus far have claimed it as the expression of their views. The *Tribune* broke forth into jubilee about it. Nothing can compare with the tranquil, placid pleasure that the *World* has in it. The *Times* has put down both feet and rejoiced on this platform. And the *Journal of Commerce* declares that its doctrines are those that it has advocated ever since it can remember! Now, it is said that misery makes strange bed-fellows. I think you will admit that liberty makes stranger. But we are all together. Do not let us go asunder. For once I am glad to belong to the great church political of all these different members. I extend the right hand of fellowship to all papers, no matter what their former course has been, that earnestly advocate these acceptable doctrines of liberty. Let us forget the past. Let us not seek the things in which we differ. Let us not divide ourselves by raising questions of the future. One step at a time is sufficient. Let Congress accept this recommendation of the President. Let the people express their approval of it in tones that shall not be mistaken. Let the policy of emancipation begin. Let Delaware, let Maryland, let Kentucky, let Missouri, let Tennessee, begin to avail themselves of this proffer. Let the heart and the pocket of the nation go with the indications of Providence. Let us make haste to reach the glorious results that are promised. And if, when we have taken one step, questions come up of how, and on what conditions, God will show us the next step, if we are only united. I tell you, the great difficulty in the way of the abolition of slavery heretofore, aside from the fact that its history was not consummated, has been, that we did not want to abolish it. We were not united to do it. And now, if this people are united in this thing, you may depend upon it, to say nothing of the emphasis that there is in numbers, that where there is a will there is a way. If you are purposed, if you are willing to sacrifice something, and if you take hold of concordant hands, and cheer each other, and avoid things that are irritating, and stand together with your faces as though you would go toward Jerusalem, God will create a new heaven and a new earth for you; a Jerusalem shall come into our midst, — a Jerusalem of prefigured liberty.

XI.

THE SUCCESS OF AMERICAN DEMOCRACY.*

"So the king of the South shall come into his kingdom, and shall return into his own land. But his sons shall be stirred up, and shall assemble a multitude of great forces: and one shall certainly come, and overflow, and pass through: then shall he return, and be stirred up even to his fortress. And the king of the South shall be moved with choler, and shall come forth and fight with him, even with the king of the North: and he shall set forth a great multitude; but the multitude shall be given into his hand. And when he hath taken away the multitude, his heart shall be lifted up; and he shall cast down many ten thousands; but he shall not be strengthened by it. For the king of the North shall return, and shall set forth a multitude greater than the former, and shall certainly come after certain years with a great army and with much riches. And in those times there shall many stand up against the king of the South; also the robbers of thy people shall exalt themselves to establish the vision: but they shall fall. So the king of the North shall come, and cast up a mount, and take the most fenced cities: and the arms of the South shall not withstand, neither his chosen people, neither shall there be any strength to withstand. But he that cometh against him shall do according to his own will, and none shall stand before him; and he shall stand in the glorious land, which by his hand shall be consumed. He shall also set his face to enter with the strength of his whole kingdom. And equality" — or conditions of equality — "shall be with him; thus shall he do." — Dan. xi. 9-17.

I do not use these words in any close historical sense. They are a very poetic and glowing description of a conflict in which, with a singular fitness to our times, both the terms North and South, and the events which were

* April 13, 1862, the anniversary Sunday of the attack on Fort Sumter.

predicted, are strikingly suggestive. And although a sharp exegesis might destroy some parts of the seeming analogy, I shall consider them as a splendid poetic imagery. As such, I think you will agree with me that it is a remarkable passage, and that it not only describes the past with great accuracy, but throws a blazing light upon the times that are to come. We are in the midst of times the most exciting; times that demand faith; times in which the teachings and prophecies of Scripture come with peculiar emphasis.

You will remember the scenes of one year ago. It was just such a bright and beautiful day as this has been. The air was full of news. These great cities boiled like caldrons. The people had learned that the guns had opened upon Fort Sumter. Treason was consummated! Our hearts yearned toward the brave garrison. We hoped that the leaders and their companions in arms would sustain the stronghold. Our hearts felt the cold breath of horror, when at last it was known that the flag of the Union had been assaulted. The forts that had belched their fire upon that flag had been built underneath its protection. They had carried it for years upon their flag-staff. The very guns that were flaming upon it had been founded and forged under its flowing folds. The men that aimed them had been born and reared under its protection. That flag had been the honored ensign of our people in their memorable struggle for independence. It had seen the British arms laid down before it. It had been honored in every land. Our men-of-war had borne it, without disgrace, to every part of the world. Nor was there a port upon the globe where men chose or dared to insult that national emblem. That inglorious wickedness was reserved to our own people! It was by American hands that it was dishonored, slit with balls, and trailed in the dust!

That a crime so unnatural and monstrous was then going on, made the anniversary of this day memorable above all Sabbaths of our history. It was an infernal insurrection against liberty, good government, and civilization, on the most sacred day of the week! We shall not soon experience a like excitement again. Although but a year ago, it seems ten years. And, in ordinary history, ten years are not so full of matter as has been this single year. It is full of events visible, but yet more full of those things that do not come under corporeal observation.

Such has been the intensity of public feeling, that it has seemed as if nothing was doing. We have chidden those in authority, and felt that due speed had not been made. But within one twelvemonth a gigantic army has been raised and drilled; all its equipments created; all the material of war produced and collected together. The cannon that now reverberate across the continent, a twelvemonth ago were sleeping ore in the mountains. The clothing of thousands was fleece upon the backs of sheep. As we look back, we can scarcely believe our own senses, that so much has been done; although, at every single hour of it, it seemed as if little was being done, — for all the speed and all the power of this great government were not so fast and eager as our thoughts and desires were.

A navy has sprung forth, almost at a word; and,

stranger still, by the skill of our inventors and naval constructors, a new era has been inaugurated in naval warfare. It is probable that forts and ships have come to the end of one dispensation, and that the old is to give place hereafter to the new.

The history of this year is the history of the common people of America. It is memorable on account of the light that it throws upon them. We are fond of talking of *American ideas.* There are such things as American ideas, distinctive, peculiar, national. Not that they were first discovered here, or that they are only entertained here; but because more than anywhere else they lie at the root of the institutions, and are working out the laws and the policies of this people.

The root idea is this: that man is the most sacred trust of God to the world; that his value is derived from his moral relations, from his divinity. Looked at in his relations to God and the eternal world, every man is so valuable that you cannot make distinction between one and another. If you measure a man by the skill that he can exhibit, and the fruit of it, there is great distinction between one and another. Men are not each worth the same thing to society. All men cannot think with a like value, nor work with a like product. And if you measure man as a producing creature — that is, in his secular relations — men are not alike valuable. But when you measure men on their spiritual side, and in their affectional relations to God and the eternal world, the lowest man is so immeasurable in value that you cannot make any practical difference between one man and another. Although, doubtless, some are vastly above others, the lowest and least goes beyond your power of conceiving, and your power of measuring. This is the root idea, which, if not recognized, is yet operative. It is the fundamental principle of our American scheme, that man is above nature. Man, by virtue of his original endowment and affiliation to the Eternal Father, is superior to every other created thing. There is nothing to be compared with man. All governments are from him and for him, and not over him and upon him. All institutions are not his masters, but his servants. All days, all ordinances, all usages, come to minister to the chief and the king, God's son, man, of whom God only is master. Therefore he is to be thoroughly enlarged, thoroughly empowered by development, and then thoroughly trusted. This is the American idea, — for we stand in contrast with the world in holding and teaching it; that men, having been once thoroughly educated, are to be absolutely trusted.

The education of the common people follows, then, as a necessity. They are to be fitted to govern. Since all things are from them and for them, they must be educated to their function, to their destiny. No pains are spared, we know, in Europe, to educate princes and nobles who are to govern. No expense is counted too great, in Europe, to prepare the governing classes for their function. America has her governing class, too; and that governing class is the whole people. It is a slower work, because it is so much larger. It is never carried so high, because there is so much more of it. It is easy to lift up a crowned class. It is not easy to lift up society from the very foundation. That is the work of centuries.

And therefore, though we have not an education so deep nor so high as it is in some other places, we have it broader than it is anywhere else in the world; and we have learned that for ordinary affairs intelligence among the common people is better than treasures of knowledge among particular classes of the people. School-books do more for this country than encyclopædias.

And so there comes up the American conception of a common people as an order of nobility, or as standing in the same place to us that orders of nobility stand to other peoples. Not that, after our educated men and men of genius are counted out, we call all that remain the common people. The whole community, top and bottom and intermediate, the strong and the weak, the rich and the poor, the leaders and the followers, constitute with us the commonwealth; in which laws spring from the people, administration conforms to their wishes, and they are made the final judges of every interest of the State.

In America there is not one single element of civilization that is not made to depend, in the end, upon public opinion. Art, law, administration, policy, reformations of morals, religious teaching, all derive, in our form of society, the most potent influence from the common people. For although the common people are educated in preconceived notions of religion, the great intuitions and instincts of the heart of man rise up afterwards, and in their turn influence back. So there is action and reaction.

It is this very thing that has led men that are educated, in Europe, to doubt the stability of our nation. Owing to a strange ignorance on their part, our glory has seemed to them our shame, and our strength has seemed to them our weakness, and our invincibility has seemed to them our disaster and defeat. This impression of Europeans has been expressed in England in language that has surprised us, and that one day will surprise them. We know more of it in England because the English language is our mother tongue, and we are more concerned to know what England thinks of us than any other nation.

But it is impossible that nations educated into sympathy with strong governments, and with the side of those that govern, should sympathize with the governed. In this country the sympathy goes with the governed, and not with the governing, as much as in other countries it goes with the governing, and not with the governed. And abroad they are measuring by a false rule, and by a home-bred and one-sided sympathy.

It is impossible for men who have not seen it to understand that there is no society possible that will bear such expansion and contraction, such strains and burdens, as a society made up of free educated common people, with democratic institutions. It has been supposed that such a society was the most unsafe, and the least capable of control of any. But whether tested by external pressure, or, as now, by the most wondrous internal evils, an educated democratic people are the strongest government that can be made on the face of the earth. In no other form of society is it so safe to set discussion at large. Nowhere else is there such safety in the midst of apparent conflagration. Nowhere else is there such entire rule, when there seems to be such entire anarchy. A foreigner would think, pending a presidential election, that the end of the world had come. The people roar and dash like an ocean. "No government," he would say, "was ever strong enough to hold such wild and tumultuous enthusiasm, and zeal, and rage." True. There is not a *government* strong enough to hold them. Nothing but self-government will do it: that will. Educate men to take care of themselves, individually and in masses, and then let the winds blow; then let the storms fall; then let excitements burn, and men will learn to move freely upon each other, as do drops of water in the ocean. Our experience from generation to generation has shown that, though we may have fantastic excitements; though the whole land may seem to have swung from its moorings on a sea of the wildest agitation, we have only to let the silent dropping paper go into the box, and that is the end of the commotion. To-day, the flames mount to heaven; and on every side you hear the most extravagant prophecies and the fiercest objurgations; and both sides know that, if they do not succeed, the end of the world will have come. But to-morrow the vote is declared, and each side go home laughing, to take hold of the plough and the spade; and they are satisfied that the nation is safe after all.

And we have come to ridicule the idea of danger from excitements. Where else was there ever a nation that could bear to have every question, no matter how fiery or how fierce, let loose to go up and down, over hill and through valley, without police or government restraint upon the absolute liberty of the common people? Where else was ever a government that could bear to allow entire free discussion? We grow strong under it. Voting is the cure of evil with us. Liberty, that is dangerous abroad, is our very safety. And since our whole future depends upon our rightly understanding this matter, — the liberty of the common people, and the glory of the common people, — and since this government of our educated common people is to be the death of slavery, and to spread over this continent an order of things for which in past experience there is no parallel, and for which men's ideas are not prepared, — we do well to take heed of this memorable year of the common people. For histories will register this year of 1861 – 62 as the year of the common people of America.

I. One year ago there fell a storm upon the great heart of the common people, which swayed it as the ocean is swayed. It has not calmed itself yet. It was that shot at the American flag that touched the national heart. No one knew before what a depth of feeling was there. We did not know how our people had clustered about that banner all their ideas of honor and patriotism and glory. We did not know how the past and future met and stood together upon that flag in the imagination of every American. In an hour all this was disclosed. And what was the manifestation of that hour? All things that separated the common people of America were at once forgotten. There rose up, with appalling majesty, the multitude of the common people. The schemes of treachery, the political webs that had been framed, went down in a moment; and the voice of the common people it was that called the government to be energetic, to take courage, and to rescue the land.

But I would not have you suppose that the common

people gave forth merely an unreasoning zeal, — a furious burst of patriotic emotion. The common people of the North had, and they still have, a clear, comprehensive, and true idea of American nationality, such as we looked for in vain in many of the leaders of past times. They had taken in the right view of national unity. They had a right view of the trust of territory held in common by all, for all, on this continent. They felt, more than any others, that Divine Providence had given to this people, not a northern part, not a middle ridge, not a southern section, but an undivided continent. They held it, not for pride, not for national vanity, not to be cut and split into warring sections, but as a sacred trust, held for sublimest ends of human happiness, in human liberty. And the instincts and intuitions of the common people it was that made this, not a struggle for sectional precedency, but a struggle for the maintenance of the great national trust, and for the establishment of American ideas over the whole American continent. And our government felt that they could lean back on the brave heart of the great intelligent people.

While, then, men of our own blood are ignorant and blind; while even to this hour the ablest statesmen in the British Parliament are declaring, though in a friendly spirit in most respects, that it were better that an amicable settlement and separation should take place, and that they should live apart who cannot live peaceably together, our common people are greater than parliaments or than ministers; and they see, and feel, and know, that God has rolled upon them a duty, not of present peace, but of future stability, national grandeur, and continental liberty.

This is the doctrine of the common people, and it will stand.

For that idea our common people are giving their sons, their blood, and their treasure, and they will continue to the uttermost to give them.

For this sake see what a common people can do. One of the most difficult things for any people to do, for any reason, is to lay aside their animosities and malignant feelings. But this great common people have laid aside every animosity, every party feeling, and all political disagreements; and for one year they have maintained an honest unity. I am more proud of the substantial unity that has been wrought out in the North, than of any battle that has been fought. It is the noblest evidence of the strength of our form of government.

The common people have given without stint their sons, their substance, and their ingenuity: and they are not weary of giving. They have consented patiently to the interruption of their industries, and to all the burdens which taxes bring. Taxes touch men in a very tender place; for human nature resides very strongly in the particular neighborhood where taxes anchor. And if anything takes hold of men and brings them to their bearings, it is the imposition of burdens that are felt in the pocket. I sometimes think that men can carry burdens on their hearts more easily than on their exchequer. But they have taken both the burdens of taxation and bereavements, they have given both blood and money; and they are willing to bear the load as long as it is necessary to secure this continent to liberty.

They have demanded of this administration which

they themselves ordained, that it should not spare them. The only thing that the people have ever been disposed to blame the government for has been, that it has not moved fast enough; that it has not done enough. "Take more; call for more; do more!" is the demand of the people upon the government.

They have accepted the most unwonted and dangerous violations of the fundamental usages of this land with implicit submission. They are a proud people, jealous of their rights; a proud people, the flash of whose eye is like blood when they are wronged in their fundamental rights; and yet, the precious writ of *habeas corpus* has been suspended, and they have consented. They have been restricted in their intercourse to a degree altogether unprecedented, and they have judged it expedient to submit.

They have submitted to the limitation of speech and discussion, — a thing most foreign to American ideas. The arrest of men without legal process or accusation, and their imprisonment and long duress without trial, — these are new in our times and in this land. And yet, under all these interruptions of our most grave and important principles and rights, the people have been calm; they have trusted their government; and they have been willing to wait.

These are dangerous things, even in extremity; but for their sakes who control the affairs of this nation, and that they might have the most unlimited power to crush the rebellion, and establish liberty, the common people, with magnanimous generosity, have yielded up these imperishable rights.

When the whole national heart beat with gratification at the arrest of men who had been at the root of this grand treachery, mark, I beseech of you, the bearing of the common people of America. If there was one thing about which they were expected to rage like wolves, it was this. Nothing in external circumstances could be more irritating and aggravating than those exhibitions of foreign feeling which came to our knowledge. I know that the diplomatic language of the two governments was very smooth and unexceptionable; and I am informed that the tone of many of the local papers of England was kind; but all the English papers that I saw, with one or two exceptions, were of such a spirit that I will characterize them only by saying that good breeding was not common where the editors of them lived. If there was one single missile more offensive than another, it was eagerly sought out. Tried on the side of revenge; tried on the side of national animosities; tried by foreign impertinence and unkindness; tried at home in the midst of treachery, in the midst of war, in the midst of troubles and burdens, and in the midst of an interrupted commerce, — mark the heroic conduct of this great American people.

Government pronounced its judgment against the feelings and expectations of the common people. Slidell and Mason were to be given up. There was silence instantly, and thoughtfulness, throughout this land. Then came acquiescence, full, cheerful, uncomplaining. I have yet to see a single paper that seriously, after the appearance of the letter of the Secretary of State, made one complaint or ill-natured remark. Such a thing was never before seen in the history of the world. Mason and Slidell might have been taken from Washington to Boston Harbor under the care of a single officer, without molestation from the common people of America. These are the common people that they are pleased to call the mob of America; but not among crowned heads and privileged classes, not among any other people on the earth, is there such stability, such order, such self-restraint, such dignity, and such sublime nobility, as there is among the educated common people of America. God bless them! Under the terrible inflictions of battle, under griefs innumerable, in the midst of desolations that go to the very heart of families, there is the same noble, patient, uncomplaining cheerfulness and devotion to this great cause.

II. The history of this year has silently developed many convictions based upon great truths. It has, in the first place, revolutionized the whole opinion of men as to the relative military power of the Free States and Slave States of America. It was an almost undisputed judgment, that the habits of the South bred prowess; that they were chivalric; that their educated men were better officers than ours; and that their common people, in the hour of battle, would be better soldiers than the laboring classes of the North. It never was our faith, it never was our belief, but that the laboring and educated common people were just as much better for military development, when the time came, as for ordinary industrial purposes. Events have justified our impressions in this regard.

Let us look, for a moment, at the line of battle. Passing by the earlier conflicts prematurely brought on, in which the advantage was, without good conduct on either side, in favor of Southern men, what is the general conclusion from that line of conflicts that subsequently followed each other almost without interruption, from Hilton Head, Beaufort, Roanoke, Newbern, Fort Henry, Fort Donelson, Somerset, Nashville, Island Number Ten, Pittsburg Landing?

Without further particularizing, what have been the general results of this series of conflicts? The rebels are swept out of the upper and eastern parts of Virginia. They have lost one portion of North Carolina. Their seaboard is almost taken from them. They have been driven from Kentucky and Missouri, and in Tennessee they are close pressed on Memphis itself. They are on the eve, apparently, of losing the great metropolis of the Southwest. And has there been one single field in which Northern endurance and courage have not been made to appear eminent over Southern? In the battle of Pittsburg Landing what a disparity there was in generalship between the North and the South! That battle was won by the soldiers. The Southwestern men had every advantage in military skill, and on our side the only advantage was that we had men who would not be beaten. Our soldiers had little help of generalship. It was hands, and not brains, that conquered there.

This matter, then, will, from this time forth, stand on different ground. It is not for the sake of vainglorying that I make these allusions. If it were not that I have a moral end in view, I should think them unseasonable; but we shall never have peace until we have respect, we shall never have respect so long as a boasting Southern effete population think that they can overmaster Northern sturdy yeomen.

When they know what Northern muscle and blows mean, they will respect them; and when they respect them, we shall be able to live in harmony with them: and not till then.

But there are many other things that have been evolved in the history of the year. There have been convictions wrought in the minds of the thinking common people that will not be easily worn out. There is coming to be a general conviction, that men brought up under the influence of slavery are contaminated to the very root, and that they cannot make good citizens of a republic. The radical nature of slavery is such as to destroy the possibility of good citizenship in the masses of men. Exceptions there are, because even in the Slave States there are large neighborhoods where slavery does not exist, and where many men are superior to their circumstances. But the average tendency of slave influences is to narrow men; to make them selfish; to unfit them for public spirit; to destroy that large patriotism from which comes the feeling of nationality.

I think there is a widening conviction, that slavery and its laws, and liberty and its institutions, cannot exist under one government. And I think that, if it were not for the impediment of supposed constitutional restrictions, there would be an almost universal disposition to sweep, as with a deluge, this gigantic evil out of our land. The feeling of the people in this matter is unmistakable. The recommendation of the President of these United States, which has been corroborated by the resolution of Congress, is one of the most memorable events of our history. The fact that a policy of emancipation has been recommended by the Chief Magistrate, and indorsed by Congress, cannot be over-estimated in importance. Old John Quincy Adams lifted his head in the grave, methinks, when that resolution was carried,—he that was almost condemned for treason because he dared to introduce in Congress a subject that looked toward emancipation. Last Friday — a day not henceforth to be counted inauspicious — was passed the memorable bill giving liberty to the slave in the District of Columbia. One might almost say, if the President had signed it, "Lord, now let thy servant depart in peace, according to thy word; for mine eyes have seen thy salvation." It is worth living for a lifetime to see the capital of our government redeemed from the stigma and shame of being a slave mart. I cannot doubt that the President of the United States will sign that bill. It shall not shake my confidence in him, but it certainly will not change my judgment that it should be signed, if he does not sign it. It would have been better if it had been signed the moment that it was received; but we have found out by experience that though Abraham Lincoln is sure, he is slow; and that though he is slow, he is sure!

I think that it is beginning to be seen that the North, for its own sake, must exert every proper constitutional influence, and every moral influence, to cleanse the South from the contamination of slavery. What gambling-houses and drinking-saloons are to the young men of a neighborhood, taking hold of their animal passions, and corrupting them where human nature is most temptable, undermining their character, and wasting their stamina, that Southern marts are to our common people. The animal parts of our nature come naturally into sympathy with the South. The Southern institution is an academy of corruption to the animal feelings of the whole people, and it will continue to be throwing back into our system elements of inflammation and trouble as long as it exists. I dread such a settlement of this controversy as will follow whenever all malignant passions and political machinations shall have swept the bad men of the North and of the South together again for future legislation.

We have begun, also, to suspect another thing, which we shall learn more and more thoroughly; and that is, that hereafter, in this nation, the North must prevail. For the North is the nation, and the South is but the fringe. The heart is here; the trunk is here; the brain is here. The most exquisite compliment ever paid to New England was in the secret scheme and machination of the leaders of the rebellion, which it was supposed would be successful. They meant to threaten secession and war, and arouse a party in the North that would unite with them, and then reconstruct in such a way as to leave New England out, and take all the rest of the nation in. Had they succeeded, they would have been in the condition of a man that should go to bed whole at night, and wake up in the morning without his head! For the brain of this nation is New England. There is not a part that does not derive its stimulus and supply from that fountain of laws and ideas. Well may they wish to exclude from their corrupt constitution and laws that part of this nation which has been the throne of God. Well may they desire to separate themselves from that portion of our country which has been the source of all that is godlike in American history. But I do not think that they will cut off our head. And hereafter I think it will be felt more and more that the North is the nation: not New England, but the whole North from ocean to ocean, — all that is comprised in the Northern loyal Free States. It is the foundation of industry; it is the school of intelligence; it is the home of civilized institutions; it is the repository of those principles which are the foundation of our political fabric; and if we hope to save the government and our peculiar ideas, it is the North that must save them, and not the South. We may just as well say it as to disguise it. Whatever may be wise or unwise, expedient or inexpedient, in times of party management, I do not hesitate to say, and I repeat it again and again, that the North is this nation, and that the North must govern it: not against the Constitution, but by the Constitution; not against law, but through law; not for selfishness, but for the well-being of the whole; not to aggrandize itself, but to enrich every State in the Union, from the North to the South, and from the East to the West. The South are prodigal sons; they are wasters; they are destroyers. The North has conservative forces; and now that she has come to govern, she will be derelict, she will forfeit every claim to respect, and she will bring the judgment of God on her head, if she hesitates to take the government, and maintain it till she has carried the principles of the American people of this continent triumphantly through.

Since, then, her ascendency means liberty, the thrift of the common people, and the progress of civilization, the North owes it to the nation itself not to yield up that ascendency. One side or the other must prevail. Let it be that side that carries forward to the future the precious legacies of the past. There go two principles looking to the future. One is represented by our flag, and all its starry folds. Liberty; democratic equality; Christianity; God, the only king; right, the only barrier and restraint; and then, God and right being respected, liberty to all, from top to bottom, and the more liberty the stronger and safer, — that is the Northern conception. And that is the precious seed that shall pierce to State after State, rolling westward her empire. What has the North done? Look at Michigan; look at Ohio; look at Indiana; look at Illinois; look at Wisconsin; look at Iowa. These are the fruits of Northern ideas. And where is the South? Look at Missouri; look at Texas. See what States she rears. And which of these shall be the seed-planter of the future? Which shall carry the victorious banner? Shall the South carry her bastard bunting, bearing the pestiferous seed of slavery, degradation, and national rottenness? or shall the North, advancing her banner, carry with her stars and stripes all that they symbolize, — God's glory in man's liberty? I think — and I thank God for it — that the great heart of this people is beginning to accept this destiny, and that it is becoming the pride of their future.

There is but one other thing that I will say, for I do not wish to weary you with too long a discussion of that which is dear to my own heart as life itself. While there have been many incidental ills and evils occasioned by the present conflict, it has had one good effect in amalgamating this heterogeneous people.

Since we have received millions from foreign lands, there have been some political jealousies toward those belonging to other nations. I think you have seen the end of that most un-American Native-Americanism. There is not one nation that has not contributed its quota to fight the battles of liberty. The blood of the Yankee has met the blood of the Irishman. Right along-side of our Curtis was the noble Sigel. Right by the side of the wounded American lay the wounded German. Two tongues met when they spoke the common words, Country, Liberty, God, and Freedom. And now there is no foreign blood among us. They are ours. They have earned their birth here. Their nativity is as if our mothers bore them and nursed them. America has received all her foreign population, now, with a more glorious adoption, and they are our kindred. God be thanked for this substantial benefit. War, with all its horrors, is not without its incidental advantages.

Is the year, then, that is just past, to have a parallel and sequence in the year that is to come? What is to be the future? What are our prospects and hopes? I am not a prophet. I cannot lift the veil from what is before us. I can only express my own judgment. Perhaps you think I am sanguine. I think I am not sanguine, though I am hopeful. And yet I have no other thought than that victory awaits us at every step. We are able to bear our share of defeat. If the blessing of liberty is too great to be purchased at so cheap a price, let God tell us the price, and we are ready to pay it. We have more sons to give. We can live lower, and on less. Our patience is scarcely drawn upon. The sources of our prosperity are hardly touched. And I think I may say for you, and the great American common people, "We will give every dollar that we are worth, every child that we have, and our own selves; we will bring all that we are, and all that we have, and offer them up freely; but this country shall be one, and undivided. We will have one Constitution, and one liberty, and that universal." The Atlantic shall sound it, and the Pacific shall echo it back, deep answering to deep, and it shall reverberate from the Lakes on the North to the unfrozen Gulf on the South, — "One nation; one Constitution; one starry banner!" Hear it, England! — one country, and indivisible. Hear it, Europe! — one people, and inseparable. One God; one hope; one baptism; one Constitution; one government; one nation; one country; one people, — cost what it may, we will have it!

XII.

CHRISTIANITY IN GOVERNMENT.*

"The spirit of the Lord is upon me, because he hath anointed me to preach the Gospel to the poor; he hath sent me to heal the broken-hearted, to preach deliverance to the captives, and recovering of sight to the blind, to set at liberty them that are bruised, to preach the acceptable year of the Lord." — Luke iv. 18, 19.

"AND he began to say unto them, This day is this scripture fulfilled in your ears."

This could mean nothing less than that he applied to himself this scripture, and accepted it as a proper description of his own work, — as a proper unfolding of the aims and intentions of his work on earth.

Consider the width and scope of this memorable passage from the prophet Isaiah. Good tidings to the poor, — by far the greatest in number of all the people in the world; healing to the broken-hearted, — the children of sorrow; deliverance to captives; instruction to the ignorant; release to those in slavery; — this he declared to be that for which he was ordained. It was not for the regeneration of society first, and from the outside; it was not for the incul-

* June 29, 1862. Slavery had been prohibited in the Territories, June 20, and the Confiscation Act was pending.

cation of an exact system of truth; it was not for the family; it was not for any objective and usually understood thing, that he came. A moral purpose, comprehending all these, and underlying them all, he announced as being the drift and the genius of his ministry. It may be said that in this annunciation our Saviour declared his congregation,—those to whom he came to preach. He gathered together, as it were, round about him, the classes to whom he intended to minister, and for whom he had a special message.

Christ declared God, then, in him, to be on the side of those hitherto despised and neglected,—the great under-class. He, as it were, set aside those whom hitherto men had esteemed and counted honorable.

The first class to whom his mission related consisted of those that were bruised,—the multitude that were in slavery, and that were beaten by cruel masters, as if they were but oxen, or hide-tough asses; men that were mere beasts of burden. The world was full of such. Almost every heathen nation had slaves. It was so in the civilized nations as well as in the savage. There was no difference as to the fact between barbaric peoples and refined. As to numbers and treatment, there were incidental differences. But slavery was almost universal; and Christ declared, "I come for the slaves."

The next class was even greater than this. It was that which was composed of the mentally blind,—the ignorant. The Gospel is a common-school Gospel. Christ came as an educator. He came to strike through the narrow and opaque human mind with that intelligence which should carry, not simply knowledge of figures and letters, but the capacity to know whatever it was necessary that men should know. His mission, then, was to the million; for then, as now, the million were made up of the ignorant. Men have always been crude and unameliorated in the mass. They have lived chiefly among the lower notions. In regard to all but one in a million since the world began, it is true that they have been but little better than mere intelligent animals. It was time that some one should look after these; for they were the most neglected and uncared for of any class of people on the face of the earth.

The next for whom he declares that he came were the captives. They may be supposed to differ from those who are bruised in bondage. They were political captives. They were men that were incarcerated. They were the wretches whom governments, for various reasons, had deprived of their natural rights. Every government of old, and not very old either, has had its camps and castles of miserable victims of jealousy, fear, cruelty, revenge, avarice, and ambition. Some have been bad, doubtless; although, if all that deserved imprisoning had gone to prison, there would hardly have been enough left to be jailers, in many periods of the world. But, in fact, captives have included some of the best blood of humanity. Some of the noblest of all the world's spirits have been the endungeoned. Prison histories will be the most affecting histories, I think, when we come to read where God educated his heroes. In that last day of exhibition and judgment, when the first shall be last and the last shall be first, when God calls for thrones and those that sat on them, as we open our eyes to behold regal splendor, what a squalid set will dodge past the light and glory of the eternal throne to hide themselves in everlasting darkness! And when God calls for dungeons and prisons, and we look to see a limping, miserable crew of hideous criminals, behold, they shall be led on by the noblest forms of martyrs! Men that are now crowned by the glorified and radiant dignity of patriots; unbribable men; men willing to do, and willing not to do, (which is a thousand times harder than to be willing to do,) for the sake of their country; men willing to go forward though it was unto death, and willing to stand still though to stand still was to live when life was the curse of existence, — they shall be found in the roll of captives. And of those who have suffered vexations and limitations and wrongs; of that great unbefriended and unjustified mass of men that in every age and nation have been the disgrace of government, and the torment of good men, — of these Christ says, "My Gospel sends me for their behoof: I came for them."

Lastly, and most comprehensively, he declared that he came for the poor. The poor have always been the least esteemed and the least estimable, judged by what they have been actually able to put forth. And in every age, and almost wholly, they have been a mere soil out of which other men's prosperities have grown. For a few classes have regarded themselves as carrying in themselves pretty much all that God could be supposed to be interested in in this world. The masses of men have always and everywhere been despised or patronized with the same kind of pitying condescension with which men patronize and pet dogs and horses. The poor are a pretty good poor, if they do not want to be anything but poor. Nobles like poor people when they will work for them, and give them no trouble. And kings say kind words to the poor if they are humble, and if they pay their taxes willingly and promptly. And so it has been with the degraded classes and with the refined classes, the world over. The poor have been a very good poor if they would stay poor, and do the duties that they were told to do, without grumbling. If they would be soil, and let other men root in them and grow strong upon them, they have been liked very well. The poor have, from the beginning, been the neglected and the undeveloped. The unlovely traits, the incongruities of disposition, the tendencies to vices, have been among them: not exclusively but largely. Whatever fruit there can be in ignorance has belonged to the masses that have been poor.

It has been a part of the universal egotism of man to assert his own superiority over those round about him. And when he unites himself to a profession, it does not take away his inclination to do this. It augments it. Professionalism narrows men. In law, in medicine, in the ministry, in art, in every profession, men are narrowed, because professionalism girds them with an iron hoop of selfishness. By as much as a man excludes others from him, by so much he is narrowed.

All classes in society have done what professions have done. The same selfishness that is in the individual develops, throws out its branches, and bears its fruit in classes. There has been a middle class, a bottom class, and a top class, and each has had the same bad peculiarity; but arrogance and pride are more developed in the upper classes than in the lower. The educated and refined classes, when they hear that God thinks of the world, suppose that he thinks of such as they are. They suppose that, when he looks upon the world, he sees the best specimens of men. I think he sees them too. I think he loves rich men, and wise men, and proud men, and selfish men. I think he loves crowned and sceptred kings. I think he loves everybody and everything that he has made. He takes care of the sparrow, and even of the worm. There is nothing in the world that God does not have a kind consideration for. And in the human family I do not think he looks upon any class and says, "You are my peculiar people." Everywhere throughout the globe God has a heart for all.

This is not to be confounded with that preference which is based upon character. What I mean is, not a preference of personal love growing out of disposition, but that general benevolence of which God speaks in Christ Jesus when he says, "He makes his sun to rise on the evil and on the good, and sends rain on the just and on the unjust."

These, then, are those to whom Christ declared that he had a mission, — the great underlying classes in society, — the unfortunate, the neglected, the unlovely, the ignorant, the undeveloped, — they whom the educated men of history have always been pleased to regard as the inferior specimens of the human family. He says, "I am commissioned and ordained to preach the Gospel to the poor, to comfort those that are in affliction, to release those that are in captivity, to bear intelligence to those that are in ignorance, to destroy the injustice of those that hold men in bondage. I am sent to proclaim the acceptable year of the Lord to all those that are low down among the inhabitants of the earth."

Why should our Saviour have chosen such a congregation? Not because he had no sympathy with the educated, the refined, and the ennobled. He had: not with the selfishness, and pride, and arrogance which refinement often breeds in men; but with the men themselves, — for a man is not any the worse in the sight of God because he is educated. In preaching for the poor and neglected classes, we sometimes are liable to leave the impression, that it is a man's misfortune not to be poor and neglected, as if there was some fault in being refined and cultured. So far from that being true, the more perfectly developed a man is, the nearer he comes to God's ideal in men. We are to strive for refinement, and educate our children to do it. It belongs not to any favorite class, but to the whole race. It is not, therefore, because God has no sympathy with the educated, that he declared that the mission of the Gospel was to the poor and the low.

Nor is it because he is ignorant of the vices and the moral loathsomeness of the masses of men. It sometimes is the case that men preach about the poor, and imprisoned, and ignorant, and think it a bright and blessed thing as long as it is merely a matter of preaching and sentimentality; but that, when they go into the midst of these classes, when the ideally poor become real poor people, when they preach among the Caffres and Hottentots, (where to induce a man to put on a shirt is evidence of his conversion, and where men are obstinate and bitter and malignant and unmanageable in proportion to their ignorance,) and when they see the mischiefs that belong to uninstructed poverty, are discouraged and disgusted. Now, our Saviour cannot be supposed to have been unacquainted with these mischiefs; and yet he looked upon the unfortunate subjects of them as a mother looks upon her child that is diseased and covered with sores. She does not love the sores, but she loves the child all the more because it needs medicament and nursing care.

Nor is it to be supposed that the Saviour meant that there was, on the part of God, any repugnance to government, to society, to justice, to moral discriminations. From everlasting to everlasting, Jehovah is a God of law, — a God that will by no means clear the guilty. God ordained these things, but he impartially regards all mankind as common children; as the members of one family, of which he is the Head and Father, and of which they are the brethren. And although we differ from each other in endless particulars, we resemble each other in yet more particulars. For each carries the line and lineament of the Father; each has the germ of future growth; each has the element of immortality. And God sees that these obscure but divine qualities unite men, and are of more importance than those incidental developments by which one surpasses another.

In providing for the whole, God aims at the lowest, not because they are more amiable or more lovely, but because he would lift up the whole. If you wanted to raise a building, it would not be wise for you to put your screws under the roof, and raise that first, thinking that the walls would follow it up.

They would not. If you wish to raise the roof of a building, put the screws under the foundation; for that which carries the foundation up an inch will carry the roof up an inch, and that which carries the foundation up a foot will carry the roof up a foot. If the top leaves of a tree begin to wither, and I wish to remedy the evil, I shall go to work, not at the top of the tree, but at the root. For he who takes care of the root of a tree takes care of the top. And in human society that system which is comprehensive enough to take care of the bottom will best take care of the top. It is folly to apply agencies at the top, supposing that they will necessarily strike down. They will not. You cannot boil a caldron downward with fuel, but you can upward. It is impossible to get a radiation from an upper class that shall enlighten a lower. The educated portion of a community is liable to be arrogant, exclusive, and dominating; and in order to raise society as a whole, there must be a moral system whose genius is to exert its forces upon those of every class. Is it not reasonable to suppose that a system that is capable of taking care of the worst, will be much more abundantly capable of taking care of the best? The Saviour came to the neglected, the despised and despoiled, the poor, the helpless. He was radical. He began at the root. He addressed himself to the bottom. He preached a Gospel that had regard, not to a few, not to the more prosperous, not to the wealthy, not to those who could make return for his efforts in their behalf, but to those who constituted the foundation of society, and who, if carried up, would be lifted by a system of moral influences that must carry up the whole of society.

If the tendency of the Gospel of Christ, then, is to be on the side of the masses of men, we might expect that history would reveal the fact; we might expect that results would show such to have been its tendency. Such has been the tendency of it from the time when the Apostles went forth from Jerusalem to preach it to this day. It may be said that the history of the preaching of the Gospel has been a history of the development of Christian democratic ideas. Since the day of Christ, the Gospel has created an era in the history of men. Even in the most corrupt periods of the Church, even in those times when the Church was aspiring to monarchy and despotism, and seeking to be universal, — even then the Gospel carried with it a democratic element. The bottom even of the Catholic Church was democratic, though the top was aristocratic. The same is true in our day of the Methodist Episcopal Church. Its government is so intensely aristocratic that the popular element is hardly felt in it; but the worship is more democratic than that of almost any other church in the world. In that Church the democratic and aristocratic elements are strangely combined. I do not say this, of course, for any purpose except to show that it is possible to unite in one system two opposite elements, by uniting them in different parts of the same organization. In the worst days, Papacy, little of the Gospel as it carried in its worship, could not help carrying with it the element of democracy. From the hour in which it was whispered by priest or bishop in the ear of living or dying men, that it pleased God to give his life, in his Son, for every human creature, it was inevitable that those men should infer that then every human being was king. It was not for the generic, but for the specific, that Christ died. He died for men, not as a mass, but as individuals. I love my children, but I never love them as a group. I always love them as individuals of that group. God loves the world, and all that it contains of men, but he loves them as individual men, and calls them by name. And the death of Christ was for men individually. And from the moment that a man hears this story, "You are of so much importance that the Lord of glory came down from heaven, and poured out his life that you might live," — from that moment he beholds his right of thrones. He is a king's son.

This democratic element of the Gospel has been strikingly manifested in the history of the past, and it is being still more strikingly manifested in the history of the present. The more the Gospel is preached, the more does it develop the great element of Christian democracy. (I am not to be understood as speaking of democracy in any party sense. I would cleanse the word from all the stains that have been brought upon it by its misuse in politics.) All things work for the welfare, the rights, the education, the empowering of the masses of men, or the common people. Schools work for the common people. Commerce works for them. Industries of every kind work for them. Inventions work for them. Competitions work for them. Quarrels of kings work for them. Quarrels of nobles work for them. The armies raised by despots to enslave their own subjects teach those subjects how to use arms, and by and by to defend their own rights. Reformations work for them, and declensions work for them. Everything runs down hill to the bottom, where the great mass of the common people are. Now, in our day, the evidence is overwhelming of that which Christ declared of himself, — that he came to preach a Gospel for mankind; not for refined classes, but for those that most need it, — the poor, the helpless, the enslaved. He is revealing it by history more astonishingly than by his Word.

All the world over, the tendency of things is, not toward the good of the few, but toward the good of the whole. The Czar of Russia is legislating steadily, not for class interest, but for universal interest. I regard Russia as one of the most extraordinary examples of this tendency in our age. Austria, that is determined not to work for Christ, is working for Christ all the time, as is shown in her recognition of certain moral principles which relate to the welfare of the common people, and in her granting to the common people certain rights and privileges. All Western Europe feels more and more the power of the common people. Even the astute Emperor of France is obliged to ask the common people if he may reign. He regards the will of the common people as a pilot regards a sand-bank or a rock, as a troublesome thing that must be steered around; and he steers around it. And where he does go, is often not where he wants to go. And when any comprehensive policy is to be pursued in England, or France, or Italy, or even great Russia, the government is obliged to sound out, as with a line and plummet, and see where the deep channels of the popular mind are, and to run in those channels. They cannot go just where they have a mind to; for although crowns govern peoples, peoples govern crowns just as much, — and they are doing it more and more in every generation.

Nor are the indications among us any less plain. Nothing in our midst can flourish that does not belong to the whole. Classes may be said to be like fountains. The water, conveyed by a secret pipe, throws itself into the air, and falls down sunned and radiant, into the upper shell. But that can hold but little, and it runs over, and the next shell catches it. Although that can hold more, it cannot hold it all, and it runs over again, and the next shell catches it. At last the big reservoir at the bottom catches the whole. That is broader and deeper than any of the basins above it. No fountain can play that undertakes to drink up its water, and give those beneath none of it. In our community that which belongs to a class is soon strangled or destroyed. In art, the man that attempts to paint to the exclusive notions of a class cannot succeed. To the life of the artist two things are necessary, — money and fame ; and he cannot get these if he paints for the few, and not for the many. As a general fact, it is only the painters for the common people that can secure eminence and support. In other words, art, without knowing what ails it, has been obliged to conform to this great democratic tendency, and work for the common people. Pleasure cannot be exclusive. Let an opera-house be built for the rich, to secure peculiar privileges to them, and it is cursed in the very method of its construction. But let it be built for the masses, to give equal privileges to all, and it thrives. For a class of a hundred men that own a million dollars each is not half so efficient in sustaining an establishment of that kind as a million men that come with their shilling apiece. It is not streams of water here and there that make the ground moist, but little drops that fall all over the surface. And it is not great streams of wealth that make communities rich, but the little drops that belong to the innumerable hands of the common people. In this land, and in every land, railroads, if they would succeed, must be not for the exclusive good of the strong and intelligent, but for the good of the common people. Learning is of no great account that goes into its cell, like a worm into its cocoon, to spin there. Learning, to be of much use, must have a tendency to spread itself among the common people. It matters not how solid or broad a man's learning may be, if he holds it for the benefit of the few, he must take an audience of a few. If he is select, he must put up with a select audience, and with the remuneration of a select audience. If a man of learning would turn his learning to a good account, as society is constituted, not here alone, but the world over, he must not be select: he must have something for all men. The books of the last thirty years might almost be set apart as books leavened with the spirit of the Gospel. In what regard? In regard to its doctrines and morals? No: in regard to its tendency to emancipate the lower classes. Take the books of Eugene Sue. I look upon them as corrupt; as blasted with moral corruption. I do not think that such a man as he is competent to write of virtue, or anything of the kind. And yet I think his novels are all the more on that account memorable, as showing what is the power of the Gospel, in that, although his characters were detestable, and his scenes were inexpressibly bad in multitudes of instances, yet that for which he painted characters and organized scenes was the release of the ignorant and the poor. He carried bad medicine to men; but, after all, he was working for them. And often bad men are found going in that direction. Take the poetry of the time of Pope and Dryden,— the hardest, the deadest, the most inhuman period of any history. Read their letters, and see what selfishness they display; how absolutely they ignore everything except class; and with what utter contempt they speak of all that is not of their class. Take the literature of the last twenty-five or thirty years. How genial it is! How it leans toward the good of the whole! It may be doctrinally wrong, it may lack moral tone, it may carry with it influences that are harmful; but, after all, its tendency is in the direction of the common good. And it is memorable to see how Christ is working through all these instrumentalities for the emancipation of men everywhere.

I remark, once more, that Christians now have in their hands a criterion by which to judge of the probable developments of the future. Having a knowledge of what was the tendency of the Gospel in the days of Christ, and of what is its tendency now, we may understand what are to be its directions and developments in human society and life: not in its immediate results, perhaps, but in its final issues. It is to bear to the masses of men their rights. It is to guard their interests. They are to be instructed, educated, empowered, ennobled by it. A man is safe just in proportion as you make much of him, and dangerous in proportion as you permit him to be little. The spirit of the world, as represented in monarchical governments, is a spirit that fears a man, and treats him as a dangerous animal. Cardinal Mazarin, looking upon men in the spirit of the institutions of his time, would have said, "They are brutes; they are ignorant and capricious; it will not do to trust them; they must be watched and controlled." A man looking upon men in the spirit of our institutions would say, "They are so ignorant, they are so circumscribed, that they are dangerous: take off their bands, and give them liberty." The way to make a man safe is to educate him, to develop him, to bring out what there is in him, to spread out his branches wider and wider; not to hold him in, not to take anything away from him. If you want to make a man safe, give him more, instead of diminishing what he has got. The more you give him, the safer he will be. The law of Christ, the spirit of our institutions, and the destiny of the time to come, is this: that men are to be made safe by being cultured; by having their faculties made broader; by being made better capable of self-government.

In view of these statements, first: the Christianity of a nation is to be measured by the condition of its lower classes. That is not the way we count; but we count wrong. In judging of the progress of Christianity, we are apt to judge by the number of churches, and ministers, and communicants, and eleemosynary institutions. These things, as having a certain validity, are not to be spoken of contemptuously; but, after all, it is not what is on the top of society, but the average condition of society at the bottom, that determines the Christianity of a nation. The condition of a nation as regards its masses will determine the spirit of that nation with reference to Christianity.

The Christlikeness of Christianity itself is to be measured, not in symbols and institutions, but in its general spirit and influence. You should recollect that religion is never church, nor priest, nor doctrine. These are mere instruments that religion employs. Religion is the unembodied spirit of truth, of devotion. It is an invisible quality which is obliged to be incarnated for practical purposes. Institutions and ordinances and usages are but the outward form which religion uses, and they often become corrupt; so that the Christianity of a community, as represented by its usages and ordinances and institutions, may be gross and infidel. Sometimes men that the Church calls infidels represent Christ better than those that are in the Church; because they represent Christ most, not who represent the word of his doctrine most, but who represent his spirit most in their dispositions, — and, above all, that spirit which brought him from heaven, to give his life a ransom for many. The spirit of any church whose sole thought is to take care of its own communicants has not that spirit. We build our churches, and get everything fixed so as to make ourselves as comfortable as possible, and gather our families in, and shut the door, and take care of those that are inside, and let those that are outside take care of themselves. We arrange all things just to our liking, and then say, "The church is in a good condition, and do not let us disturb it." And so the church sings its own lullaby; and the minister puts his foot on it and rocks it, that it may go to sleep in peace. Its own ease and enjoyment seem to be the aim of the church; and if you bring before it questions of duty, the evils that abound in the community, and the claims of men outside of its pale, you are charged with being a disturber of the church, and with bringing into it topics that make discord among the brethren. The ideal of a prosperous church, often, is a church that acts on a principle of spiritual selfishness.

Property is good when a normal use is made of it; but when a man employs property as an instrument of selfishness, and becomes a miser and an avaricious man, then he does not make a normal use of it. Love of praise is right in certain degrees; but an inordinate love of praise is not right. A taste for art is highly commendable where a man seeks it for the refinement of other men; but it is far less so where a man seeks it for his own refinement. A man holds religion in the true spirit, when he holds it for the benefit of those about him, but not when he holds it for his own individual benefit. And a church is corrupted when it wants Christianity for its own peace, and not for the amelioration of persons that are not members of it.

When a light-house keeper, on a stormy, dark, tempestuous night, is told to go into his attic and take care of the lantern, why does he receive such instruction? Because the ocean-burdened ship afar off, and a long way from home, is coming upon the coast. He is to do it, because wind-driven craft are creeping toward the land, and need the guidance of the light. It is for the sake of the imperilled mariner that he is sent to take care of the lantern. But suppose he should say, "I am instructed to take care of this light"; and should put up the shutters, saying, "The wind shall not blow this light out"; and should hang curtains over all the cracks, saying, "I will keep out every breath of air"! The light is safe, and it illumines the little room in which it burns; but on the sea it is dark. He might just as well let the light go out; for the only object in keeping it is that those on the deep who are approaching the shore may be directed by it.

Now, churches are God's light-houses, and he says to them, "Shine out for the poor, the ignorant, the wretched, the neglected: let your light so shine before men, that they may see your good works, and glorify your Father which is in heaven." But men say, "No, do not let it shine out." If the minister undertakes to shed its rays upon the evils of society, they say, "Take care, or you will do mischief. If you discuss that ragged abolition question in the pulpit, you will disturb the peace of the church; and then do you suppose we can sell our pews? Why do you not preach the blessed Gospel of peace, instead of preaching a gospel that is all the time leading to discrepancies and troubles? If you will not disturb the church, you shall thrive, and our pews will be filled with fashion and quality; but if you insist upon introducing agitating subjects continually, you will destroy your own prospects, and our pews will be empty or filled with an ordinary class of people." My Master was rejected when he was upon earth. When men beheld him, there was no comeliness in him. And as long as Christ comes to an unregenerated and wicked world, there will be men of infidel selfishness and ambition and pride that will look upon him and say, "There is no comeliness in him." Such men do not like a Christ that turns things bottom side up.

The integrity of a church is to be judged, not by

a vagrant, unregulated, random, malignant, agitating spirit, but by its spirit toward the poor in its own and every neighborhood. The church that, following the example of Christ, writes on its banner, "We are sent to preach the Gospel to the poor; we are sent to open the prison door; to give seeing to the blind; to set at liberty those that are bruised; to carry confusion to wrong, and rescue and release to the wronged," — the church that writes that on its banner has the spirit of the Gospel. If you have that spirit, you are Christ's indeed, but not otherwise.

The condition of a nation is to be measured by the moral condition of the bottom, and not of the top. Ah! my friends, we can perhaps bear measuring better than any other nation; but we cannot bear it. There are many things in which we stand above all other nations. There are in our midst some of the ripest fruits of Christian culture. The general spirit of intelligence among our people, and of our democratic institutions, takes into consideration to a considerable extent the welfare of the whole. There are in the developments of the age not a few auspicious signs that may well give us hope for the future. But remember that there are influences opposed to Christian democratic tendencies in every nation. As long as there is selfishness in the bosom of men, as long as men are willing to put down everything that hinders their own personal aggrandizement, so long there is opposition to these tendencies in things political, as well as in things ecclesiastical; and it is only the regenerating power of the Gospel that will transform selfishness, and that will bring safety to our times and people.

I know that we have revivals of religion. I thank God for the great revivals of '57–8. They were much reviled because they did not teach men to set the slaves free; because, when a man was converted, he was not made an abolitionist. It would be as reasonable to revile dew because it did not act like rain. In a time of drought I would rather have a rain that would soak the ground two feet; but if I could not have that, a rain that would soak the ground three inches would be better than nothing; and if I could have nothing but dew, I would be glad even of that, because that would keep the plants from exuding their juices and withering away. There are different qualities of revivals of religion: some are far better than others; but there is nothing so bad in spiritual things as moral death.

The tendency which inspires the passage which I have read, and which was the text of our Saviour, will exist in varying degrees of imperfection and weakness and irregularity; but it is the characteristic feature of the Gospel wherever it goes.

I cannot make a specific application of this subject to all the questions that are arising now; but two things I can say. The first is this: that, as a matter of doctrine, it is important that you should have the spirit of benevolence which Christ had, and which his words teach you to have, by which the rights of all men, clear down to the bottom of society, are made dear and sacred. When you have that spirit, you will generally have a criterion by which to judge of what is right in specific cases. If you have not that spirit which shall lead you to desire the welfare of the masses of men, you will be arrogant and proud and selfish and worldly and corrupt; but if you have it, it will become an interpreter to you as to your duty toward your fellows.

The other thing is this: we are drifting now right on to days of trial. The very masses of this people, for whom the Gospel is a shield and mountain of blessing, are themselves turning against the poorer than they, and manifesting toward the African disgust and contempt. Those in our midst who have lately fled from the oppression of crowns and sceptres—peasants of Europe who have come to this country that they might secure the rights of freemen—are turning to crush those beneath them, as they were crushed by their tyrannical lords. The swaying masses are giving way to fears of a destruction of their interests by competition, and turning around to wrong God's poor, just as they have been wronged. They thunder when they look up, and blast when they look down. They rage against oppression upward, and practise it downward. The great State of Illinois has voted that no more black men shall come within her borders. A black man can have no sort of status or privilege there. And petitions are being circulated in other States with the view of preventing the blacks from entering those States. There seems to be a crusade getting up against the African. A party seems to be forming on this basis, and preparing to appeal to the worst and bitterest passions of men. It has not the groundwork of a single honorable principle. It is made of the very elements of hell. Its only basis is, hatred of the negro. That is its capital; and, as long as there is facile communication between the infernal pit and the human heart, it will not lack capital. They who belong to this party want to wrest the government from its present hands by playing upon this one feeling, — the hatred of the people to the African.

I do not say that the black man is to be received into equality with yourselves in marriage, and in other respects, and that he shall walk in society in the same conditions that you do. I would not take away that liberty which you already have with reference to white people. You go with whom you please; but you are kind to all men. You seek the companionship of such as are congenial to you; but you recognize the rights of all men. Not everybody goes into your parlor; but everybody is treated with respect by you. You have a right not to receive the low and ignorant on an equal footing with yourself; but you have no right to trample upon them. I do not say that the African is your equal; but this I say: God made the African, God made "niggers," Christ died for "niggers," and they will rise in the last day, and you and they will stand together to give account for all the deeds done in the body. They are a part of the human family, and God loves them, and that great law of eternal love which is supreme in heaven, and which God himself never violates, is binding upon you in respect to them. And in this day, when corrupt party leaders are ready to sacrifice and tread down the rights of the poor, I stand up to say, in the name of the Lord Jesus Christ, that he came for them, and that, if you lay the hand of harm upon them, God will not hold you guiltless.

I bethink me of that sentence which Christ spake,— "The first shall be last, and the last shall be first."

In that great day of reckoning, there shall stand up many and many a slave, transcendent, and O how radiant! All that was earthly will be gone. Nothing will be seen but the tried and patient spirit that through long injury clung to Jesus, and sang and prayed in its own poor way, and clomb up to heaven, and there emerged in sweet emancipation. Over against him, squat like a toad, shall stand the master, that here was haughty and high and honored. And while the master hops his way down to everlasting shame, the slave, that was a beast of burden here, now developed into the fair proportions of inward life, and standing in glory, shall shine like the stars of the firmament.

XIII.

SPEAKING EVIL OF DIGNITIES.*

"They are not afraid to speak evil of dignities." — 2 Peter ii. 10.

IN this passage the Apostle is setting forth the attributes of bad men. Among the marks of their evil life is the fact that they are living in passionate indulgences; that they scorn the restraint of those that have moral authority over them; that they are filled with pride and conceit; and that they have a habit of evil-speaking of those who are in power. The term translated *dignities* signifies glories or eminences. It may include, and it does, doubtless, more than magistrates. It reaches up into the spiritual realm. But it certainly includes officers of civil government. Our observation will teach us that there was great need that the Scriptures should enjoin upon men obedience, respect, and honor toward those who bear rule, and also abstinence from needless reproach and causeless revilings.

There are many reasons why we, in our time, should have our attention called to this matter of

* July 16, 1862. During the period of dissatisfaction after the disastrous defeats of McClellan on the Peninsula, ending July 1.

duty. It is the duty of the minister of the Gospel to preach on every side of political life. I do not say that he *may;* I say that he *must.* That man is not a shepherd of his flock who fails to teach that flock how to apply moral truth to every phase of ordinary practical duty.

As our community is organized, as we are related to government, we stand exactly in antithesis to those to whom the Gospel was first preached. It was the duty of the Roman citizen not to make the laws, not to make officers, and not to hold either lawmakers or laws or officers under criticism, or in any sense under responsibility. His duty was a virtuous life as a citizen, and obedience to the constituted powers.

The same Providence that made every government hitherto has ordained that under which we live. And the fundamental principle of that government is that all authority is from the citizen, and that all officers are responsible to the citizen. It is your duty to make laws, and to make the administrators of laws. It is your duty to take care of the state, and to think for it.

Now there are laid, in our day, upon every single Christian citizen obligations and duties which he cannot well discharge without ethical light. From whom shall he derive that light? From any one that can give it to him. But from whom has he a right to demand it? From those whose province it is to teach men how to apply moral truth to the conduct of their practical life. And therefore, in our government, and in the circumstances under which we live, the minister of the Gospel not only may, but must, teach men how to conduct themselves Christianly in the management of political affairs. It is a branch of that duty which I am now to discharge, — to teach you how to conduct yourselves toward those who are in authority.

We live amidst great excitements, which are tending to arouse the passions of men; and should public disasters come, or should long disappointment follow our great exertions, and we be withheld from the realization of our most ardent wishes, we shall find ourselves surrounded by men that will lay no restrictions on their tongues, and there will be in us many feelings which will seek improper methods of expression. Let me, therefore, beforehand put you upon your guard in the use of your tongue.

We are liable to mistake in the performance of duty; for, as I have intimated, under our government it is the duty of the citizen to consider the conduct of officers, to debate the propriety of their measures, and to judge matters of law, policy, and administration. I hold that the great intelligent common people are the tribunal before which, in the end, all these things must come, — yea, and morals and religion themselves; for, in the evolution of God's providence, the Church is being held responsible, not merely for the public sentiment of single churches, but for that great public sentiment which exists outside of churches, and which is made by them. We need, therefore, instruction to lead us to do our duty, and — so far as we are set to judge — to criticise and condemn; and to lead us, also, to avoid the peculiar temptations which are incident to the discharge of our duties toward those in trust.

Let me point, then, first, to some of the dangers to which we are liable.

We are in danger of inconsiderate reproach, inconsiderate evil-speaking, of men in public stations. It is taken for granted, by many, that those who are not of our side are of course marks for any shafts that we may be pleased to send at them. It is taken for granted that we are to defend those whom we have put in power, and to lose no opportunity of attacking those whose election we opposed.

The common laws of morality among neighbors, and certainly Christian canons, are almost dispensed with in that zeal and eagerness and inconsiderateness with which we inveigh against men that are discharging public functions, and that are not of our party nor of our interest. Men take up things hastily, without proof. If any evil thing reported of those in authority goes in the line of their prejudices, that is enough to give it credence with them. Now, to tell a thing for true which you do not know to be true, is to tell a lie; and if you do it often, you make yourself a liar. And there is no lie that is so bad as a lie that is told against the reputation of a man. It is not enough that you say, "I heard it." If you only heard it, then you must report it as a thing heard. But, after you have told it without qualification, to put in the plea, "I supposed it was true," or "I did not know but it was true," is no justification for a heinous offence against good morals. And there is great laxness of honor, and certainly of justice, in the sentences which we are accustomed to pronounce, not only in our thoughts, but in our utterances, upon men that are in public places. We are ready to believe evil. Often men are anxious to hear things against those who are not of their choice. They feel a sort of enmity toward them, and they are glad, therefore, of an opportunity to speak against them. Hence they contravene that fundamental law of charity which is laid down in the thirteenth of Corinthians. They do rejoice in finding evil and iniquity in another. It is sweeter than honey to their taste to find out some reportable thing prejudicial to men in authority.

We are prone to employ unweighed language. We indulge in terms that are unwarrantable, except when applied to absolute crimes, toward men who are guilty of no crime, simply because we happen to dislike them. Language may sometimes be strong in its application to men where it is morally descriptive of their conduct, or where it conveys high moral judgment. There are no terms, however broad and strong they may be, that are so justifiable as terms of high Christian feeling, even if they be condemnatory. But more often our untempered language springs from our passions. It is temper that speaks. Sometimes one would be led to suppose that eminent men were incarnate fiends, by the descriptions given of them. Everything hateful is attributed to them. They are almost stripped of human attributes. How, at last, are men's names associated with all that is most abhorred! How does the imagination go on, kindling as it goes, forever picturing them as monsters! There are men in this nation — some that are in office, and many that are not — who are, as it were, but hones to give a sharp edge to men's tempers and passions. And yet, when we come to see these very much abused men, how unlike they are, frequently, from that which we have been taught to suppose them to be. Let a familiar instance be recalled from history. Do you not remember the whirlwind of the times of Andrew Jackson? Do you not remember how terrible was the bitterness that was felt against him? Turn back to the papers that describe his administration and personal conduct. Was there ever an adjective expressive of bitterness, was there ever language of violence, that was not employed to heap obloquy on him? Years have passed away. He has gone to his rest. We have formed different judgments. We have separated good from evil. And how does the whole community look back and fervently wish that we might have one good month of his stalwart will, to drive on this languid, lagging war to victory! O for Andrew Jackson! And yet I remember the day when I should have as soon thought of invoking the Devil as him! And are we never to learn wisdom by these constant mistakes? Are we never to cease to ridicule and exaggerate the faults of those, or the supposed faults of those, who are elevated to places of authority, where they are assailable by the tongues of all men? Are we never to learn how prone we are to overcolor and overcharge?

The habit is sometimes indulged of invading the sanctity of the private life of public men. This is peculiarly ungenerous. For they are placed before men so as to be searched by all eyes; and they are helpless of concealment. Their private character and personal habits are almost the only refuge that is left to them; and if these are invaded, they are robbed indeed. Men in public places are for the most part unable to enter into controversy, or make any defence against attacks upon their private motives and personal conduct, and therefore it is the less honorable to make such attacks.

The only exception that I can imagine is that where, by a gross and infectious immorality, public men are damaging the public safety and welfare. Even under such circumstances exposition is seldom required under our elective system, where men should apply the corrective by the use of the vote rather than by the use of the tongue. I warn you, therefore, that it is unjust, ungenerous, and to the last degree wicked, to follow men in public places with persecution that touches their motives and private character. Their policy is open to all men's inquisition: their motives are in their own souls, and with their God.

Men are tempted to unjust language in regard to those who conduct public affairs, because it is very natural to suppose that public managers are responsible for all the hinderances, and lets, and delays, and misfortunes of those affairs. We avenge our own selfish misfortunes upon those that we suppose are in some way connected with them. For we always want some one to blame; and we always see to it that that "some one" is not ourselves. It was the custom of the Jewish priest to select two goats. One he slew, using its blood for various sprinklings. The other he laid his hand on, in the sight of the people, when it became the scapegoat for all their sins, and was hooted and driven into the wilderness. But what did the goat care for their execrations, when he could start for the grass of the wilderness, and get out of their way? When we want something on which to heap our sins and faults, we usually take public men, and they are our scapegoats, — only there is no wilderness into which they can run and browse. The disposition to blame, to find fault, to relieve ourselves by complaining of others, is a disposition that is universal. It is more or less partaken of by us all.

We sympathize easily with fault-finders. There is a bad spot in the human mind, which is gratified by hearing evil reported of men. There are few who are sweet-minded enough to hate the tidings of evil in respect to others. And those who are advanced to publicity, those who are set in the magistracy, are particularly liable to be objects of reproach and abuse. In our form of government every officer is a successful man among several that are rejected. When a man is raised to any public place, there is not only a disappointed party, but there are individuals grievously disappointed; and there are various reasons, quite disconnected from his administration, why many men on every side should employ their tongues in detraction of him. There are many who, loving to hear evil of men, are quickly caught by sympathy with those who are evil-speakers; and then they soon become evil-speakers too.

There are many reasons why we should be very scrupulous in this regard.

In the first place, our public magistrates represent the whole welfare of the nation, and whatever lowers their dignity and authority, in some measure injures the entire public. Besides, in speaking against a magistrate, you are speaking not alone against that magistrate, but also against the interests that he holds in his hands and represents.

Not only is a citizen bound to elevate to the magistracy those who are to bear rule, but, having done this, he is bound to help them in discharging their duty.

For public sentiment is to public officers what water is to the wheel of the mill. Where there is no public sentiment, an officer stands *in vacuo*. It is impossible for a law to be executed among you which is not concurrent with your wish. It is impossible for any judge, representative, or civil magistrate to thoroughly carry out any policy to which he is not incited, and in which he is not helped by the sympathy and encouragement of the community. Your duty is to assist, and not to criticise; and that duty can never be conjoined with a bitter, name-calling, reviling, censorious spirit.

We are to bear in mind, also, how different a public trust is from what it seems to be to those outside who have never tried it. Consider how easy it is for people to preach who never have any preaching to do! How easy it is for people to bring up children who never had any to bring up! How easy it is for poor folks to spend rich people's money! How easy it is for men out of office to tell people that are in office what they ought to do! There is a universal conceit and arrogance in this respect.

It is no small thing for a man to stand in the centre of practical public duty. It is very different from standing in a private sphere. Elements are so many, interests are so conflicting, there are so many contrary minds that are drawing hither and thither, that except in rare instances, where a man has a dominant will, following a clear and discriminating judgment, it becomes operose and burdensome to discharge public duties. We ought to remember this. It will qualify, somewhat, our severe words of condemnation.

It is especially to be considered how different is practical administration from moral speculation about duty. I recognize the necessity of moral speculation. I hold that it is the duty of every ethical teacher to raise up a theological idea of right and duty, and to maintain before the mind an ultimate standard of perfection. Although, when we attempt to realize the truth, we never shall bring practice up to the full ideal of the truth, yet, by maintaining that ideal clear and strong in authority, we shall bring practice further up toward it than we otherwise should. Writers and preachers and teachers are to demand the utmost purity, the utmost truth, and the utmost honor. When they demand perfection in the application of a moral principle to any common state of human affairs, they forget that the incarnation of a principle is a gradual thing; that it grows; that it cannot take place in an hour. You can preach broadly the doctrine of liberty to all men; but if you undertake to administer the process of giving liberty to all men, you meet with ten thousand conditions that you have not taken into consideration, and that you are obliged to settle. In theory, you are not obliged to touch them. It is right and proper for you to say that liberty is every man's birthright, and that every man has a right to it; but when you undertake to secure this right to every man, you will encounter difficulties innumerable which will hinder the immediate consummation of your purpose. We need moral speculation. The world cannot go too far in that direction. You will go higher if you aim at perfection than if you have before you a lower standard. But it must not be forgotten that the most that we can justly expect of men in places of trust, who are dealing with practical things, is, that they shall take a moral principle and carry it as far as they can under the circumstances. It is the duty of all who are outside of public affairs to bear this in mind. For it is very easy, as I have found, to preach; and, as I have also found, it is not so easy to practice. It is very easy to tell men what to do when you have no responsibility. Advice is very easy to give, and usually very useless, in such cases. And we are to remember that men are not necessarily delinquent, or deserving of censure, because they fail to carry out in practice the fulness of that which they have themselves held as an ideal principle.

We are to consider, too, how exceedingly burdened public men often are, and that what seems to us to be delinquency in duty may be owing to the fact that they have reached the limit of their power of execution. We are to consider how perplexed a man may be as to what is his duty; how he may be tied up by precedent; how he may be overruled by law; how many casuistical questions may come in to unsettle him. "It is always right," it is said, "to be true." That does not touch the question. The question often is, What is true? It is said that it is always safe to be right. Why, yes, only tell me what is right, and I do not thank any man to insure me that it is safe to be right. The trouble is in ten thousand delicate situations in which a man may be placed. What is right? — there is where the rub comes; and to repeat, and sound, and roll over and over again, these declarations of the safety of following right and truth, amounts to nothing. The trouble is to know what is true and what is right, in any practical conjunction of affairs.

These cautions must not, however, be deemed a dissuasion from a Christian citizen's duty of vigilance and free criticism. They are only meant to put you on your guard, and teach you that you are judges, and not advocates; and that all public men come to the bar of your mind for a just judgment, as a man comes to the bar of a court for the just judgment of the bench. Not with your passions, not with your interests, not with a careless tongue, but with conscientiousness, with broad, kind, sweet feelings, must you look upon those who bear rule among you. Judge them with a righteous judgment.

There are some who are so disgusted with the abuse of the tongue that they urge acquiescence in things as they are. They would have magistrates regarded and treated as men acting under the authority of God. It is said, "Receive them; obey them; let them alone: they are God's ministers." Some of them contrive to serve two masters, then! I admit that some magistrates are of God; but I do not believe that every magistrate is. I believe that government is of God; but I do not believe that every man that wields the power of government is of God in any such sense that he is to be set free from our just inquisition and judgment. Nothing could be more ruinous, both to the public magistrate himself and to the public welfare, than any doctrine that teaches us to have a superstitious regard for him, and to abstain from measuring his conduct, and from a proper and just use of the tongue respecting it. You are solemnly bound to hold all men to account whom you place in authority. To do this is the only safeguard under our institutions. Fatal would be that day in which the people should be taught to let men alone that were advanced to office and responsibility. Even excessive and harsh judgments, with all their faults, are better than no judgment at all; but just judgment is better yet. We should fearlessly apply to public men the highest standards of measurement in character and conduct and policy. We should judge them, and they should know that we judge them, and they should fear our judgment because we judge them with a scrupulous care to be accurate, with the utmost caution in receiving the elements of fact on which we base our conclusions. If there was a Christian public sentiment, — and by this I mean, not a public sentiment formed by nominal Christians, but a public sentiment formed by the use of Christian standards of judgment, — if there was such a public sentiment, there is not a magistrate in the land that could stand against it for a day, or an hour. Its justness would be its terribleness. And such a public sentiment there ought to be, both as a terror to evil-doers in office and as a praise and encouragement to those occupying places of trust who seek to do well.

While, therefore, I do not dissuade you from the use of your rightful prerogatives, or from your duty, in this regard, I do dissuade you from rashness, haste, and ill-natured and untempered judgments. Bear with those that are in authority. Uphold their hands. Give them as much confidence as it is possible for you to give. Do not trust them unwarrantably, beyond measure, or indiscriminately; and yet it must needs be that you should trust them.

Nor should you withhold trust because men do not realize your full ideal of what is right and noble.

Men are what they are; and you must take them with all their faults and limitations and inexperiences. You must take them for just what they are, and make the best of it.

Meanwhile, there is a Christian duty of prayer for all that are in authority, which was never, it seems to me, so much obligatory as now. I am impressed, I am oppressed, with the critical position in which we are every day, more and more. I love my country. I love her noble institutions. I love the radical ideas from which those institutions sprung. It seems to me that American ideas — not the base and refuse stuff that has sometimes passed under that term, but in verity *American ideas* — come nearer to the Gospel of truth in civil institutions and processes than anything that the earth has ever before known. My heart swells when I look on this broad continent, and see what God means for us, if we are faithful and true to our privileges; when I think what a fair and mighty form this nation will present when it comprises the whole of this vast expanse, when State shall touch State from one extremity to the other, when an electric chain of patriotism shall run over all these mountains and through all these valleys, and when from ocean to ocean there shall be but one people, with one glorious career of liberty. But it seems to me that we are coming into imminent peril. I never felt that we were so much in jeopardy as now. I never felt that we were so liable to lose by slowness, by languid caution, by an unreasoning fear of possible evil, and by indifference to the real evils that are crowding about us, as now. Every single month that this war goes on brings us into greater and greater danger. Every month, from this time out, is against us, and in favor of rebellion. Unless we can, erelong, bring this gigantic struggle to a close, we are rent asunder, and rent into, not two nations, but more than you can count upon your hand, with a clouded future, with warring elements innumerable, with endless strifes and quarrels between States, with I know not what grinding and clashing. Sometimes, in storms on the sea, ships are suddenly struck, and all the things that have not been securely fastened — crockery, and furniture, and various stores — are thrown from their places by the jerking power of the waves, and then they roll from side to side in strange mingling and confusion. Horrible indeed would be the grinding and clashing of the mixed contents of our ship of state, if this continent should be rocked by the fierce storm that now threatens it. I regard it as only next to utter destruction for this nation to be rent asunder. It is for my safety, now, that I declare that there must be no separation. It is for your safety. And therefore I feel more solemnly than ever that we should avoid all careless speech, all unjust criticism, and, above all, the language of impatience and passion, and surround those that bear rule with our prayers. They should be made to feel, not only that they are watched by this people, but that they are impelled by the pulsations of its great heart. Never before were there such duties resting upon men. Never before was there a day when so much might be done, or when so much might be lost by not doing. Let us not withhold confidence, nor give it in any such way as to abet or help wickedness. We must not only stand, but make other men stand. We must not stand, but advance; and we must not only advance ourselves, but make other men advance.

But, meanwhile, to some there are no means of speaking. O yes, there are. When in storms masters of vessels cannot make their crew hear, they stand on the quarter-deck and shout through a trumpet; and the trumpet takes his words, and, enlarged, they roll out fourfold. God's ear is the speaking-trumpet through which we are to speak to men. Pray in the morning, at noon, and at night. Pray much for the government, much for your President, and much for the generals of our army; and every word that you utter will be heard. You that have children or friends on the battle-field, pray, and your pleadings shall enter the ear of God, and he shall answer them in his providence. Pray for the Chief Magistrate of this nation; pray for the leaders of our soldiers; pray for this land; pray for the cause of men and the cause of Christ that are bound up in the welfare of this land. If we are to be rent asunder, let the sad spectacle be hid from my eyes. May God permit me to die or ever I shall see this land destroyed. I have no further mission, and no further wish to live, if ruin is coming upon it. Give me my whole native land, with not one acre clipped, not one State lost; give her to me from the cool North to the warm South, from the eastern ocean to the western; give me all of it, and not less than all, unmutilated, symmetrical, with an auspicious future opening, and all influences of evil averted,— give me my native land so, and I can spend and be spent for her. But if she is to be rent asunder, and rent asunder that there may be erected another infernal government, whose foundation-stone, as its would-be founders boastingly declare, is to be the oppression of men, then may it be hid from my eyes.

But it shall not be, — *it shall not be!* There are unrolling, I would fain believe, in the mysterious ways of God, decrees of liberty; and we shall have our emancipation. We that now are fevered with war shall yet be healed of our trouble, and have rest. We are like patients on whom is some imposthume which fills the body with racking pains, and who, when at last the gathering ulcer bursts and discharges its contents, come again to quiet, and sweet sleep, and peace. When that terrific boil, slavery, bursts and discharges its foul contents, there will be peace upon this continent. Until it does, you will have no peace.

XIV.

NATIONAL INJUSTICE AND PENALTY.*

"Blessed be thou, Lord God of Israel, our Father, for ever and ever. Thine, O Lord, is the greatness, and the power, and the glory, and the victory, and the majesty; for all that is in the heaven and in the earth is thine; thine is the kingdom, O Lord, and thou art exalted as head above all. Both riches and honor come of thee, and thou reignest over all; and in thine hand is power and might; and in thine hand it is to make great, and to give strength unto all. Now, therefore, our God, we thank thee, and praise thy glorious name." — 1 Chron. xxix. 10 - 13.

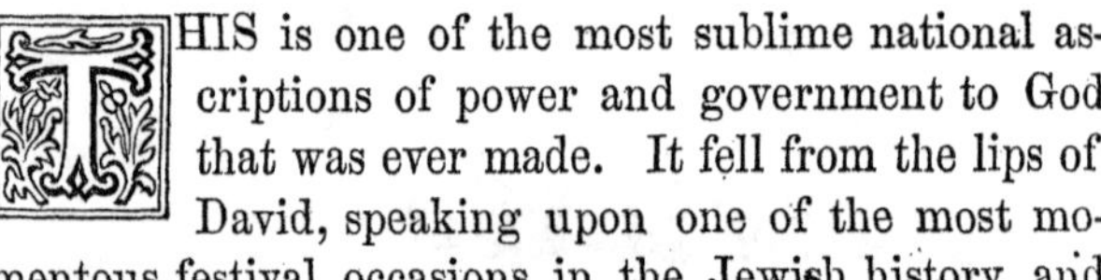

THIS is one of the most sublime national ascriptions of power and government to God that was ever made. It fell from the lips of David, speaking upon one of the most momentous festival occasions in the Jewish history, and became, by acceptance, the sentiment of the whole people. They declared their faith in God's supremacy and government over the affairs, not only of individuals, but of nations. They recognized and acknowledged, not only their dependence upon God personally, but also their dependence upon him for national prosperity and glory. It is the uniform doctrine

* September 28, 1862. Emancipation was proclaimed six days before; the *habeas corpus* suspended four days before; Lee had retreated after Antietam, Bragg was still strong in Kentucky, and men's minds were deeply exercised over the question of the President's War Powers.

of the Bible, that God has a government over this world, which includes in it both the government of individuals and the government of communities of individuals. This doctrine is not peculiar either to Christianity or to Judaism. All nations that have attained any degree of civilization have substantially held this great truth, that the world is governed by God, and that not only the affairs of individuals, but the affairs of societies also, were supervised and provided for under the Divine government. But in the sacred Word the government of God over nations is taught with more intelligence, with more discrimination, with a clearer revelation of the principles on which that government stands, than ever it was taught elsewhere. All religions recognize the fact of government. It is a peculiarity of the Christian faith, in its antecedents, and in its own self, that it reveals the ground and methods of the Divine moral government over the world.

It is important to know that the government of God over nations is conducted by an administration of natural laws. There are many who have thought that God governed as an absolute monarch, looking at such things as pleased him, and rewarding them by a direct personal volition, and looking at such things as displeased him, and punishing them by a direct personal volition. There are many who revolt from the moral government of a Being of whom it is taught that he interjects his own volitions upon the stated laws of nature. And the progress of science reveals the fact more and more plainly that there is not any interference with natural law. It equally lays the foundation for the better exposition of the doctrine of the Divine government, — namely, that it is a government over this world through natural laws, and by a Divine administration of them. It is said that natural laws are stated and immutable. That is very well for a popular expression, but it will not bear examination. For there is nothing that is less immutable than a law; nothing that is adapted to have more elasticity; nothing that may be more endlessly varied by the degree of intelligence that you bring to bear upon it, and the advantage which you choose to take of it. An ignorant and stupid man, standing in the scope of a natural law, makes nothing of it. An intelligent and wise man, by using it, makes the fields fruitful, covers the hillsides with thrifty orchards, and fills the valleys with beautiful gardens. And the difference between a stupid and ignorant man and a wise and intelligent man is simply the difference of the control that they bring to bear upon natural laws, and the use to which they put them. And the difference between civilization and barbarism is the difference between knowing how to use natural laws and not knowing how to use them. And as men grow toward manhood, they come more and more to know what natural laws are, and how to use them, and how, by using them, to obtain benefit. How much more, then, shall He that made man know how to use natural law! It is supposed that God made laws as a machine which he does not dare to put his finger into, lest he shall stop the machine, or bruise his finger; and that he therefore stands behind the world, saying, "I have built this world, and put laws into it, and wound it up, and I cannot touch it." It is not so. God manages natural laws just as man manages natural laws, only with supreme intelligence and with unerring accuracy. A government of natural law is the best government on which volition can be brought to bear. For the Divine scheme is so large and so broad that there is not a thought nor a wish to be executed that God cannot execute better through changes of law than by direct, overt omnipotence. And there is no occasion to interject volitions, and set aside natural law.

This does not diminish, it augments immeasurably, the efficiency and certainty of the Divine government over men. If the Divine government depended upon a single being's thought and continuity of attention, it might be imagined at least that there would be remissness or weariness and slumbering, — though He that keeps Israel never slumbers nor sleeps. If God's government is one of appointed laws that have no remission and never cease their agency, if there are treasured in them great penalties and great rewards, if the government of natural law is self-executing, and if God gives it power to roll on and distribute mercies and curses, according as they are, one or the other, fit and proper, then the system of administration is one from which there is no escape.

Now God's government over nations is a government through natural laws. It is universal. It is unvarying. It is immutable. It is not to be escaped.

The administration of God over nations is conducted substantially upon the same great principles as that over individuals. A nation is but an aggregation of individuals. There is more in national life than there is in any individual life; but men individually carry with them into civil federation every law and necessity that they have as individuals. They leave nothing behind. They take on additional obligations, and come under some additional laws; but they leave off nothing. And the administration of government that prevails over individuals prevails over them as much when they are aggregated into societies as when they stand alone. It is true that the conditions and the methods of evolution in nations differ from those in individual life. The life of an individual is quickly sped. Whatever takes place with regard to a man must take place in a period of some eighty years. And if an individual is indolent, his indolence very soon makes its penalty appear. Drunkenness in a man does not wait through many generations. The penalty must appear during his life, or it cannot be a penalty. The penalty of dishonesty and dishonor comes quickly to a man. For the circle in which an individual moves is small, and he comes to the result of his conduct soon. But a nation is made up of millions of individuals, that splice each other and overlap generations, so that the punishment of a nation does not come, as does that of an individual, during the lifetime of any one, but during the lifetime of the whole nation. The period is prolonged. For drunkenness cannot be produced in a nation, as in an individual, to-day or to-morrow. It takes a longer time to make a nation drunk than it does to make a man drunk. A long process must be gone through before a nation can be debauched. The space of some generations is required for that. It is not until an evil habit is established that the penalty begins to inure. And so in respect to national dishonesty, a nation is not made dishonest, as a man is, in a day. A hundred men may become dishonest, and they may be steadily infecting a hundred others with dishonesty; and these may spread their desolating principles to a whole generation; but it takes a great while before so large a life as that of a nation, with its myriad individuals, acting and counteracting, becomes so corrupted as to begin to reap the fruits of the great law of reward and of punishment.

As a nation is complex, as it is made up of successive men, as it requires long periods for the evolution of anything, good or bad, the reward or the penalty will not be immediate. The good or the evil comes to a nation according to its periods of life, just as it does to an individual. When the time comes, the remuneration comes to the nation, just as certainly as it does to the individual, although it takes it longer to move, because there is so much more of national life than of individual life, and because the adjusting processes require so much more space and time in the life of a nation than in the life of an individual.

A nation, like an individual, is held to responsibility for its obedience to physical laws. The laws that relate to an individual man's body, and that vindicate themselves in the case of an individual, also relate to the physical condition of a race or a nation. A nation is held to responsibility for the violation or observance of social laws, or laws of intelligence, of industry, of frugality, of morals, of piety. It takes longer to make a nation accountable than an individual. But in its longer period a nation is held accountable for just exactly the same things that an individual is. For a million men have no right, because they are a million, to do what each individual one of them has no right to do, against a natural law.

The observance or violation of moral principles in civil affairs is, if possible, even more signally rewarded or punished in national life than in individual life. Honor, truth, justice, fairness, fidelity to obligation, moderation of desire, magnanimity, — these are more in a nation than in an individual. They are, therefore, more obviously rewarded in a nation than in an individual, and their opposites more obviously punished. If this be so, nowhere so much in the world as in our land ought Christian citizens to be taught to consider the facts and principles that bear on national life, as well as those bearing on their own individual life.

You are part of a family, and you know that the welfare of that family concerns your individual welfare. You are part of the city or town where you live, and I need not say to you that you have your dividend of the public welfare, good or bad. You are members of the great civil society, you are members of the body politic of this nation; and while the welfare of the nation is made up in part of what you contribute to it, your welfare is in part made up of the nation itself. And no Christian minister that understands his duty in America can fail to indoctrinate his people in respect to their Christian duties as citizens. Though as Christians you examine your own hearts and your own consciences, though as Christian communicants you strive to cast out evil thoughts and desires from your mind, that does not fulfil your duty. You are bound, as a part of your fealty to Christ, to think also of national character, of national morals, and of national welfare. And as we have come to a time in which, in the most signal manner, God is making to appear his great retributive government of nations, I propose to mark out some of those features of Divine government that are now displaying themselves toward this nation, and in our affairs.

If it is possible for a nation to sin, it must be when it has been led systematically to violate all the natural rights of a whole race or people; and American slavery, by the very definition of our jurists, is the deprivation of men of every natural right. For the American doctrine of slavery is no analogue or derivative of the Hebrew or any mild form of slavery. It is the extremest and worst form of the Roman doctrine of slavery; the harshest that the world has ever seen. It is a dehumanizing of men. It is the deliberate taking of men, and putting them in the place of cattle or chattels, and violating every one of their natural rights. Now, if this was done by an individual, we might suppose that that individual, in due time, would be punished. If it was done by a small community, we might suppose that that community would be punished. And if there is a moral government, if God is just, and if he rewards or punishes nations in this world, it is not possible for a nation systematically to violate every natural right of four millions of people, and go unpunished. If that can be done, — if a nation can deny every single principle of the Decalogue, and every moral canon, as applied to a whole people, from generation to generation, and God take no account of it, — then I do not blame men for saying that there is no God. I do not stand here to say that if the Bible does not condemn slavery, I will throw the Bible away. I make no such extravagant declaration as that. There are reasons why you cannot throw the Bible away. It clings to you; it is a part of your life; it is woven into your memory of father and mother, and of your childhood; and you cannot throw it away. But this I do say: that if you teach that a nation of thirty millions of men may, by their organic laws, systematically violate the natural rights of four millions of men for twenty-five years, for fifty years, for seventy-five years, for a hundred years, and no sort of retribution follow, then do not blame men for saying that in that case there is no moral government over the affairs of this world.

Suppose a man could drink a quart of whiskey before breakfast, another quart before dinner, and another before supper, but never reel, and do it for forty years, for sixty years, and never be drunk, what headway should I make with young men in impressing upon their minds the danger of drinking whiskey? It would not be dangerous if it did not make men drunk. And if men can perpetrate every violation of natural law upon a whole race, from generation to generation, and no penalty follow, then there is no testimony of God against such wickedness, and it is not wicked.

On the other hand, if they do it, and every step of doing is marked either by the intimation of penalty or the actual disclosure of it, and if that penalty is graded so that you can trace it from step to step, and so that he that is blind can feel it, if he cannot see it, then there is no casuistry about slavery, or about Scripture or textual authority against slavery. Then no man can get rid of the doctrine of God's judgment against slavery, and that there is a moral government which makes it penal to violate the rights of men.

Let us look at it a little in this light, and see if there is any testimony, under God's great moral government, on the subject of the sinfulness of slavery.

1. There is no right more universal, and more sacred, because lying so near to the root of existence, than the right of men to their own labor. It is primal. But the very first step of slavery is to deny that right. There are four millions of men, women, and children, to-day, to whom is denied the right to their own labor, — the right to direct it or to have the fruits of it. Now you may reason as cunningly as you please, and tell me that it is better that it should be so, and that the slaves are better off where they are, and I will point to every State where slavery has denied to the slave the right to his own labor, and will show that in that very spot God has blighted and cursed the soil. Every Slave State that has had exacted and enforced labor has itself felt the blight and curse of slavery in its agriculture. What is the land in Virginia worth to-day? It is worn out and abandoned. If it were not for slave-breeding, old slave-tilled Virginia would not now be a Slave State. It is not on account of her tobacco, it is not on account of her cereals, it is because Virginians sell their own blood in the market, that she is a Slave State. It is only by doing that, that she can make profit on slaves now. Her agriculture is killed. Her soil is wasted. You may track slavery through North Carolina, through South Carolina, through Georgia, through Alabama, through Mississippi, through Louisiana; and I do not tell any secret, or state that which any man doubts, when I say that the agriculture of slavery is an exhausting agriculture, and that it wears

out every part of the country that it touches. The work of the slave carries the punishment of the master. The master takes away his right to his labor, and the slave turns round and says, "I curse the soil." The soil is cursed, and it is a witness of God.

2. Slavery violates the social and family rights of men. For the law of slavery is that every man in slavery is his master's, and not his own. Of course, therefore, every woman follows the same law. And there is no such thing as the right of marriage. There is a form of marriage which is observed with more or less decency under different circumstances; but there is neither the doctrine nor the impression, throughout slavery, that, when a man is once married, his wife is sacred to him forever. Sale is divorce; and the general law is that, when a man is sold ten miles from the plantation where his wife is owned, he is free to take another. The Church never thinks of disciplining him if he does, nor the woman if she takes a second or a third husband.

Now if anything is fundamental in this world, it is marriage; but if anything is violated systematically and inevitably, it is the right of marriage in men that do not own either their wives or their children in any way whatever. Is there any testimony on this subject? Has God visited such a monstrous violation of natural and moral law with any punishment? Yes, in destroying the sacredness of the family relation. The virtue of the family estate is sapped throughout the South. I know what I speak. It is not a matter into which you can go in detail; but the great sanctities and purities of wedded life are universally violated in the South. Talk about amalgamation as one of the hateful abolitionist doctrines! Amalgamation is never unpopular until it has been made lawful; and then men hate it like perdition. But just so long as it is concubinage, adultery, and fornication, it is the most popular doctrine in the whole South. And I know that the very foundation of the virtue of the young men throughout the South is perpetually sapped and undermined. I believe that nowhere are women more virtuous than there; and nowhere do they suffer more than there. And in God's great revealing day, when the anguish of wives' hearts and mothers' hearts, when all that they have been made to suffer by the contaminations which they have seen brought by slavery into their families, shall be revealed, O how dreadful will then appear God's witness and punishment of that vile system! Those who take away from the slave the fundamental right of matrimony, and of the family, are punished by the undermining of the virtue and purity of their own households.

3. Slavery makes ignorance indispensable to the slave; because where there is knowledge, every faculty is a wheel set in motion. The more complex the machinery of a man's mind is, the more needful it is to have a skilful engineer to manage and keep it in repair, and the more fuel it requires to run it; while the less complex it is, the nearer the man is to an animal, the easier it is to manage it and keep it in repair, and supply its wants. As long as man lives only in bone and muscle, he asks nothing but pork and corn-meal. As long as he is an ox, he chews ox-fodder. When he becomes a man, he eats man's food. And the difference between a slave and a man is the difference between fodder and food. The moment you give

a man a heart, he must have something for his heart; the moment you give him imagination, he must have some opportunity, some scope, some leisure, for his imagination; the moment you give him reason, he must have food for his reason; and as you augment a man in civilization, and make more and more of him, there must be a larger space, more room, for him. And so, when you give slaves intelligence, you make them so voluminous that a man cannot afford to provide for a hundred of them; and it is not safe to let them provide for themselves. The only way, therefore, to make slavery profitable, is to keep the slave ignorant.

Now, is there no punishment for this wrong? If a man shuts the door of knowledge against his fellow-man, is there no testimony of God against it? Is it no sin to rob manhood of knowledge? Is it no crime to take from man the liberty of being what God made him to be? I hold that there is no other crime in the calendar to be compared with that. The man that robs a bank in New York commits a slight offence compared with that which he commits who robs a human being of the right to open his own mind before God and man. And what is the punishment of that? The white man says to the slave, "You shall not know anything"; and the slave says to the white man, "Massa, *you* shall not know anything," — and he does not! For the great mass of the white men of the South are profoundly ignorant, and must remain ignorant, for the reason that you cannot have schools where there is a legalized system of ignorance. Where there is a system of enforced ignorance that deprives four millions of men of knowledge, you cannot also have a system of forced intelligence that shall diffuse knowledge among the remainder of the population, as the free schools of the North do among our population. The necessity of keeping the slave ignorant is the necessity of keeping the major part of the white people at the South ignorant. They are ignorant, and ignorant they will remain while slavery remains; and God bears witness that he punishes this exclusion of knowledge from the slave.

4. Slavery, taking away from man his rights, and degrading him to be a thing of bargain and sale, avenges itself by making human life unsacred wherever slavery prevails. It begins by lowering the idea of manhood, and by making slave-life of no account, except for purposes of traffic. The punishment is that, in lowering the idea of manhood, and making life of no account in respect to four millions of men, it does the same things in respect to all mankind. And where is life so cheap, and where can a man be killed so easily and with so little disturbance of society, as in the Southern States? And where slavery is the most rancorous, not only are duels, riots, assassinations, and bloody broils most frequent, but the whole of social life is low and barbarous. And it is reasonable that life should be cheaper there than in civilized communities, because it is a great deal more to kill a virtuous, noble-minded man than a barbarian! There are some men such that if you kill one, you kill a thousand men; and there are some men of whom you might kill a thousand, and then not kill more than one. Influences proceed together by elective affinities; and thus a system that for the sake of slavery lowers the doctrine of manhood, lowers it about all

men. Thus it punishes itself, and carries the penalty in its own nature.

5. Yet more terrible is another aspect. Slavery, while admitted to be an evil, and regretted, might consist with correct civil ideas. It did in the beginning. Till within my remembrance, Christian men and statesmen in the South admitted that slavery was an evil, deprecated its existence, and hoped for its decline and its extinction; and it was quite compatible with the existence of slavery that these men held right doctrines about men and government. But a change came, and the doctrine that now exists throughout the South on the subject of slavery is, that slavery is right, and that it is the right of the strong and the intelligent to take away from the weak and the ignorant every civil right, and every personal right, and to subject and subdue them to their own will. That is now claimed by the South as a right. Well, what has been the penalty? The assumption of the right to denude four millions of men of their rights, has avenged itself by rolling back and corrupting every political theory and every political idea throughout the South. Every thinking man there has been corrupted to the core by this doctrine of slavery. And I aver without fear of contradiction, that the South have set themselves free from democracy and republicanism. They are neither republican nor democratic. They are aristocratic, and are verging close upon monarchy. And slavery has punished them. As an instrument in the hand of God, it has been turned upon them for their punishment. They have been punished as with a whip of scorpions. They have held a doctrine that justified them in taking every civil and every natural

right away from their fellow-men, and God has punished them by turning them back to the barbaric periods, and driving them upon the waste and now abandoned doctrines of Europe. And the States of the South, — you know where they are. They are four hundred years back of where you stand, and they are going back. They have already got the other side of the Reformation, and they are on the way to the Red Sea, and God will thrust them in!

6. As with States, so with the Federal government. I might cite innumerable instances of penalty that have accompanied the opening and progress of this system of slavery. The Federal government has tolerated slavery, and it has experienced, and is experiencing, punishment therefor. In the inception of this government, when independent States were being persuaded to coalesce, and to form one great nation, the dread of weakness was so great that men consented to act by sight, and not by faith.

A cooper goes to work to make a wine-cask. He prepares the staves, and begins to set them up. This one is sound, and he sets it up; that one is sound, and he sets that up; he runs around the circle, till he comes to the last three or four staves, when he takes them up, and finds that they are worm-eaten and bored in every direction. He says, "I am afraid that I shall not make my barrel if I do not put them in: I know they are poor, that the wine will leak out, and that I shall have a terrible time to save it, but I must make up my barrel, and these are all that I have." So he puts them in, and drives down the hoops; and when the wine is put in it runs out, and then follows a system of tinkering, and driving in a chip here, and a sliver there. But in spite of all that he can do, the wine leaks away. And, after infinite trials and vexations, he finds that the wine is all gone, and that the barrel is good for nothing. What should he have done? He should have thrown out those worm-eaten staves, and made the barrel smaller.

Now, because they were afraid that South Carolina — that rottenest of rotten staves — would not come in, the framers of our government admitted slavery, the worm-eating devastation of this country. Suppose they had said, "We will have a Union and have freedom in it, and only those that consent to the exclusion of slavery shall be admitted," — suppose they had said this, and made their barrel smaller, and made it sound, is there any doubt as to what the issue would have been? But they were so afraid of weakness that they wished to make the barrel large, and they put in worm-eaten staves; and the result is that there has not been one single weakness in this government that has not followed directly from the mischief of slavery in it. We were a homogeneous people. We had opportunities on this continent, and elements of prosperity, such as no nation ever possessed. There never was launched such a people on such a sphere as this. And the great and only cause of weakness and trouble in the Federal government has been slavery. And the agitations and disturbances and sufferings through which we have passed have been so many penalties and punishments which God has infixed upon the wickedness that included slavery in this government. We have had a head full of sound teeth. Slavery is the only tooth that has ached. Every other one has been true to its function.

It has been said that resistance to slavery has been the cause of all our national troubles. That is as if a wise physiologist should say that the resistance of the principle of health in a man's body to disease was the cause of fevers, and that the way not to have fevers was to lie down and let the disease go through its course. Yes, there has been conscience enough to make resistance, thank God. If it had not been for that, we should have been corrupted through and through, and the very marrow would have been rotten before this time.

For a period of fifty years, on pleas of national peace, for the sake of harmony and prosperity, the loyal and free States have declined to maintain the policy of liberty, and have permitted slavery to augment from an acknowledged evil to a dominant power, — from a thing permitted to a despotic influence. We have, for a period of fifty years, had a race of statesmen, bribed and corrupted, who have perpetually said, "Let us not disturb the prosperity of this great nation." O, how they have laughed at and scorned the men that sounded out God's denunciations and woes against such monstrous iniquity! and how they have uttered in the ears of a credulous public the declaration, "This nation, this Government, this Constitution, — are they not more precious than the *isms* of the abolitionists?" In other words, when God's law demanded justice, they have said, "Commercial prosperity is more than God's law." When once a man, that never, I fear, will say so good a thing again, said that there was a higher law than legislators ever passed, the whole nation — not excepting ministers in pulpits, who have, I hope, learned better things by this time — derided the idea that there could be a higher law. And such has been the state of things in the midst of which politicians in this country have been trained, and which has brought the original principles of justice and equity to contempt. The ruling spirit of the nation has been a commercial spirit, and that in its lowest forms.

Has there been any penalty? What has been the result of the last fifty years of peace-making? Go to Sharpsburg; go into Virginia, where battles have been fought; go along the swamps of the Chickahominy; go through Kentucky and Missouri, where war like a sirocco has desolated everything; go where the land rocks and reels with earthquakes and convulsions,—and read the lessons of peace that we have been taught. For in these days we are reaping what we have sowed. These things are the fruit of the seed that we have planted. You would have peace, and you see what you have got. If you had stood up before, manfully, and listened betimes, and resisted the evil that threatened the very life of the nation, you would not have come to this pass. You were warned, you were exhorted, innumerable witnesses foretold what the result must be, and behold it has come upon you!

I beg you still further to take notice of some remarkable facts.

If there is any State in this Union that has suffered more severely than another, it is Virginia. If there is any State that has sinned against light and knowledge, it is Virginia. She knew better; and she has been desolated, skinned, peeled, stripped bare. Famine now sweeps with outspread wings over her plains, and desolation grins in her valleys, that a few months ago were as lovely as paradise.

Virginia was dragooned out of the nation. When the convention was elected, it was elected by the people in favor of the Union. They assembled in Richmond. There was a conspiracy of slave-traders, who, in connection with some desperate politicians, instituted a terrorism; and that convention was dragooned to a secret vote that took the State out of the Union, by that corruptest, guiltiest, and most accursed class of men, slave-traders, who are hated of men, of God, and the devil. And that State, which was the keystone of the arch, and which permitted herself to fall out, has had the most terrible punishment. Is there no lesson in that? Is that an accidental fact?

Consider, again, the strange part that has been played in this conflict by Southern women. A woman always goes with her whole heart, whether for the good or for the bad. Women are the best and the worst things that God ever made! And they have been true to their nature in this conflict. Southern men have been tame and cool in comparison with the fury of Southern women. Now, admit that they were blinded. A man that steps off from a precipice is not saved because he is blindfolded. A man that walks in fire is not saved because he thought it was water. I suppose that of the male population of the South between the ages of fifteen and fifty, a majority will be utterly cut off before this war ends. To a great extent, Southern households are to be stripped of those that are their heads, and the South is to be a realm in which woman shall be deprived of her natural protector, and bear unutterable woes of poverty and sorrow and murder and rapine. She has taken such an unfortunate position in this war, for slavery, and she has sinned against such great light, that God is bringing down upon her head condign punishment.

We, too, are suffering in the North, and in the same way that we ought to. I accept the punishment. It is measured with an even hand all over the country. Every man that should have voted right, and did not, is having, or is yet to have, a part in the sufferings caused by this struggle. Every State that, for the sake of its manufactories, has refused to do the right thing, has suffered, and shall suffer. For I call you more specially to take notice, that the North has suffered to the extent to which she has winked at slavery for the sake of commerce. Why is it that the State of Connecticut — my State — the State in which I was born and bred, which I love with an unfaltering love, and of which I have been so often ashamed — has been so servile, so radically Democratic, in the sense of that Democracy which means pandering to slavery, — why is it, but that she has established petty manufactories along the shore, and that her great market has been South? Why has the manufacturing North been so largely pro-slavery? Why has the policy of freedom been so often betrayed and paralyzed by the merchants of New York and Philadelphia, and Boston and Pittsburg? Commerce has bribed them. And what is the result? You have been making money out of slavery. A part of my support comes out of slavery. I do not deny this. I know that I eat sugar and wear cotton that have been produced by the unrequited labor of slaves. I know that this evil of slavery has gone through every fibre of the whole North. And while I blame the North, I take part of the blame on my own head. I put part of it on your head. I distribute it to every State. I am not making complaint against the South distinctively, but against the nation. And by the time you have paid two thousand million dollars of taxes, and have but just begun, I think that the Lord will have got back pretty much all that the North has made out of slavery! God is a great tax-gatherer; he is out now on that errand; and he will have a prosperous time!

I call you still further to take notice, that every nation and people on the globe that has had any political or pecuniary connection with this monstrous evil is being made to suffer. God is pouring out the vial of his wrath; and bearing witness, tremendous witness, by war, against slavery, and against the cruel wickedness of men that perpetuate it. The South suffers, the North suffers, and, next to this nation, England suffers, because, next to this nation, she is guilty. England? why, there is not a better-tongued people in the world. England? I honor her old history; I honor her struggles for liberty; I honor her stalwart valor in the present day. And yet the commercial classes of England have thriven, and made their wealth and built their palaces, out of slave labor. And to-day there is mourning in the factories of England, there is famine in her streets, and the commercial classes are demanding that the ports of the South shall be opened. And now that government, which has already winked at wickedness on account of the necessity of obtaining cotton, is yielding, and is considering whether it is not necessary for her to commit another monstrous wickedness. God punishes England, because England has had to do with slavery. And he is punishing France. France suffers less, but France is suffering. Find me a nation whose welfare has depended on cotton or sugar, and I will find you a nation that is suffering in consequence of this war.

Are these facts accidental? The condition of the South, of the North, and of foreign countries, in their relations to the war, — are these accidental? Is there any such thing as a divine witness? Are there any such things as indications of a moral government, and of punishments accruing from the transgression of moral laws?

What then, I ask, in conclusion, is infidelity in our day? It is refusing to hear God's voice, and to believe God's testimony in his providence. There are plenty of men who believe in Genesis, and Chronicles, and the Psalms, and Isaiah, and Daniel, and Ezekiel, and Matthew, and the other Evangelists, and the rest of the New Testament, clear down to the Apocalypse; there are plenty of men who believe in the letter of Scripture; and there are plenty of men who believe everything that God said four thousand years ago; but the Lord God Almighty is walking forth at this time in clouds and thunder such as never rocked Sinai. His voice is in all the land, and in all the earth, and those men that refuse to hear God in his own time, and in the language of the events that are taking place, are infidels. And the infidelity is greater in your case than it could be in the case of any other people; because to believe in slavery, to refuse to believe in liberty, and to be unwilling to believe that God rewards liberty and punishes slavery, against your education, against your historic ideas, against all the canons of your political structure, against the natural sympathies of the heart, — that is a monstrous infidelity. No man can be such an infidel by disbelieving the Bible as you can by standing and looking upon the current events of this age, and refusing to believe that God is bearing witness against oppression and in favor of liberty. Take care. You are in more danger on that point, just now, than on any other. Because things are coming to a crisis. We are about to move in gigantic force in one way or the other; and it is necessary that we should fall back on some great principle. Henceforth, let us refuse to take guidance and direction from the counsels of cunning men or weaving politicians. It is time for us to fall back from the counsels of men, and strike some great immutable principle of God.

What, then, is to be our policy for the future? What are we to do? One class of men will say, "The remedy for all these evils is to gather together about twenty secessionists, and about twenty abolitionists, and hang them!" But I will tell you what hanging abolitionists will do. It will do just exactly what would be done if, when a terrible disease had broken out on a ship, the crew should kick the doctors overboard, and the medicine after them. The disease would stay on board, and only the cure would go overboard. You may rage as much as you please, but the men who labor to bring back the voices of the founders of this Union; the men whose faith touches the original principles of God's Word; the men that are in sympathy with Luther; the men that breathe the breath that fanned the flame of the Revolution; the men that walk in the spirit of the old Puritans; the men that are like the first framers of this model republic, — they are the men, if there be any medicine yet, by whose hand God will send a cure. Hang them? that was the medicine that the Jews had when they crucified Christ. The Lord of glory was put upon an ignominious tree, and they thought that they would have peace in Jerusalem! And where is Jerusalem? Where are the Jews? They are a by-word and a hissing to the earth. And you, the children of men that came here for liberty; you, that heard only the doctrines of liberty from your mother's lips, and drank it with her milk; you, in whose make every thread and every fibre was spun from the golden fleece of liberty, — can you stand in any doubt as to what the remedy is for such times as these? It is to repent of past days, to break away from the past, and to call God to witness that in time to come we will consecrate, individually and nationally, every energy to repair the mischief of slavery, to do it away utterly, and to establish the reign of universal liberty. That is the path of safety. And blessed be God, he has sent a porter. He has opened the door by the hand of the President. He has lifted the silver trumpet of liberty, and the blast is blown that rolls through the forest, and goes along the mountain-side, and spreads wide over the prairies. It is known on the hither ocean, and on the thither; and the waves of the Pacific, and the waves of the Atlantic, lift themselves up, and sound together notes of gladness because that policy is enunciated which cannot be taken back. As long as it was a question whether the President meant to declare emancipation, as Commander-in-chief of the army and navy of the United

States, as a military necessity, — as long as there was any doubt on this subject, the North was in danger of being divided into two parties, one attempting to make him proclaim liberty, and the other attempting to make him stand up for slavery. He has taken his choice between them. And there can be but two parties in the North, one of whom shall go for liberty, the government, and the President, and the other for the South, for treachery, and for slavery. The foundation of all opposition is knocked out.

I know it is said that the President is not the government; that the Constitution is the government. What! a sheepish parchment a government! I should think it was a very fit one for some such men as I often see and hear! What is a government in our country? It is a body of living men, ordained by the people, who administer public affairs according to the laws that are written in the Constitution and the statute-books. The government consists of living men that are administering, in a certain method, the affairs of the nation. It is not a dry writing or a book. President Lincoln and his Cabinet, the heads of the executive departments, are the government. And men must take their choice whether they will go against their government or go with it. Mouthing traitors will pretend to go with the government while they are undermining it, and honest men will go with it, — and you know that the honest men in the North are yet a large majority. I thank God that the lines are drawn. There is nothing so demoralizing as equivocal neutrality, and nothing so bad. And since the President has taken ground, since the administration and government are now fixed on the side of liberty, the old original wisdom of our Constitution, and the doctrine of our fathers, we are going to have the Union as it never was, but as it was meant to be. The Union as it was meant to be, and not the Union as it was, is to be our doctrine; because the Union as it was, was a monstrous outrage on your rights, and on mine. The Union as it was guaranteed me the right of speech, to be paid for by my life in Virginia and Carolina and Georgia and Alabama and Mississippi and Louisiana and Arkansas and Missouri. I could not have gone to either of those States and spoken the words that I have spoken to-night without praising God to-morrow morning in another world. Am I to celebrate the Union as it was, which was a practical violation of the great canons of the Constitution, of the great principles of the Bills of Rights, and of the great doctrines of the Declaration of Independence? Slavery had corrupted it, and made it to be practically an abominable thing in many of its usages. But the Union as it was to be, the Union as it was in the intent of the framers of it, — let that come back; and, so far as it is twisted out of shape, let the twists be taken out, so that it shall stand just exactly plumb to the line of the Constitution. Then we shall have the Union that is to be, and the Union that we want.

And now, my Christian friends, if the whole Church of the Christian North and the loyal North, if the ministers and the members of the churches, and all that are religiously inclined throughout the North, will be pleased to make this a matter of religious conviction, and if they will assume that God has come to judgment with this nation, and will for their future policy ask, not, "Mr. Seward, what wilt thou have me to do?" nor, "Mr. Seymour, what wilt thou have me to do?" nor even, "Mr. Lincoln, what wilt thou have me to do?" but, "Lord, what wilt thou have me to do?" — if the Christian public of the North will settle their duty in the light of eternity, and according to the principles of God's Word, and if they will take the slave, and bear him to Calvary, and lay him down under the cross of Him that gave his life for the poor and wretched, and if then, as the sacred drops fall from the wounded side upon his beaten and bruised body, kneeling down, they will say, "Jesus, what wilt thou have me to do for this injured and oppressed one?" and will settle it there, and under that influence, I have no fear.

We shall see struggles, and go through deep and bitter trials yet; but the future is bright. For where Christ sits is daylight and morning. And if the whole Christian public of the North set their faces toward God, and move toward him, they will move away from night, and toward the day, — a day that, when it shall once have arisen on this continent, shall know no setting, — a day of Christian liberty, — the harbinger of universal freedom to a world regenerated. God grant it.

And as for me, I am determined, by that same help that has been vouchsafed to me from the beginning, to preach a Gospel of liberty among you, and to bear witness for liberty, as founded in religion, to all this nation. I will not be intimidated. I shall not be persuaded. Come weal or come woe, — whether we are defeated and cast back again, or whether we go forward immediately to the prosperity of an ascertained and settled liberty, — as long as I have life and health, and strength and breath, I will use them first and last, and chiefly and only, for the enunciation of that Gospel which brings release to the captive, and liberty to man. There is no power even in hell, though you bring its legions and its monstrosities upon the earth, that for one single moment will hinder or turn back this testimony that God made man to be free. I will preach it for the sewing-woman; I will preach it for the poor day-laborer; I will preach it for the white man and for the black man; I will preach it for all in this land; I will preach it for the oppressed of other lands, — for the Irishman, for the Dane, for the Englishman, for the Frenchman, for the struggling Italian, and for the Hungarian; I will preach it for every man. For God hath made all nations of one blood, and to dwell together. I own the brotherhood. I accept every man as my brother, inheriting my right. And as long as I claim for myself liberty, I will assert it for other men, I will live for it, and I will die for it.

I see that this is not my own individual inspiration. I am moved to this because it is in the heart, because it is the public sentiment of States and communities. I am but the mouthpiece of millions of men; and I say to those that meditate treachery and tyranny, Beware! God has come to judgment, but he has come to a judgment by which he will purify his people, and make them a peculiar people, zealous of good works. We shall see a glorious Union. We shall see a restored Constitution. We shall see a liberty in whose bright day Georgia and Massachusetts shall shake hands that never shall be separated again. There is love yet to be raked open. Now there is fierceness of hatred; but there shall come concord, fellowship, and union, that no foreign influence can break, and no home trouble shall ever mar again. We shall live to see a better day.

XV.

THE GROUND AND FORMS OF GOVERNMENT.*

"That the hypocrite reign not, lest the people be ensnared." — Job xxxiv. 30.

THE whole context from the seventeenth verse is worthy of reading.

"Shall even he that hateth right govern? and wilt thou condemn him that is most just? Is it fit to say to a king, Thou art wicked? and to princes, Ye are ungodly? How much less to him that accepteth not the persons of princes, nor regardeth the rich more than the poor? for they all are the work of his hands."

God is the greatest democrat in the universe. He does not regard ranks, nor conditions, nor degrees; and he says that the highest rich man is just like the lowest poor man, and that a king is no better than the humblest of his subjects. They are all alike before the throne of God. As you go toward heaven, you go toward the true divine democracy.

"In a moment shall they die, and the people shall be troubled at midnight, and pass away: and the mighty shall be taken away without hand. For his eyes are upon the

* November 22, 1862.

ways of man, and he seeth all his goings. There is no darkness nor shadow of death, where the workers of iniquity may hide themselves" — from God. "For he will not lay upon man more than right, that he should enter into judgment with God. He shall break in pieces mighty men without number, and set others in their stead. Therefore he knoweth their works, and he overturneth them in the night, so that they are destroyed. He striketh them as wicked men in the open sight of others; because they turned back from him, and would not consider any of his ways: so that they cause the cry of the poor to come unto him, and he heareth the cry of the afflicted. When he giveth quietness, who then can make trouble? and when he hideth his face, who then can behold him? whether it be done against a nation, or against a man only: that the hypocrite reign not, lest the people be ensnared."

It is affirmed that Job was written at some period between Abraham and Moses. It is the oldest portion, or at least one of the oldest portions, of the sacred writings. And yet, old as it is, the world-long controversy whether God governed the world by a moral law, with rewards and penalties, had begun when it was written. The whole passage read is a fine assertion of the fact of Divine government, and with shades and applications that would seem to make it the transcript of God's procedure in our own time.

The fault of all expectations and arguments as to the existence of a moral government over human affairs is apt to be that men seek for the evidences of a moral government where they are not most eminent. For the Divine government is distributed through many different departments of life. A part of it appears in the individual. A part of it follows him into the family. A part of it belongs to his commercial, and a part of it to his civil life. And we are to gather the results of any moral course, not alone in an individual fate, but in the collective fate of all the individuals represented in the household, in their business, and in their civil estate. And the results of God's moral administration appear partly in the individual, partly in the household, partly in the affairs of commerce, and partly in national histories. But man's life, taken comprehensively, bears witness to nothing, if not to the moral government of God, which rewards right conduct, truth, honor, virtue, manhood, and duty, and punishes the reverse. And history has been written in vain, if history has not taught this. But it has not been written in vain, and it does teach this. A man in civil government is just as much a subject of the divine moral government as a man in his individual relations.

Civil governments are said to be of God. All government is ordained of God; and civil governments are so, not as by revelation and ordination, but because the nature of man necessitates government. God did not create man, and then command a government over him, but he created man with a necessity and instinct of government, and then left that instinct and necessity to develop themselves. God made men to need clothes, but he never cut out a pattern for them to make their clothes by. He left them to choose their own raiment. God made appetite, but he never made a bill of fare. He left men to pick out their own food. God made man's necessity for government, and then let him alone, and that necessity of government wrought out civil governments.

There has been a law, also, in these; for governments are not accidental. Governments are always the legitimate outworkings of the condition of those governed; and there cannot, for any prolonged period, be a government that is not, in the nature of things, adapted to those under it. If there is an absolute monarchy, it is an indication that there is a state of the people that requires an absolute monarchy. If there is an intermediate, or aristocratic government, it is an indication that the state of the people is such as to necessitate that government. If there is a continuous and strong republican government, or self-government in any form, it is because there was a condition of the people that wrought it out. For governments are not arbitrary. They are the effect of which the moral state of the people is the cause. Therefore we are not to rail against any form of government, as if it were itself a monstrous wrong. Governments are shadows that nations and peoples themselves cast; and they usually measure in some degree the proportions of the peoples or nations that cast them.

The lowest conditions of men always induce strong governments; they always induce governments of force rather than of motive; and for the reason that men in an undeveloped and ignorant state are unsusceptible of motive. They do not think much. Their moral sense is inchoate, and you cannot address many motives to it. That part of their life is superstitious rather than religious, and it leads to the introduction of superstitious motives into government. And in proportion as men are in condition like animals, you must harness and whip them as you do animals. You cannot govern them in any other way. We act upon this principle in our households; for the little child, before it has learned to use its reason and its moral sense, is governed through the skin. And just in proportion as it is redeemed from animalism, and carried up toward intelligence and moral sense, a moral and intellectual government is introduced in the place of a physical government. You cannot govern a child of four years as you can a man of forty, simply because those motives which influence the developed nature of the man have no effect on the undeveloped nature of the child. And so it is in governments. While men are low and brutal and savage, while they have possession of but a part of themselves, it is not possible to govern them in any way except with reference to their condition.

The middle state will result in government by orders and classes. It will emancipate such as are strong and intelligent, and leave the ignorant yet under strong government. When all men are ignorant, you will have absolute monarchies; when a part are intelligent and the rest are ignorant, you will have aristocracies; and when the whole are intelligent, you will have democracies, or republican governments. One of these three is inevitable. The people determine what the government shall be. If they are brutal, there will be tyrannies; if they are partly civilized and partly uncivilized, there will be aristocracies; if they are wholly civilized, there will be democracies. Governments necessitate themselves, and adapt themselves to the people.

Let us look a little at this order of governments, as founded upon the character of the people.

Strong governments belong to the undeveloped and

weak. It is so of necessity, and it is so by right. If it is wrong to have monarchies when they are required, it is still more wrong to have people that can be governed by nothing but monarchies. So long as people are crude and undeveloped, you can govern them in no other way than by strong and compulsory means. There were attempts made early at self-governments, but they all failed ignominiously, for the reason that the people were not prepared to govern themselves. The Jewish nation has been called a commonwealth. That there were in its legislation elements of a commonwealth, there can be no doubt; but in point of fact the government of the Jewish people never did amount to anything more than a strong government. It was either a government of chiefs over tribes, or a government of priests, under the name of theocracy. And it was a strong government, whatever the form might be.

Just as far as ignorance and passion and rudeness exist in a community, they impede self-government, or even make it impossible. And where the people are not prepared or qualified to govern themselves, absolute governments are just as certain now as ever before. Government is not a thing to be chosen, except so far as necessity is itself choice. Adaptation is a kind of generic choice. It is supposed that we have outgrown monarchical governments. We have been taught, since the days of the spelling-book and the old "Columbian Orator," that this nation could not be governed by a monarchy. It depends upon how ignorant and how wicked you are. Large portions of this nation cannot be governed by anything but a monarchy now, and there is danger that erelong such will be the case with the whole nation unless there is a change. For as ignorance disappears, so disappear monarchies; and as ignorance comes back, so inevitably come back monarchies. August laughs at the idea of March, and says, "We have no frost; we have warm nights and glowing days, and there shall be no more frosts." And September says it, only with a fainter voice. And October begins to feel pinching frosts. And as the days grow shorter, and the nights grow longer, and November and December come in, the reign of winter again ensues. And there is a January to every August, as there is an April to every January. And there are just such revolutions in the history of the world. You can have Pharaohs again, if you want them, — though I pray God that there may be a Red Sea for every one of them! You can have dynasties again by just letting the people become adapted to them by ignorance, by unvirtue, by a want of self-restraint, by pampered self-indulgence, or by pride growing out of monstrous prosperity. Every step toward declension from moral character is a written invitation for tyranny to come back, — and it never lingers long nor hesitates when invited.

Whenever, from any cause, large portions of any community become barbarous, they necessitate monarchies, and the prevailing governments must either grow strong, or fail entirely; for there can be no self-government except where there is virtue, intelligence, and moral worth.

Strong governments, then, belong to the first conditions of the world, to the lowest states of human life; and they are not good as compared with better governments, but good as compared with nothing at all.

The process of civilization, with all its manifold powers, acts first, of course, upon the strongest natures. In strong governments there will be, if they be at all good, a tendency to improve. This tendency usually shows itself first, not in masses, but in single instances; and when educating influences begin to bear upon a community, the most susceptible are first affected; the men with the strongest minds, with the most intellection, with the richest natures, with the best parts, are earliest developed. The word *aristocrat* comes from a Greek word that signifies *the best.* And in the progress of the development of national life the first men that are educated, and that begin to have the power that comes from education, are men that by original endowment are the best men, the most intellectual men, the men of the most brain and substance.

The second result is that such men become incapable of enduring an arbitrary government. As long as men are ignorant, and deficient in will, they are incompetent to resist a strong government, and, like the masses around them, they submit to it; but as they begin to think, and have will-power, they begin to resist the government, and it slides off, and begins to distribute its power, and an aristocracy comes in as the first transition from an absolute government, so that there will be a monarch, with a class, as in England, or a class without a monarch, as in some of the ancient nations. Under such circumstances, the government is called the government of the best men over the masses, or of the few over the many. And this is a natural and inevitable transition state from strong government to self-government. It holds a middle place between a government *over* the people and a government *from* the people. It includes, in some degree, the elements of both. And the same reason that compels the crown to divide its power with the higher classes will go on steadily, compelling these higher classes to admit fresh sections into their upper circle. There is a tendency in governments to work toward the republican form. That is to say, where governments are wisely and efficiently administered, men more and more learn the art and acquire the capacity of governing, and become themselves depositaries of governmental power.

In all Europe there is a steady progress toward the last great form of civil government, — namely, republican government, or government of the people by the people. I know it is said that the English government is the best government on the earth. Very likely it may be the best in the intermediate period; but it is not standing still in that period. If there is one thing more certain than another, it is that, as the popular element increases, that government recedes from aristocracy and monarchy toward republicanism. There may be a nominal king. I do not object to that. Names do not change anything. I would as lief have a man or a woman (I would rather have a woman, on an average!) to be called king or queen as to have a man to be called president. And as to the class of nobility, there have been periods when they, or when the nobility combined with the monarch, were adapted to the conditions of the people; but as the people are themselves becoming intelligent, they are tending toward a state of things that will inevitably make them partners of the great governing power. England is working toward self-government.

The republican form of government is the noblest and the best, as it is the latest. It is the latest because it demands the highest conditions for its existence. Self-government by the whole people is the teleologic idea. It is to be the final government of the world. As to whether the world is ripe enough to develop such a government, which shall be able to maintain itself through any considerable number of generations, it is useless to speculate.

But the process of developing a good and stable republican government may go through ages. It is not a settled fact at all, that, because we have come into a republican government, this nation is going to live and be perfected in it; because it is often the case that one government rises up and works out one or two elements of the great scheme which God is developing in this world, and then dissolves, and that the next government takes up and carries forward that which the first began. It may be that the work which we have begun is to be taken up and carried forward by a government that is to succeed this. Yet there is a counter analogy to this, — the fact that God is giving to nations that have declined, and wellnigh lost their national life, rejuvenescence. We see what was never before seen, — a nation, after having died, come to life again. Italy has found resurrection, and is growing strong. Spain has been resuscitated, and is growing strong. Even Austria is coming up from senility, and seems to be growing strong. Nations now seem to have a recuperative power. And two things are possible in respect to our own people. Having taken the first steps in the demonstration of the great doctrine of the government of the people by the people, our whole national life may collapse, and new nations may come up and carry on that doctrine in its later development; or, having gone through one period of our growth, we may renew our youth, and go on again in the same grand and divine experiment of government which we have wrought out thus far.

And let me say here, that republican governments cannot be had by any mere legislation. They must be the effect of compelling causes. Government is an outworking of the spirit of the people, and it holds a constant relation to their actual condition.

If men are ignorant, or morally low, even under republics, they will cease to be self-governing. They will be led by cunning men, who will gain power over them by courting their passions, and lead them, not according to the decisions and judgments of the masses, but according to the schemes and plans of those who acquire a surreptitious influence over them.

This is the meaning of our text, "That the hypocrite reign not, lest the people be ensnared." Under republican governments it is possible for men to be ensnared by cunning men, and, while they seem to be controlling their own destinies, to be themselves absolutely controlled and guided and governed.

There will always be large classes of men whose spirit and training will cause them to be antagonistic to self-government. Proud and haughty natures are the perpetual enemies of republicanism. There are institutions in society — some of them religious institutions — that nourish the spirit of governing. Even the teaching of God's supremacy, and of a certain delegation of Divine authority to those who teach it, comes to be an inculcation of government in such a sense as to train men to the love of governing. Always, in every republican government, there are large elements which tend away from that government toward a strong government.

Yet, in spite of all delays and retrocessions and plottings, unquestionably the human race are developing right on toward this final and best form of government. In every generation tyranny contracts its sphere; and now we see the beginnings of the preparation for a higher type of government. Despotisms are becoming constitutional monarchies, constitutional monarchies are becoming aristocracies, and aristocracies are becoming republican governments. And the tendency of the whole world at present, in every one of its departments, is to develop the common people. Almost every influence that is working in the world now, judging it from hundred years to hundred years, is flowing in one direction; and that direction is toward the emancipation and elevation and education and empowering of the great mass of mankind.

The tendency of religion is in this direction. It has worked out one vein, and hierarchies have had their day. It is taking on more democratic forms, and it will take them on from this time forth.

The spirit of missions has had an important and unsuspected democratic influence. The attempt of Christian nations, at a vast expense, and with great trouble, to civilize poor, miserable barbarians, has been itself a testimony to the worth of poor, miserable barbarians. It has had a tendency to increase in the popular estimation the value of a man without regard to his accidents, without regard to his condition or circumstances. Man, merely as a creature of God and an heir of immortality, has risen in the market. Before Christianity was revealed, do you suppose any nation on earth were such fools as to spend millions of annual dollars to civilize barbarians? Before the time of Christ, it was an offence punishable with slavery or death to be a foreigner. If a mariner was shipwrecked upon a foreign coast, he was put to death or made a slave, on the charge of being a foreigner. Clear down to the days of the Apostles, to be a foreigner was to be nothing at all. The Greeks did not recognize human existence except as Greek existence. They counted all the rest of the world as trash, literally and truly. They learned no languages but their own. The Greek tongue prevailed in Greece, and there was not another language spoken there. The Greeks scorned to learn any language but their own. They called other languages *noises*. The Greek tongue was considered a language articulate, having sense and philosophy and reason, and all other nations besides the Greeks were said to *make noises*, in distinction from speaking. And their contempt of other peoples, previous to the setting forth of the Gospel,—how does it stand in contrast with the spirit of modern Christian nations! For England and France and Germany and America are sending out, every year, scores and scores of men elected and consecrated to the work of evangelization abroad. They give their lives freely to that work, and countless treasures are raised at home for their sustenance while they are ministering to barbarians in other lands. What a witness is this to the value of man! What a thing is worth, is to be measured by what men will do and suffer for it. And silently, imperceptibly, and unconsciously, missions have become democratic, and have raised in the estimation of the world the worth of man; — not this man or that man; not a man of this nation, or a man of that nation; not a civilized man; not a man of genius; not a man of skill; not a man of learning; but man with just the original attributes that God gave him. Religious influences, for two thousand years, have been meliorating laws and policies and governments so as to bring them more on the side of the people.

And now, at last, almost all the great causes of human conduct are working in that direction. If you examine the tendency of inventions and mechanic arts, you shall find that, although they work for all men, they do not work half so much for the rich, the strong, and the wise, as they do for the poor, the weak, and the ignorant. When steam was invented, it was the poor man's invention; for it has elevated the poor man ten degrees where it has the rich man one. Now the poor man can travel the world over. Once, only the rich man could do it; but steam has made them equal. The rich man always could wear fine fabrics. The poor man could not, till steam made manufacturing cheap. The rich man always could have luxuries. The poor man could not, till art and science were applied to domestic institutions and common life; and then he could. Now the poor man has better food than the rich man used to have, and he knows better how to cook it than the rich man once did. There is not a truckman in New York that does not live better than Alexander lived. There is not a seamstress that does not have on her table things that would have made Queen Elizabeth stare. Take the bill of provender, I was going to say, of Shakespeare's time. You might almost call it fodder, it was so coarse, and so much like animals' food. We should think ourselves treated worse than the prisoners at Sing Sing, if we had to live as the royalty did three or four hundred years ago. They would have been glad to live as our poor people live now, who are clothed better than they were, who have better houses than they had, and whose instruments of labor necessitate less drudgery than theirs did. For every machine, although when first invented it seems to supersede the laborer, has the effect to raise the laborer one step higher. Every time an iron muscle is invented, it gives emancipation to human muscle. Every time you enslave a machine, — a slave that you have a right to hold in bondage, — you set free ten thousand slaves that ought not to be held in bondage. And these are revolutionizing forces that you cannot get around. You might as well undertake to change the course of the Gulf Stream as to undertake to arrest their tendency.

And that which is true of art is also true of literature. If you go back to the time of Sterne and Swift, you shall not find, I had almost said, a single generous, humanitarian sentiment in their writings. One thing is certain, — that down to the time of Cowper, the English literature (that part which comprised the poems particularly) was filled with a supercilious contempt for the common people. The boors, the peasants, the yeomen, were considered as mats on which fine people might rub their feet and clean their shoes; as good for nothing in themselves, and serviceable only by reason of their relation to the upper classes. And the spirit of humanity, the appreciation of human worth under a rough exterior, and, above all, the desire for the welfare of every man, — these sprang up within the last hundred years. Our literature has been growing purer. Nor is it so with ours alone; for the French literature has improved as well as ours. I do not know that the French have as many Tract Societies as we have. But if it is religious to aim to develop the poor, and to create a powerful tendency toward humanity and self-sacrifice and purity, then such writers as Victor Hugo are religious writers. They are not spiritual writers, but they are religious, in that they are aiming toward the evangelization of the masses of men. And the literature of the globe to-day is humane, at least, if it is not spiritual.

If you go from literature to art, you find this still more remarkably illustrated. The days are waning in which royalty, aristocrats, and rich men can be said to be the chief patrons of art; and he that would be exalted as an artist must humble himself, and accept the divine idea of the grandeur of the common people, and not disdain their sympathy and their patronage. I do not object to those who painted the Virgin Mary and the child Jesus; but I think the Virgin Mary and the child Jesus are more to us than they were to those that painted them. What are they to us? Mother and child. Mary and Jesus were for a particular age. Mother and child are universal. They are something that comes home to every household and every heart. And the Madonna and her child are more to us, I say, than they were to those that painted them. And though I do not object to the painting of antique subjects, the subjects of past days, unquestionably the living schools are to be the schools that feel themselves called to work for the common people, and in the direction of true and Christian democracy.

Once a picture was significant of almost royal possessions. It is becoming less and less significant of wealth. Indeed, I think that pictures are less apt to be found where there is sudden wealth, than where there is real culture and good taste in comparative poverty. More and more every year pictures are coming to be owned by persons of moderate and slender means, because they have an appetite for beauty, and must have beauty to feed it. One flower in the room of a seamstress who looks at it every other stitch, is worth more than the garden of a king which he disdains to walk in. So there is a love of art beginning to develop in the common people. And all things are tending to make it possible for the common people to gratify their taste in this direction.

Once nobody could own a book unless he had a fortune. Now a man that cannot afford to own a book ought to die; he is too poor to live! It is the cheapest thing there is. Rum and reading are the two cheapest commodities of the globe!

Take one single invention, — photography. The world will never die after this. It will live in shadow. We shall have our uncles and aunts, our fathers and mothers, our children, and our children in every year's stage; and we can keep them. What a shadowy army is marching, in the shape of photographic portraits, to the next generation! O that it could have been so in days past! My mother died when I was but a small child, and I do not remember to have ever seen her face. And as there was no pencil that could afford to limn her, I have never seen a likeness of her. Would to God that I could see some picture of my mother! No picture that hangs on prince's wall, or in gallery, would I not give, if I might choose, for a faithful portrait of my mother. Give me that above all other pictures under God's canopy. My children are richer than I was when I was a child. The child of the poorest man in this congregation is richer than the child of the richest man was then.

And not only is photography enabling us to preserve our friends, but it is bringing the whole world to a man's door. You can look upon the monuments of Egypt, and at the same time toast your feet at your own fire. All the palaces of the globe are brought to you, as are also the mountains and rivers of distant countries. The very battle-field of Antietam was here almost as soon as the news of the battle reached us; and before the dead were buried, we had portrayed their mangled and swollen forms.

And not only is photography taking representations of all the natural and artificial wonders of the globe, so that the poorest man can have the shadowy portrait of everything on earth; but it is taking even the secrets of the sun and moon.

And these are but single instances of elements

which are, as we see, working to make rich and strong men richer and stronger, to be sure, but working ten thousand times more to make the poor and the weak rich and strong.

And as in respect to these elements, so in respect to learning and education. Always the rich have been able to educate their children. Not always have the poor been able to do it. But now everything is working toward the education of the common people.

So that at this time, while governments are ameliorating, while absolute monarchies are changing to constitutional monarchies, while constitutional monarchies are becoming aristocracies, while aristocracies are more and more diffusing themselves, and sharing their power with the masses, while all tendencies are toward self-government in political forms, — at this time, while these things are taking place, religion and art and learning and science and inventions are co-operating. There is one direction to all these forces. God's hand, like a sign-board, is pointing toward democracy, and saying to the nations of the earth, "This is the way: walk ye in it." The road is very muddy in some spots, and the march will be slow, but the march will be one way; and though it may be like the march into summer out of winter, or like the march of Israel out of Egypt into the promised land, summer and the promised land — self-government — will at last be reached.

Let us look, then, in the light of these remarks, at some of the relations of our own times to this tendency.

The first thing to which I will call your attention

is that extraordinary contrast which exists between this country and the other countries of the world,—the most extraordinary, I think, that was ever exhibited under the sun. Europe, starting from a point of abject despotism, has, for the last two hundred years, been steadily unfolding, and throwing off its cerements, and working its limbs, and preparing its feet for marching. Nay, it has begun to march. And though its way is through revolutions and through blood, though it is held back by reactions and retrocessions, yet, on the whole, judged by long periods of time, the progress of Europe has been from barbarism to Christian civilization; from absolute monarchies, up through constitutional monarchies and aristocracies, toward governments by the people. And all tendencies, however much they may have seemed to thwart these things, have really worked for them. Europe began at the point of despotism, and she has gone toward republicanism until she has all but grasped it.

How was it with America? We began at the point of Christian democracy. There never was so democratic a people as we were. There never was a nation with such developments of republican ideas. And we have steadily marched in the opposite direction. We have gone right away from democracy toward aristocracy. We have tended more and more to deny the natural rights of man, and set the strong over the weak (the white strong over the black weak), and to found a new dynasty, most hateful and odious, until we are poisoned in the very veins of our national life, in every part of our governmental policy.

And while Europe has been going in one direction,

we have met her, going in the other, she bearing the dark emblem of despotism, which has grown brighter and brighter until it has almost emerged into the glorious light of liberty, and we bearing a blazing torch kindled from the very altar of God, which has grown dimmer and dimmer till it has almost sunk into Egyptian darkness. There never was another such contrast.

That tendency has been met, and, in so far as the free Northern States are concerned, turned back, but only just in time for their redemption. But the attempt to recover ourselves has led to a conflict between these opposite elements such as never before raged. For this war is a war of ideas; it is a war of fundamental principles; it is a war of absolute influences; it is a war between the spirit of absolute government, as developed by the necessities of a servile society, and the spirit of self-government as developed by the condition of an intelligent population.

Now there can hardly be a doubt as to the final issue. God's intention is too plainly indicated to leave any doubt as to the ultimate state of the world. But whether that state is to exist in our day, in our children's time, or in remote ages, no man can tell. We know which side, after tumultuous struggles, shall have the victory, but whether that victory shall be delayed through generations, or whether it shall be achieved at once, we do not know.

Yet, let us take a hopeful view. Let us hope that we shall be found adequate to the exigencies which have come upon us. Let us not be bribed nor betrayed. There is no question but that the right is with us. Every principle of justice and humanity that has been developed in the past cries out to us of the North to go forward. Every analogy of God's providence calls out to us to advance courageously. Every aspiration of the human soul urges us, who are on the side of universal liberty, the liberty of all men, not to yield, not to compromise, but to maintain our stand to the bitter end, and to the glorious victory therein.

I believe that this nation will not flinch, and that it will stand. Yet I do not know the power of the Devil. His minions, his hypocritical agents, are abroad. I do not disguise my opinion on this subject, any more than on any other. I believe the opposition that has arisen against the administration and the government is the meanest and most hypocritical that ever existed. I would sooner pluck off my right arm than give countenance to it in any way. There was a time when I felt that all party spirit was being laid aside, and that all parties were being united to sustain the administration in the prosecution of this glorious war in the cause of universal humanity. I was in favor of sinking all political considerations, and standing by those men that best stood by the government. But since the enemy has sown tares among us, and an opposition has been formed, God do so to me, and more also, if I strike hands except with him who is openly and avowedly for liberty, and liberty for every man. I would denounce my own brother, I would denounce my own father, if he were ranged on the side of these enemies of their country and of freedom. I love my God and my fellow-men more than any man that carries my blood in his veins. And however much men may have been my friends, however much I would have been glad to help men into places of power, once let them stand on the side of those detestable hypocrites who are undermining with specious pretences the cause of liberty, and who, by infamous guises, are feigning friendship for an administration which they mean to destroy, God do so to me, and more also, if I touch them, except with the besom or with the rod of destruction.

But, although in the main I hope, let us be prepared for the worst. We have materials for a terrible conflict among ourselves. It is not the fault of those who invite them that we have not revolutionary outbreaks in our midst. I have no doubt that there are men in New York who would inaugurate blood, murder, and revolution, if they dared. The only thing which holds them back is a sneaking prudence. But for that we should have another era of massacre such as Paris saw in the days of the French Revolution. There are men in our midst who are so wicked that they do not need to go to hell! They carry it with them; it is in them; and they are their own devil! And these are the men, unquestionably, that are first and foremost as plotters in that specious, sinuous friendship that would go to the administration, and say, "How art thou, my brother?" while it plunges the dagger under the fifth rib. Be not found in their counsels. O my soul, come not into their secrets. It is not a safe thing for a man that keeps well to his God and his country to keep such company. Take care whom you go with. And when you go to vote, vote so strong for liberty that there shall not be any danger in your vote.* Throw it as far as you can toward God's throne, toward God's providence, toward the destiny of the

* The reference is to the then pending State election of New York.

race, toward the final results of Christianity. Throw it away from glozing, deceitful, selfish man. Go with the stanchest principles. Go back to the days when we had Franklins and Jeffersons and Washingtons, and take their utterances, and follow their precepts. The only way for us to escape troubles innumerable, I think, is to fight out this battle which we have entered upon, with courage and energy, and to the very last. You never will have another war so cheap as this. Suppose you should make peace with the South by sliding these unprincipled and subtle politicians into power, — suppose you should compel the weak hands of the government to yield to a compromise with the South, — do you suppose that would bring peace in your day?

From the moment that they get on their feet again, every election in the North will turn upon whether one State or another shall not go over to the Southern interest; and there will be a fight between Northern and Southern interests, and you will have to vote under the menace of arms, and hold your ground by force, or go down before threats. And when it comes to threatening, the South is worth a hundred of you. When it comes to knuckling, you are worth a hundred of the South! You are on your feet now, and I advise you to keep there. Your hands are out, with your hearts behind them, and I advise you to keep them out. There has never been a sight more despicable than that of Northern doughfaces in the presence of Southern slave-drivers; and now that Northern manhood is emancipated, and you are standing up, I beseech of you in the name of God and humanity, do not put yourself again into bondage and servility.

Money, — will that buy you? Then stand for liberty. A slave made free will purchase a hundred dollars' worth at your factory where a slave in bondage will purchase one dollar's worth. What does a slave want? How many combs will he buy? How many mirrors? How much glass? How many pianos? How many harps? How many books? How many harnesses? How many whips? One in the hands of a single man is enough for forty slaves. Freedom will diminish exports immensely. Why? Because, when the slaves were slaves, they lived on the least conceivable quantity of everything, and there was a great surplus for exporting. But the moment you make them free, they will become consumers to a much greater degree than they have been. If you must have a money motive, I advocate freedom on this ground. Freedom promotes commerce and manufactures. There is not a farmer to whom, if his plough could speak, it would not say, "Go for freedom, — it will make me bright"; there is not a mechanic to whom his every tool, if it could speak, would not say, "Vote for freedom, — it will make me lively"; there is not a ship-builder to whom every ship in his yard, if it could speak, would not say, "Work for freedom, — it will make me merry on the wave"; there is not a manufacturer to whom his machinery, if it could speak, would not say, "Encourage freedom, — it will make me musical."

All the factories in New England, if they could vote, would vote for freedom, — except cat-o'-nine-tail factories; I believe they would vote for slavery. No; they would turn about and go to making horsewhips, and, on second thought, vote for freedom! Every interest of agriculture, commerce, and manufactures, every industrial interest of the North, will be abundantly profited by a policy of liberty. As civilization increases among men, it makes them more, and multiplies their necessities. When a man is a savage, he has but one or two faculties to feed; but when he becomes civilized, he has a great many more mouths open and calling for food. For the more the human mind is developed, the more numerous are its wants which must be supplied. And blessed is that nation which has to supply the wants of a civilized people. They are great consumers.

It is supposed that the natural state of a man is simplicity. No, it is complexity. The natural state of a man is like that of a tree. And what is the last state of an oak, but to divide and subdivide, and spread out infinite branches on every side? The first state of a man, like the first state of a tree, may be simplicity, and he may be, as it were, a single whip; but as he begins to grow he will throw out branches, and these branches will throw out other branches, and those will throw out others, and he will take in more by root and leaf. Every interest that makes money and intelligence pleads for a policy of liberty.

And since there is a necessity for it, since by the voice of the highest officer of the nation it has been declared that emancipation is a military necessity, let us stand by that which we have got. Let us not fall back one single step in this great conflict, in which thus far God has so gloriously led us. For if this nation falls to pieces in your day, or in your child's day, will it come together again? No hand has ever yet restored the Phidian marbles. No architect has ever rebuilt Athens. The Acropolis is dishevelled and rent, a monument of her death, and a memorial of her past glory. But it is easier to bring together shattered temples than it will be to bring together the shattered principles of this great temple of liberty which has been reared in this country, if you permit it to be rent. It is a doctrine of devils, this doctrine of division. While you have the power, hold the nation together. Weld it. Secure the unity of this people, voluntary at the North, and compelled at the South. One government, one Constitution, one political doctrine which makes all men free and equal,— that shall be the glory of the continent; that shall be the prophecy of the future; that shall bring down the blessing of God, against which all the machinations of the Devil shall not prevail.

XVI.

OUR GOOD PROGRESS AND PROSPECTS.*

" And the spirit cried, and rent him sore, and came out of him: and he was as one dead; insomuch that many said, He is dead. But Jesus took him by the hand, and lifted him up; and he arose." — Mark ix. 26, 27.

IT was the peculiarity of demoniac possession that the evil spirit seated at the centre of the victim's life dispossessed his will, and acted through all his organs by the infernal volition of the usurper. Thus, every sense and every function was controlled by this demoniac influence. The sight, the hearing, the touch, the reason, and all the voluntary powers, were subject to its control.

This nation has been possessed of the Devil. Like those of old, it seated itself at the centre of life and volition. It lodged at the vital centre of government. It held in its grasp the great nerve of commerce. It controlled the nation's great heart and brain. It managed its eyes, its tongue, its hand. This nation saw and tasted and heard and felt what its demon told it to.

We read that the evil was of long standing in the case from which we have selected our text; that the

* Thanksgiving Day, November 27, 1862.

victim grew worse ; that no one could cure him ; that the demon had subjected its wretched object of persecution to numberless torments.

The parent declared that this demon "teareth him." And so hath it done with us. All the causes of trouble together for fifty years, in this nation, have not been so rending as this one demon.

"He foameth, and gnasheth with his teeth," the father said. This is painted to the life. We have seen it in Congress, in legislatures, in caucuses. Wherever the Southern temper has been, there was foaming and gnashing of teeth.

"Ofttimes," saith the father, "it hath cast him into the fire, and into the waters, to destroy him." By sea and by land, slavery has kept us on fire, leading us into war with weaker nations, laying schemes for filibustering, prompting the robbery of coveted islands and isthmuses, and agitating the world with Ostend manifestoes, which were so many diplomatic bombs, filled with destructive material.

When the demon saw Christ, "straightway the spirit tare him ; and he fell on the ground, and wallowed, foaming." Whenever the foul fiend of slavery has been met with the truths of the Christian religion, it has gone into paroxysms of fury in like manner. The mildest enunciation of the sublime and eternal truth of a higher law, of a law of unchangeable right, that overshadows legislatures and silently annuls their evil, that surrounds justice and liberty with the everlasting safeguards of God's decrees, — the enunciation in the mildest form of this supereminent truth on which God's government stands, set half a continent foaming and wallowing.

At length the day of deliverance came to this possessed child. But what tyrant ever forsook his power peaceably? The foul spirit that could not remain was determined, if possible, that nothing else should ever come after it. Impelled by the mysterious and irresistible words, "Come out," it rent the victim sore, and "he was as one dead."

And now the divine exorcism has been spoken. God has said to slavery, "Come out of the Union, and enter no more into it"; and, mad and spiteful, it is wasting the whole South, and threatening to burn its cities, to desolate its fields, to efface its civilization, and to leave the land as a wilderness.

There is an exquisite pathos in the rest of the narrative. Men who only looked upon the outside of things said, "He is dead," — because he had got well. "But Jesus took him by the hand, and lifted him up, and he arose."

Yes, after the spasm, the convulsion, the death-swoon, in this fair, demonized South, there shall come a better hour. A Saviour shall reach forth his hand; industry shall revive; schools shall shine; churches, with a pure religion, shall arise; and on the demoniac ruins shall stand health, strength, peace, reason, conscience, and love.

But one more circumstance demands our notice. The friends of this miserable victim had sought relief even from the disciples of Christ; but they could not heal him. Neither could the temple priests nor the Jewish exorcists or physicians; for none of them had the skill or courage to hit the root of the evil. They were putting plasters behind the head of the man that had the devil inside of him. They were giving him gentle physics and mild deobstruents. They were attempting to treat the devil by the skin, who sat in the very centre of the heart and brain. And, of course, they could not cast him out. No medicine could loose his tongue, or free his eyes, or give quiet to his brain, till the foul spirit at the heart was expelled. They tried remedies; they employed persuasive arguments; they sought, doubtless, by every ingenious device, to cure the mischief, and to keep the devil in him; — in short, they were conservatives! Superficial, unthorough, timid, foolish, — that it is to be conservative. Wherever there is a mere question of facts, a man may be conservative, or may be radical, and may be right or wrong, as the case may be; but in all cases which turn on a moral truth, a man is a fool that is a conservative, and no man is wise but a radical. Since the times are showing it so loudly, we may dare to speak out at last, and say so. The moment the blow was struck at the root, no more need was there of medicine or of palliatives. When the cause of the evil was removed, all the symptoms ran away too; for when God and the Devil stand face to face, one or the other must utterly fail. There is no ground for compromise or peace between them.

Without a doubt, there were a great many Pharisees and priests and statesmen of the temple, who disapproved of this rash act of exorcism, as they deemed it. "There," said they, "see how the victim is convulsed!" And when he lay half dead, they said, "Did we not tell you so? See what your meddling has done!" For then, as now, there were men who would rather see the strength which the Devil inspires in men and nations, than that weakness which Christ brings, and out of which God ordains strength that shall never be overthrown.

A second time has this nation been called, by its magistrates, in the midst of war, to celebrate a day of thanksgiving. As if the elements had heard the message, and sympathized, this morning has broken fair. The storm has passed. The sun is out. There is not a cloud in the heavens. And yet many there be that say, "What have we to be thankful for?" Thousands of families are in mourning. A great nation is beating itself with war-blows. Every day, taxes, like emerging coral reefs, are shallowing the waters, and hemming us in. Business is disturbed. The nation is in convulsion. Foreign peoples are looking on, some in sympathy, some doubtful, and some saying, eagerly, "Liberty is dead!" "Is this a time," say many, "for thanksgiving?" But this is only the outside. If God gives us faith to pierce to the centre, and see what is really going on; if God shall let us see what the dying of slavery is, and that Christ is helping us by blessed exorcism; if he will interpret to us what this weakness portends which lies between demoniac possession and self-possession, and enable us to comprehend that it is like the prelude to a sweet sleep such as crises bring on a fevered patient; if he shall reveal to us the fiery fever on the one side, and on the other rest and health, — then we shall find more reason for thanksgiving than ever before on any day of the two hundred and forty and more years since this anniversary was begun upon these shores. Those that look with the senses, to-day, perhaps shall find little occasion for thanksgiving; but I declare my faith that never in one of all the years that have marched in procession since the Pilgrims' feet made this soil sacred, has there been a thanksgiving day with such deep and all-comprehending reasons for thanksgiving.

But that we may help those who receive their impressions largely through the senses, let us first recapitulate some of the grounds and causes of gladness and thanksgiving that are material.

I. We take notice of the blessings of the season; and earliest and best of these, I call you to take notice of, and to give God thanks for, the prevalence of universal health throughout the whole loyal North, almost without exception. For continuous months, and ever since this mighty struggle began, no desolating pestilence, no wasting disease, has been among us. It is to be noted, too, that for two years the scourge of the tropics has been mostly withheld. This is the greater mercy, since our unacclimated soldiers have been open to its invisible sword, which no skill can parry, and no shield can ward off. It is true that this year a few have fallen; but how few! Among them was the ardent and enthusiastic Mitchel, who died at his post, in the ripeness of years, with his armor on, and fortunate, thrice fortunate, that the door of heaven opened to him, not from among the stars, where he loved to wander, but from among Christ's poor and helpless disciples, whom he was beginning to teach, inspire, instruct, and defend. It might be glorious to enter into rest from the martyr's stake, or from the field of battle, whose hoarse music melts strangely on many an ear into the entrancing melodies of heaven; it might enkindle our imaginations more to conceive of one taken from the astronomer's chair, where he had been found in the morning, after having kept nightly watch, passing, with reason and philosophy, from orb to orb, into brighter spheres, as from glory to glory; but better, far better, nobler, and more sublime, was his going, who walked through the valley and the shadow of death from out of the lowest door on earth, — that very door of the poor through which his Master came into the world; and who, all the way from the plantations of Beaufort to the throne of God, heard airy voices exultingly say, "Inasmuch as ye did it unto the least of these, ye did it unto the King." Rest! Thy sun arose and forgot to set. It went not down; but from very noon rose into the unhorizoned heaven.

II. Through this year of health, God has made such harvests as seldom have waved across the earth. The muster of the harvest-fields has been more wonderful than any other gatherings. The poor have not anywhere cried for bread among us. Armies have been easily fed. Commerce has felt her strength revived by the abundance of the crops. Orchards have drooped to the earth and kissed the ground with the fruit which came thence. Vines have given joy to the vintage. Corn and wheat glut the canals, and overburden the engines of every road. Our warehouses are full of food. Nay, we give our breasts to the poor of other lands. Though at war, and suffering grievous burdens, we feed the cotton-spinners of Lancashire and the silk-weavers of Lyons.

III. By this sovereign mercy of God, in the seasons, labor has been made abundant and remunerative among us. While the government pays liberally those that are in the army, their withdrawal has enhanced the value of the services of those that work at home. And so it has come to pass, in this day of general disturbance, in this time of war, that there never before came to us an autumn when so much labor was so well paid. And, on the whole, the poor are going into the winter on a footing much beyond the common average in the preparation made for their comfort and support.

IV. Now let a stranger go through New England, through New York, through Pennsylvania, through Ohio, through the great States of the Northwest, and would he know that it was a time of war, if he heard no one speak, and if he received no messages except those which came by the sight of his eye? By the languishing of the field, by the emptiness of the granary, by the cattle gone, by the usual tokens of unthrift, would he know that there was war on this great half-hemisphere? Tokens there are, in that there are many eyes that drop tears, many hearts that ache, and many churches that lack both pastors and principal men; but on the side of physical society, there are almost no tokens of war among us. And yet, for nearly two years, it has been steadily pulling at our tendons, and draining our veins.

V. Meanwhile, schools are open, and little scholars throng the valleys; and all through the Free States there is no sign of war in the school-house. Academies are open. Churches are open, and their musical bells give consolation up and down through all the Free States. And still papers fly, books are read, business thrives, and the fields give their bounty. Nothing to be thankful for? There never was a spectacle more sublime than that which it has pleased God to make manifest in the superabundant prosperity of the great thriving North in the midst of its convulsion and trouble and war.

With these remarks, we pass to other considerations. In the survey of the year, we must dismiss from our minds the partialities and prejudices that have colored the thick-flying events of the day, and rise, now, at last, to the more comprehensive views of the truths that underlie them. We must have a clear estimate of our real condition and prospects, of what is the meaning of things that have happened, and of what is the tendency of things that stand prophesying, and see if we cannot find, in the great exhibitions that are to be witnessed by the understanding and by faith, abundant occasion for thanksgiving over and above physical reasons.

This nation has passed through the period of the evolution of slavery and its nature, and the experiment is ended. Slavery has had time to develop its nature upon a better field than it ever before occupied in the history of the world. It has had a chance to develop itself in the midst of Christianity, in the midst of civilization, in the midst of the inspirations of civil liberty; not under a despotism, but under a republican government, and under a policy, too, that gave to it, every year, or decade of years, all the healthy blood necessary to repair the wastes which its own nature made. If ever there was a field on which the experiment of the full, inevitable nature of slavery could be developed, that field has been in this land.

In the beginning, slavery seemed to be an accident of our country; and the experiment of its spread, of its relations to industry, and, afterwards, of its relations to morals, to political economy, and to government, was for a long time doubtful. It is not doubtful any more. The experiment has been wrought out, and there is no more doubt as to the essential nature of slavery. There are some that still pretend that it is good, and good in such a nation as this; but they are either men that do not think at all, or that, at heart, believe in tyranny. The results can never be again concealed or covered up.

The effect of slavery on the slaves may yet be a matter of speculation, or even of sentiment; but the effect of slavery on the master can no longer be a matter of speculation, and it never was a matter of sentiment. While many point to the condition of the African as a test of the virus of the system, we may differ from them so far as to say that the first effects upon the African, peradventure, may be good. I do not doubt that, when a ship-load of natives are brought from Central Africa to America, and placed where they come under the influence of even the low civilization that inheres in the masters, there will be a certain skin-deep benefit accruing to them from it. The mischief is not that it does not begin to do the slave good, but that, as soon as it begins to sprout him, it will not let him grow. It germinates him, and then cuts him off at the root. The slave is used as grass, to be browsed on; that which is required being a strong root and a quick growth.

But that is no longer a matter of prime importance.. The effect of slavery on the white citizen is not a matter of speculation any more. It is patent; it is undeniable; there it is; war has revealed it, never to be concealed again; and we know that men who live under the influences of a system of slavery are men in whom patriotism cannot inhere, in whom public spirit cannot exist, and in whom nationality cannot be present. If there has been one thing brought to the surface and made apparent, it is that the spirit of slavery has cut up the spirit of nationality and patriotism, root and branch. It was supposed that the South, full of lordly natures, was more impulsively patriotic than the calculating North; but in the time of trial, the North, that was supposed to be actuated by paltry and mercenary feelings, has been found standing nobly careless of loss, and giving up everything she had rather than see one hair fall from the head of nationality; and the patriotism of the South, that has always boasted of her chivalric feelings, snapped like a pipe-stem. With the exception of some localities in the mountainous portion of Tennessee (and let her not be overlooked), where, practically, slavery is almost unknown, the whole South went down, when the wind of rebellion struck them, as rotten trees before a hurricane. Slavery had rotted them; and war made it manifest.

Men, on going out in the morning after a violent storm has raged through the night, and seeing mighty trees that have been laid prostrate, say, "The storm overthrew them." Not so. Go and look at the stump. See how for twenty years rot has been inside. There is a ring of health on the outside, but inside all is disease; and the storm only discloses what the rot within has done. The tree has long been decayed, and it has only needed a little puff to overthrow it.

The effect of slavery upon intelligence and religion is also now apparent. We have learned that the central policy which slavery makes indispensable for its own continuance corrupts religion, and prevents education. It is not an experimental matter any longer: it is a fact. You can have intelligence wasting slavery; you can have intelligence as the cause of the cure of slavery; but if slavery is to exist as the accepted centre of any political system, it is indispensable that the slaves should be ignorant. Why? Because every single step of intelligence opens a door of want. If a master owns twenty men, and is obliged to feed them, he cannot afford more than one mouth to each. That is as much as he wants to supply. But if you begin to educate a slave, you increase the number of his mouths; and his physical mouth is the least expensive of them all. And twenty men thoroughly waked up in their faculties are more than any one man could ever feed. If you educate slaves, you make them better workmen; but you at the same time make the expense of maintaining them so onerous that you break the back of the system. So, if slavery is preserved and made profitable, ignorance must prevail throughout the Slave States; and if you must have night for the slave, where are you going to get daylight for the white man? If there are no means of enlightenment for the million little pickaninny Africans, where are the means of enlightenment for the other million pickaninny white children? It is in point of fact, as it is in point of philosophy, true, that where there is darkness enough to keep a slave a brute, there will be darkness enough to keep a white man next to a brute. It is the ignorance of the white people of the South, essential to the existence of slavery, that has been wrought into that fulminating powder which has blown up the nation; and we know it.

When the soldiers come back from the war, there will be five hundred thousand men who will say, "Southern men do not know anything; they are ignorant, wasteful, shiftless, miserable fellows."

It cannot be denied that, as an element of political economy, slavery utterly disturbs the balance of affairs in every Slave State; for, although much money is made by slave labor, and although the slaveholding States, many of them, are rich, the question is not as to their wealth, but as to where that wealth is lodged.

If there has fallen, on an average, a foot of snow over all the State, every man's sleigh can run along the road. But suppose a foot of snow has fallen over all the State, and the winds have blown it into one or two valleys, who can get through it, or travel on it? Now, prosperous wealth falls evenly over the whole community, and into the hands of the many; but when the wealth of the community is possessed by a few men, it blocks up the road, and there is no facility of travel.

And in regard to the Southern States, we know — it is a matter, not of speculation, but of statistics — that, where slave labor produces great wealth, it produces great wealth in the hands of the few, and not in the hands of the many; and that where a thousand men are so rich that they wade knee-deep in money, fifty thousand are so poor that they barely have the necessaries of life. It is said that the Southern soldiers are better than ours, because they have been used to getting along on next to nothing, eating little, and having but the coarsest and poorest food at that.

Slavery makes not only aristocracy, but plutocracy,

which is the most dangerous kind of aristocracy. It is a patent fact, and not a matter of speculation, that it gives into the hands of a few the power of a whole State. We may not have suspected it before; we may not have deduced it from any philosophical premises; but now we see it, — that the South has been controlled by a few men. In each State a few men have shaped the policy of that State. And so it comes to pass, in the South, that by reason of this plutocracy one or two hands govern all the rest of the hands. One hand in Georgia is as strong as a thousand in New York, so far as the management of public affairs is concerned. What would you think of voting, if one man could cast a thousand votes? And yet there are men there of whom this is substantially true. Their sole will is worth ten thousand votes. It always has been so, and it will always continue to be so, as long as this system is perpetuated.

Where this disproportioned power exists, even in the Free States, it is dangerous; but when it is held by men that scoff at the fundamental ideas of American institutions, — by men that deny and deride the natural rights of mankind, — by men that laugh to scorn the principle of universal liberty, — and, above all, by men that foam at the mouth and detestingly curse the conception of political equality, — when this disproportioned political power, which pevails by reason of slavery, is held by such men, it is dangerous beyond anything that the mind can conceive. And it strikes like a hammer at the Capitol with the weight of whole States.

These things have been found out. We knew that something was the matter; but we did not know what.

The patient was sick. Dr. Clay has been giving him the rhubarb of compromise, and Dr. Webster has been giving him some diluents and aperients; but nothing seemed to set him up. And when, at last, they had got him on his back, we called in the surgeon, whose name is War, who took his surgical knife, the sword, and cut him open. And now we see what is the matter. He is rotten in the kidneys, rotten in the stomach, rotten in the liver, rotten in the lungs, rotten in the heart, rotten in the brain. Now sew him up, and let him go!

It is no small thing to have been able to dissect this affair down to the very vitals, and make report of the case, so that we know that it is not merely Abolitionists telling lies about slavery, that very good thing, but that slavery is in its own self an ulcer.

We have found out, still further, that Slave States and Free States, on account of the discordance in the essential nature of their respective institutions, cannot coexist under one constitution or government. I do not say theoretically that we have found this out, but practically. There are two inferences from one premiss. Both the North and the South have at last come to one conclusion, — namely, that there cannot be under one government two sections, one a slaveholding, and the other a free-labor section. The South, which is always more philosophical than the much-educated North, long ago found it out; and it began this rebellion with the declaration that the North and the South, whose ideas and institutions were so different, could not live together under the same government. "It is impossible," said the South, with one voice, "for Free States and Slave

States to be longer controlled by one constitution or set of laws." And what was their inference? Secession. The premiss that they laid down was, that the Slave States and the Free States could not coexist under the same government. And their conclusion was secession. The North denied both the premises and the conclusion; but after seventeen months of war the North have at last come to the same premiss. And what is their inference? Emancipation. Here, then, the North and the South are agreed. They both accept it as a settled fact, that slavery and liberty cannot coexist under one government. One says, "Slavery or liberty must yield"; and the other says, "Amen; that is so." "Therefore," says the South, "Secession!" "Therefore," says the North, "Emancipation!" The argument is fairly put. The question is now being tried. The judge that is trying it is the sword; and by nothing but the sword is it to be adjudicated.

But stop and think one moment, what a stride has been taken; what an overthrowing there has been of old prejudices; what an opening up there has been of the understanding of the nation; what a mighty advance there has been in political truth. What seer could have prophesied these things? Looking upon us two years ago, with our miserable quiddling arguments and plausible reasonings, not Jeremiah, nor Ezekiel, nor Daniel, nor any Apocalyptic prophet, could have persuaded you that now the North would stand where it is, and be so radical as it is, in the full belief that there can be no such thing as the coexistence of slavery and liberty under the same government. But this is the universal conviction. There is no dissension about it. None? None among sensible men! We are all coming to this common ground, that there is a radical oppugnancy between slavery and its ideas and institutions, and liberty and its ideas and institutions.

It is a great thing to have brought the nation to this point; for now we have simplified the whole matter, and the question is, Shall nationality be destroyed? Shall the continent be given up to double and divided empire? or shall government, liberty, and right maintain ascendency, and assert authority over this nation? The sword is to determine that question, — and I have no doubt which way.

Let other men, therefore, find no argument of thanks and of gratitude; but as for me, from the very fulness of my heart, I say, to-day, — and I would lift it up, if I could, upon the chant of more angels than filled the heaven at the advent of the Saviour, — "Glory to God in the highest, and" — erelong — "peace on earth, good-will toward men." First and chiefest, those for whom Christ felt most and deepest were the poor, the dumb, the blind, the unfriended.

Passing from this end of the experiment, let us find a moment's occasion for thanksgiving and grateful feeling in the result of the great and critical test which has been passed upon republican government. We have reason to be thankful, to-day, that the system of republican government on which all our hopes depended, and upon which so much of the hope of the nations of the world rested, has not been found wanting. Our institutions have been put to the test, and they have stood it. Down on the stormy sea this nation has at last made its trial-trip, and it has come back, and the engineers are prepared to report that, though some screws have started, and although there may be some modifications and changes necessary, yet, in the main, the experiment has been a grand success, and republican institutions are not a failure.

Our government is peculiar and complex. Its two great characterizing features are the sovereignty of individual States, and the sovereignty of the nation over these States, — the independence of local interests, and the nationality of them all, confederated under one government. This government, when we look at it in comparison with any other government on the earth, and judge it by the things that it has been called to do and to suffer, affords us occasion for admiration and gratitude. For stability and power and — what you may perhaps be surprised to hear me say — speed, this republican government has surpassed any other government in the world. Though I have not hesitated to censure men, not excepting my own friends, for what seemed to me criminal delay on their part, — for the love I bear to my country is greater than the love I bear to any man on the globe; although I have been free to chide wherever I thought rebuke was merited; — yet, notwithstanding our government may have been guilty of tardiness in some respects, if you measure its speed by that of a monarchy, it has been marvellous, and almost beyond parallel. If it is measured by our own ideal of what a republican government is competent to do, if it is criticised by the test of its own capacity, then I blame it. But if it is criticised and measured by any other government, I say that there has never been a government since the world began whose stability and power not only, but whose speed in bringing its vast resources to bear upon a given object, has equalled that of the republican government of America. Where have you ever found a government that was made up so completely as this has been of the people themselves?

In that great pine-tree that stands on the topmost point of the mountain; that defies the seasons; that sings its harsh and weird melody through all the blasts of winter and all the storms of summer; and that, the year round, holds out its branches undepopulated and ever green, — in that tree there is not one single fibre, from the root to the highest twig, that does not go to make up the tree, and that does not minister to the strength by which it resists the tempests of summer and winter.

And so, in this government, there is not one single man who is not a fibre to make it stiff in trunk and strong in branch. And it is the vital connection among the whole of the people, as represented in the States and in the nation, that gives to this government a power such as no other government ever possessed.

Where before were so many men ever rolled up so easily? Where before was so large an army, so utterly ignorant of the use of arms and all military affairs, ever so quickly trained into valiant soldiers? Where before were munitions of war ever so abundantly and speedily created? Why, the foundry that yesterday knew only how to cast stoves, to-day knows how to cast fifteen-inch guns. The factory that yesterday knew only how to make buttons, to-day knows how to make bombs. The stone that yesterday knew only how to grind scythes for cutting grass and grain, to-day knows how to grind swords for fighting the rebels. And many an enterprising establishment that has heretofore devoted its energies to producing the necessities of a community at peace, is now engaged in the production of the things that are required by a community at war. And the vast resources of the nation have been developed with a suddenness and on a scale such as were never known to any monarchy. Napoleon, even in the palmy days of his grandeur, could not have raised and equipped such an army as this nation has raised and equipped, and done it so quickly as this nation has done it. And where before has there ever been a campaign like that which our government is carrying on? The disastrous Russian campaign, perhaps, came somewhat near equalling it; but that did not equal it. If you take into account the enormous length of the line of fire that stretches from Eastern Virginia to Western Missouri, and the extent of the naval warfare that reaches clear down to the Gulf, and along to the coast of Texas, there never has been such a campaign maintained so easily as that which is being carried on by this democratic, republican government of America.

Not only that: I call your attention to the nature of the people that are reared under a government and its institutions, as one of the evidences of the kind of government and institutions that rears them. I think that one of the tests of a people is their capacity of taxation, and their willingness to be taxed. The capacity of this people for taxation is boundless.

If I am rightly informed, when the engineers laid out the system of water-works that supplies Brooklyn,

— and could supply New York if necessary, — they intended to bring the water from the several connected ponds far back on the island; but, in going out to these ponds, they found the surface-springs on the way so rich and numerous, that, before they had tapped their great reservoirs, they had all that would be needed for a year or two in the city.

I think it is very much so with taxation among us. We have only touched the surface-springs. They do not go very deep; and yet they supply the demand. Never was there a nation with such unbounded liberty, with such unlimited prosperity, and with such immense wealth that the government could avail itself of by taxation. And how patiently the people have submitted! A few rebellious distillers there are, who would fain lift up their *spirits* against it; but the great people are accepting taxation, not only with extraordinary patience, but with gladness. In this matter, the legislators were the cowards, and the people had to urge them to make the law deep, broad, and stringent enough.

That is not all. A people may submit to taxation in patience, and yet not have faith in their rulers. The test of a people is in their readiness to trust their government. All Europe said, when the Trent affair had touched the pride and inflamed the feelings of our people, "There must be war in the Northern States; the wild, fierce, ungovernable democracy there must rise against their rulers, if those rulers do anything but maintain the step that they have taken." The government, by its Secretary of State, simply said, "We are in the wrong, and we cheerfully make reparation." The ship was given up, the men were released from Fort Warren, and there was not the lisp of a murmur. This great people said, "If the rulers whom we have chosen think that that is right, we are satisfied; so go down pride! go down anger!" — and they went down.

And that is not all. The government, for more than a year, has been attempting to follow conservative counsels. There are a great many men that have all along been railing at the radicals. Had you not better wait till you have seen what radicals can do? We have had a conservative policy, that would not, when the government property at Charleston and Pensacola was seized, do anything to recover it. We had a conservative President, who would not exert his authority and power to enforce the laws of the land, and who would not, though advised to do it by conservative statesmen, take any efficient steps for the relief of the immortal Anderson when he had taken possession of Fort Sumter. Conservative counsels prevailed then, and conservative counsels have prevailed since. When the bombardment of Sumter forced something to be done, it was conservative counsel that said, "Call for only seventy-five thousand men." It was conservative counsel that said, "Put sugar-plums into your guns, and with them put down the rebellion." We have had conservative generals; and we have had a conservative campaign,* made up of mud, death, and nothing! And the great conservative wisdom which we have been obliged to follow has consisted in putting a snuffer over the President, and saying, "Let not your light shine; it will disturb the spirits of

* On the "Peninsula."

darkness." But, at last, Mr. Lincoln has risen up and said, "Enough of such nonsense! I declare that, if this rebellion does not get away with itself before the first of January, the slaves shall be free!" And it was under the same impulse that led him to take that stand, — an impulse, I will not say from external influences, but I would rather feel, from the inspiration of God's providence, that is leading him, without a doubt, in a way that he knows not of, — it was under that same impulse that, when the armies were paralyzed, Mr. Lincoln said, "Come down thou here!" to the man to whom he had said, "Go up thou there." He came down, and the President has put in authority men who are supposed to mean war, in making war; and now the face of the whole army is as if it would go towards Jerusalem. And you may depend upon it that, at last, you will see something done by radical counsel. There are a few deriding papers and politicians that are complaining of radicalism; but they are like the Jewish doctors who wanted to cure the man with the devil in him, by putting plasters on the outside. Christ said to the foul spirit, "Come out of him"; and he rent him sore, and came out of him, and he fell down as one dead; and when he got up, he had not a devil in him. We have put up, for seventeen long months, with the dilatoriness of conservatism, hoping that there was some mysterious plan which would at last be brought to light, and evolve something; but the people have found out that there is no wisdom in conservatism, and that radicalism is what we want, — a radicalism which shall strike at the root of the evil, and so end the rebellion. And under this inspiration we have come upon a new era.

And I call you to notice that this great people, under all these discouraging and aggravating circumstances, have borne patiently with their government and trusted their rulers. Where before was there ever a people wise enough, and patient enough, and self-governed enough, to do this? And now, when Europe says, "Republicanism is at end," I say, God grant that it may always end by showing a people so patient, so courageous, so self-sacrificing, so trustful toward government, and so determined, through good report and through evil report, to maintain nationality on the basis of liberty.

I will say but one word upon my next point. We have great occasion for thanksgiving, that the people have stood a moral test in the most remarkable manner. It is peculiarly gratifying to me, who have always believed in the essential, though latent, heroism of our Puritan stock, and of the whole loyal population, to see this heroism developed, in spite of the charge which has been made against us abroad, that we were a trafficking people, without heroism, and incompetent to act for an idea. We have, for two whole years, stood putting every material interest at jeopardy; we have laid all our external prospects in the scale; we have seen industry in our midst comparatively stopped; and yet, up to this hour, we have said, "Come weal or come woe, let us fight this thing out for the sake of liberty and justice." And we have not turned back nor flinched. We have gone forward, and advanced further and further toward the idea of universal freedom on this continent.

How has it been with England, — antislavery England! Half a million of ladies in England, including every principal woman there, excepting the illustrious Queen, whose relation to the state forbade her doing it, signed a letter to Mrs. Stowe, beseeching that this country would take immediate action in reference to slavery, and do away this great and crying evil. And the English press has thundered and thundered at us, never ceasing to throw up in our face the reproach that we wore the black scarf of slavery, and that oppression was a disgraceful blot upon our shield. And when the time of trial came, and, for the sake of liberty, we and England alike were called to stand and suffer, we, with every month, grew more and more antislavery, more and more disinterested, more and more heroic, and more and more determined that we would never give up the central ideas of nationality and liberty, though we should suffer the loss of all things in our efforts to maintain them; and England has apostatized. The public sentiment of England has rapidly become proslavery. What is the matter? England, that has been so boastful of what she did in the West Indies, and that has prided herself so much on her antislavery principles, snapped in two the moment the test was brought to bear upon her, and went over to the Southern side. And her whole sympathy, with the exception of a few honorable men, — and may their numbers increase, and their influence grow strong as the attraction of the heavenly bodies, — her whole sympathy, with these exceptions, when her factories and ships, when her commerce and manufacturing, were touched, was transferred from antislavery to slavery; and from that time she has stood forth as a proslavery nation. And this money-loving, slave-ridden, paltry, mean

Yankee nation, in the time of her trial, stood up in her Gethsemane, sweating great drops of blood, and said, "Lord, if thou be willing, remove this cup from me; nevertheless, not my will, but thine, be done." I point to monarchy in no less an illustrious nation than Old England, and to republicanism in this country, and say, Behold the two under the same temptations, and see what a free government makes a people do, and what a monarchy lets them do.

I cannot close this discourse without mentioning another, and to me very touching, reason of thanksgiving. For the last twenty-five years, the great bugbear with which all agitation on the slavery question was sought to be repressed was, that, if any great movement should be made toward liberty, there was no cruelty, no rapine, no robbery, no crime too awful to be imagined, that would not be committed by the emancipated or rebellious slaves. And now I desire, in this house of God, and in the presence of his praying people, to give thanks to him, that four millions of heathen — poor, despised, despoiled, much-suffering, and long-outraged — have been put on the tantalizing edge of emancipation, and held there for two years, where they could see their prayers for freedom almost answered, and that they have behaved themselves so discreetly, so patiently, and so Christianly, that there can be neither in the North nor in the South any just cause of offence. And the strongest argument to-day why they should be emancipated is, that they deserve emancipation who behave themselves so well. Where has there been one servile insurrection, or one atrocious murder, by the hand of slaves? There have been thousands of murders by the hands of their masters, but none by theirs, though they have suffered the most aggravating wrongs.

General Mitchel told me that, when he held a hundred and fifty miles of the Tennessee River, he was enabled to do it because he had intelligent slaves in his employ who kept him advised of the movements of the enemy. As a reward for their fidelity, he gave his pledge of honor that they should not be returned to slavery; but when he was called to another field, Buell gave them right back into the hands of their masters, — and the sufferings of many of them are over now! Hundreds and thousands of atrocities, such as white flesh could not bear, have been practised upon these poor creatures; and yet, where can you find a single instance in which they have shown themselves bloodthirsty or revengeful? And is this fact no argument for thanksgiving? It is to me, for our sakes, for their sakes, and for the sake of their masters; for, though I am not second to any man in zeal to put down the rebellion, it is not because I hate the white men of the South. They are my brethren yet. They are blood of my blood, and bone of my bone. Alienated they may be from me, but not I from them. Wrong they are, but what would become of us if wrong voided love and kindness? Do we not live upon perpetual kindness toward sinners? I remember the days that are gone, and I cast my imagination forward to days that are to come, when this poison that drives fever and insanity through the veins of the South shall be purged away, when slavery shall be exorcised, and when they shall sit clothed and in their right minds at the feet of Jesus.

Do not you suppose that there will be times of joy and prosperity such as the sun never shone upon, when the undivided nation, cured of its mischief, shall, every Sabbath-day, lift itself up, and, in the voice of unnumbered worshippers, praise God for liberty, for virtue, and for religion? I hail the good conduct of these poor, dusky children as contributing to our prosperity, to theirs, and to that of their masters.

My friends, it is hard, on one account, to preach on Thanksgiving-day. I preach against attractions that increase with every delaying moment; and I am warned, already, not to attempt to exhaust the topics that I have enumerated, lest, long before I could do that, I should exhaust your patience. Join with me, then, in thanksgiving. Now, reminded and stirred up, lay aside that sceptical inquiry, "What have we to give thanks for to-day?" For many things in the skies, for many things on the soil, for much in the government, for much in the army, for heroic examples, for martyrs that must be illustrious as long as there is a written history in America, for good conduct among the poor and the weak and among the rich and the strong, for the whole indication of God's providence toward our future nationality, let us give thanks to God, and let us join, as with one voice, in singing praise to God for all the kindness that he has shown us. We will sing "America"; and in order to get the key, let us take up a contribution for the poor!

XVII.

LIBERTY UNDER LAWS.*

"For, brethren, ye have been called unto liberty: only use not liberty for an occasion to the flesh, but by love serve one another." — Gal. v. 13.

T has been said, usually, that this and like passages were metaphorical, and signified simply spiritual liberty. They include that; but they neither begin nor end with it.

The Apostle is not discussing, either, the question of personal liberty. That is but an inference and special application of a larger right than even civil and political liberty, — a right that lies back of all society and all individual volition, and depends in nothing upon men's opinions or arrangements, but stands in the Divine arrangement, in the creative decree.

What, then, is liberty, — the source or fountain of which all other liberties are but streams or defluctions ?

There can be no such thing as absolute liberty, — that is, the liberty of acting according to our own wishes, without hindrance and without limitation ; for man is created to act by means of certain laws.

* December 28, 1862, while the Emancipation Proclamation was expected.

Above all creatures on earth, man is placed under many and exacting laws. He is surrounded, he is walled in, he is domed and circuited by laws; and every one of them is imperative. And it is the law of the animal creation, that, as you augment being, you augment law. For there is no power, there is no faculty, in man, that is not relative to some law which it represents outside of him. And all laws of matter external to his own self are imperative upon him. And there is no such thing as liberty, in the largest sense, in the physical world. You are at liberty to go where you please, provided you please to go where natural laws will let you; but if a man, on the top of one mountain, pleases to walk through the air to the next one, can he? He is at liberty to try; but he will fall over the precipice below if he undertakes it. Has a man liberty to do as he pleases? Let him walk on water. He has no such liberty. Our liberty is hedged in by natural law. There is no step that you can take without asking permission of laws, — and how many there are of them! How many of them touch us at every point! I am a focal centre; and laws of light, laws of electricity, laws of gravitation, and social laws are running in on me perpetually, from every direction; and I am the creature of them all, and I am obliged to submit to them all. I cannot help myself. And there is no such thing as real and absolute liberty in this regard.

All laws of our physical body, of every organ of that body, must be observed. Thus, the eye has its law; and a man has liberty of sight only through obedience to that law. The ear has its law; the tongue has its law; the heart has its law; the lungs have their law. There is a law that belongs to each particular function of the physical organization. And there is no liberty in a man except in obedience to those laws. Every faculty of the mind is a definite power, moving within fixed limits toward ends that cannot be varied. Thus, you cannot feel with the faculty that is made for thinking, and you cannot think with the faculty that is made for feeling, any more than you can digest food with the lungs, and breathe with the stomach. You cannot transpose functions from one faculty to another. You have received your mind, with its faculties, each of which has its inward law, impressed upon it of God; and the liberty that you have is a liberty which is obliged to take into account, not only the laws of the physical world, but also the laws of your body, and of all the faculties of your body. And the laws of society itself, as well as the laws developed through experience, are as binding and imperative as the laws of nature, expressed in the material world, or in us. No creature is so harnessed by imperative and absolute laws as man; and therefore, than this vague but popular idea that liberty means doing just what you please, nothing can be further from the truth. No creature that God made on the earth has so little liberty to do what he pleases as man. You cannot use your arm except according to its muscles. You cannot use your foot except according to its organization. You cannot use any organ of the body except within the circuit of its appointed natural law. You cannot use the mind nor the affections except according to their own laws. There is no liberty except inside of certain boundaries.

The only liberty, then, that a man has, is the liberty to use himself, in all his powers, according to the laws which God has imposed on those powers. The only liberty in this world is the liberty to be unhindered in obeying natural laws. Our directions, our tendencies, and therefore our duties, are all expressed in the laws that God has made; and when we come to those laws we are bound to obey them; and if anybody hinders us, then our liberties begin. As toward God, liberty means obedience to laws; and it is only when we are disputed in the right of this obedience by men, that we begin to get an idea of liberty. We have a right to obey God, whether he speaks on Sinai, or in muscle or bone or faculty, or any other way. It is our liberty to unfold natural laws, and to follow them.

This may seem but a very narrow possession. It is so only in words, not in reality. It seems as though a man were shut up when you say that he can do nothing but obey a fixed natural law. The first thought suggested by the statement is that the liberty just to obey a law is a liberty so restricted as to be almost no liberty at all. That depends upon what the law includes. Take an example or two. You can do nothing in vision except what the laws of vision allow you to do; but how much there is that can be done in obedience to those laws. In a whole lifetime you cannot see all that there is to be seen. You must, if you use your ear, do it according to the acoustic law; and yet, in obeying that law, what a liberty is opened up! A man would need to be far older than Methuselah to exhaust sound in all its varieties and combinations.

This, then, is the sovereignty of man. It is the doctrine of the individual upon a Christian basis. It is the right of every man over his own mind, heart, and body; over his time, movements, and relations to the physical world. It is the sovereignty of every man over himself. It is his right to have and hold and use himself according to the laws that God made. That is his liberty; and if any one attempts to take it away from him, he attempts to deprive him of so much of his liberty. If he does not know how to use himself thus, he loses by his ignorance so much of his liberty.

This sovereignty has seldom been exercised by, or even revealed to, the mass of men in the world. Man has been rigidly hindered and hampered by civil and secular impositions as to his body. Men have not been allowed to exercise their natural physical capacities according to the law of their own development. It has been in this respect as it was in Egypt in respect to business. It was ordained what calling a man should follow. If he was born of a priest, he had a right only to be a priest. If he was born of a mechanic, he was bound to be a mechanic. He could not elect, according to the formal law of adaptation, what pursuit he would engage in, where he would go, or what he would be. Laws have divided men, cut them up into classes, and set apart to some much, to others less, to others still less, and to others almost nothing except the crumbs that fall from the table of the more favored. And it is no small thing to say to every human being on the earth, "God gave you the right to develop your body, and all that pertains to it, according to the law that is in you, and not according to the law that happens to be in the civil society where you are."

You have that liberty. Do not you like the practice of law? You can preach, if you please, and if you are competent. Do not you like the pulpit? Nothing hinders you from turning to the store. Are you a turner? and do you find that you are thrown into a business that does not suit you? Go to the forge, if you like. Nobody stands in the way of your doing it. Are you at the forge? and do you say, "I am better adapted for a seaman"? Then why do you not go on the deck? Are you on the deck? and do you say, "Farming is that to which I am best suited"? Then there is no authority or custom to prevent you from going on a farm. Do you say, "I am too far north"? Then go to the tropics: they are free to you. Or if you say, "I am too near the equatorial zone of unhealth," then it is your privilege to go to the frigid zone, if you choose.

It seems a small thing to say that a man has a right to develop his bodily life according to the laws of the body; but that declaration in Georgia or Alabama would work a revolution in less than twenty-four hours. There are some four millions of men that, if you should say to them, "You have a right to develop your body according to natural law," would inaugurate a servile revolution in a moment. For we are in such an exquisite state in this country, that to fall back on Divine law and original equity is to overthrow civil law. And yet against civil law, and by the authority of the Gospel, I declare to every man that lives on the face of the earth, "You are called to liberty." And as long as the Bible is held in the hands, not of priests, but of freemen, just so long it will be interpreted so as to sound a trumpet-call to every living man on earth, saying: "You have a right to go wherever the laws of your being permit you to go, and to do whatever those laws permit you to do." If a man is born black as midnight, — if his face is as if all the stars of darkness had kissed him, — still, if he is born with the tongue of an orator, he has God's permission and God's ordination to be an orator; and nobody has a right to say to him, "You shall not." If a man has an artificer's skill in his hand, he has a right to cut and carve, whether it be machinery or statue or what not; and nobody has a right to say to him, "You shall not follow out the law that is infixed in your organization and your constitution." And this is what I consider to be the most atrocious thing in that most atrocious, heaven-abhorred and hell-beloved system of slavery. What? that it gives a man coarse clothes? John wore camel's hair and a leathern girdle, and he was well enough off. Is it because it gives a man coarse food? Thousands of you would be better off if you ate coarse food. Is it because in its workings men are under-fed or under-clothed? Or, are they happy because they are over-clothed and over-fed? Why, my pigs are happy, that have the liberty to grunt as much as they please, that have all they want to eat, and that have plenty of straw to lie on. And men defend slavery on the ground that the black men of the South are well fed and clothed, and are apparently happy in their condition; but the fact that they have enough to eat and to wear, and that they can sing, is no evidence that they have all the rights of their manhood. I say that they have a right to listen to the voice of God in their faculties and organization, and to follow out the laws that God has wrought in them. And that we have four millions of men before whom we stand in all the majesty of local and national law, and say: "You shall not come up into yourself; you shall not have the liberty to be what God made you able to be; you shall not be free to obey the laws of your being," — this is to go at right angles to Divine decrees; it is to contravene God's creative idea.

Man has been robbed, likewise, of his mind, — that is, of his education. An uneducated mind is like undug ore. Iron on my farm is nothing. When I have dug it out, and smelted it, and purified it, and when it has been made into a sword, into knives, into utensils or machinery of any sort, then the mineral has been educated. Now a man is nothing but a mine of undug faculties. The first step in education consists in digging them out in the rough, preparatory to bringing them to their perfect form. When a man is first born, he is like an acorn. But in an acorn — that is, in its possible future — there is timber. In a bushel of acorns there are ships, there are dwellings, there are curiously carved cornices and statues. And when men are born, they are born into philosophers, into statesmen, into orators, into patriots, into wise men, — provided that, being born, they are planted, and developed, and given an opportunity to grow to that which God thought of when he created them. But the belief of the human race has been that the man who knew much was a very dangerous creature. The heresy of five thousand years out of six, and of five hundred more, and of a hundred more besides, has been that knowledge was dangerous for the common people.

There are walking-sticks that are made for seats as well as walking-sticks. When they are shut up, they are like walking-sticks, and they cannot stand of themselves; but if you open them, there sprout out legs, that enable them not only to stand, but to support a man's weight. An uneducated man is like an unopened walking-stick of this kind. He cannot stand alone. He needs to lean on some king or government. It is not until he has been taken and educated and expanded that he can hold himself up. And it is this idea of developing that which God has put in every man, so that he can stand alone, that is the foundation of self-government, — the only divine government in this world. There are in each individual man all the faculties that are necessary, if they are balanced and co-ordinated, to make him a perfect being in his social organization; and education means merely the opening up of a man, and giving him all his legs to stand on, and all his hands to help himself with. Those who govern men, and who maintain themselves by governing men, want men to need some one to lean on, and to take care of them; and therefore they do not want them opened up. Just that which they do not like is to have every man capable of standing of himself; for their interest demands a state of things in which one head shall think for a million heads, and one hand shall rule for a million hands. And it has been, since time began, the heresy that education was to be feared. Priests have been afraid, and prime ministers and princes and kings have been afraid, of education. And yet to every man belongs the liberty of having the fullest development of all that God put into the making of the human mind. We are called to liberty. It is a part of the design of that system which lies under the foundations of society, that every man has a right to the full use of every faculty of his mind according to the law that God established in that faculty.

But man has been yet worse robbed in soul than even in body and mind. He has had presented to him false gods of every kind for his worship. And by the most rigorous despotism and the most fearful threatenings, he has been forbidden to find his own way to God, and compelled to accept the gods that were fashioned for him. And when the true God has been revealed at length, after many generations, the way to the true God has been hedged up, and worship and obedience have been prescribed, and men have had no liberty of going their own way, but have been obliged to walk the priests' and the church's way. And man's whole ethical life has been framed and imposed upon him without his consent, and without appeal from it. And although much of the religion and ethics that has been taught has belonged to the true system, much of it has not. And nowhere else has man been so trained to be a coward as in maintaining his right to fashion his own ethical life, to worship and to find God in his own way; while nowhere else has sounded out so loudly the sweet voice of the Gospel, saying, "Ye are called unto liberty."

I think men in this world, for the most part, have been much like orphans, to whom has been bequeathed a large estate, but whose fraudulent executor or guardian has kept them ignorant of their parents, their possessions, and their rights, and bound them out in every direction to ignominious callings. God's great brood of orphan children have been in the hands of the Devil as their executor; and he has kept them from knowing anything about their Father, of their inheritance, or of the liberty that belongs to them. And the Gospel has come in to rip up the old settlement, expose the fraud, and bring the orphans back to their property and privileges again. And the voice of our text, the voice of the providence of God, to-day, is, " Ye are called to liberty."

Let us, then, see how this call of the Gospel acts. Christ brought liberty to men. That is, in the first instance, he established his true place in creation as a child of God; he told him what he was, and he treated him as if he was such. While the humiliation of Christ, — not merely his being born in the likeness of a man, but his selecting for his parentage the lowest class in society, and his being born under circumstances indicative of the most impoverished condition, — while this certainly illustrates the design of God, and was meant to, and to do still more that is left out of sight, it determines man's place in creation. Christ came into the world among men that had no adventitious value. There was not, of those with whom he mingled during the first ten years of his earthly life, a man that could be proud on account of his clothes, his grounds, his house, his privileges, his honors, or his titles. Christ was born in the midst of men, and he lived for thirty years among men, that had absolutely nothing but their own individual selves. He associated with men, not because they were wise, educated, large men, not because they were privileged or titled men, but simply because they were men. For he wished to teach us that the lowest man on earth is a child of God. And if this is true of the lowest, how much more eminently is it true of everything higher than the lowest! He began at the bottom of life, and stuck close to the bottom of life, where there was simply man, and nothing else. And he bore witness by every word that he spoke, and by every deed that he performed, that man, low, base, undeveloped, least and lowest, is yet God's child. He is a child of eternity. He came hither from thence, and he goes thither again. He was God-wrought, and he feels a yearning for his parentage, and seeks again the source from which he came. And he cannot be measured by anything in this world. No latitudes drawn from the earth's surface can gird a man, and no longitudes can belt him. Take the lines of infinity, and measure him with them; take God's dwelling-place, and measure him by its instruments; measure him by nothing else but these. Take the meanest, the most imbruted creature; take the blackest slave that, overworked and outworked, is kicked out to die under the frosty hedge, and whose bones even the crows do not wait to pick, and there is not a star that nightly blazes in the heavens, and speaks of God, that shall not burn to the socket, and go out, before the spirit in that poor, low, miserable, brutish thing shall cease to flame up bright as God's own crown. The poorest creature, the lowest creature, the meanest creature, is immortal, is an eternal heir of God, and bears a spark of divinity within him. This revelation of what a man is, in and of his own nature, without any regard to his circumstances, is the key-note of civilization, and the key-note of the liberties of states and of communities that shall be permanent and normal and philosophical.

It is no small thing for a man to know that. Why, a slave that knows it and sings it, a slave that dreams of heaven and chants of Christ, is richer than is the richest master that has no God but the Devil, and stands higher in the sight of angels than he. For as angels come with God's blessings down to men, methinks they fly but a little way before they reach the spirits of some of those sainted old slaves, and that then they descend

> "Nine times the space that measures day and night
> To mortal men,"

and at last come to the master. And the difference lies in the simple fact that the former have in them Christ, the hope of glory. And the man who has that has done his march, and is ready to enter into his rest, and to ascend the throne which he has inherited.

You know the story of Williams, the missionary among the Indians, who, it was supposed, was a kidnapped Bourbon, sent off by some usurper of the throne, and who afterwards found out that he was of the stock of royalty, and spent part of his life in trying to collate the facts and make the chain of evidence complete that he was descended from the loins of kings, and was the rightful heir to the throne of France. It was not so, I suppose; but suppose it had been so, think how, when the idea dawned upon him in his forest travels; how, when he came to take fact after fact, and put them together, and prove that he was of royal blood, and a monarch entitled to all the treasures of the empire, how he must have felt a heart-swell, though he might have deemed it best to continue a missionary! I know not how it would have been with him, but I know how it would have been with me. If I had learned that I was born to human titles, and to all those regalities, and if I had chosen to be a missionary, I would have been a royal missionary, and I would have given the people among whom I moved to understand that a king stooped when I stooped.

Now Christ comes and whispers in the ears of men, saying: "You are an exiled child of royalty; you are an heir, through Jesus Christ, to an eternal inheritance, and thrones and dominions and crowns are yours." He says it to the poorest, the meanest, and the lowest, and fixes a man in the knowledge of his Father, his titles, his dignity, and his destiny. And what a liberty is there!

Christ restores and enforces the right of a man to use all his nature according to the law which God has fixed in every part of that nature, without hindrance from without. He does this by his Gospel; and I am entitled to preach that Gospel. But suppose I undertake to preach the Gospel in Georgia, in full, — not the letter which kills, but the spirit which makes alive? Men want me to do it. I am frequently asked why I do not do it. They exhort me, with a fidelity and a pathos that do not fail to touch me, to preach the Gospel! And I have made up my mind that I will. And to-day I begin by declaring, in the words of this passage, "*Ye have been called unto liberty.*" Hear it, every Calmuck, every Tartar, every Chinaman, every Japanese, every Italian, every Austrian, every Russian serf, every Frenchman; hear it, among the mountain fastnesses of Norway and Sweden, through England, and along the German coast; hear it in the islands of the sea;

hear it, ye denizens of the forests of America; hear it, ye slaves on every plantation throughout the bounds of the land; everywhere, in all the earth, hear the Gospel,—"YE HAVE BEEN CALLED UNTO LIBERTY!" And if you ask me, "What is that liberty?" I declare that it is the right of every man who is born into this world to use every power, every faculty of his being, according to the law that God has fixed in that power and in that faculty, and not according to any external imposition of man. This is the liberty to which you are called. And do you want me to preach the Gospel any more? [VOICES: Amen! Amen!] "And let all the people say, Amen." The time is coming when these truths of Christ shall flame out, and when men shall understand that preaching the Gospel does not mean preaching genuflexions and days and ordinances and abstract doctrines, and that there is a truth of the Gospel that carries emancipation through and through, right to the soul, right to the heart, and that makes every man that lives on the globe a son of God, and therefore impossible to be a slave.

But, more in detail, Christ has given to every one of us liberty of thought and liberty of belief. It is not irresponsible liberty of thought that we are called to. We have no liberty of thinking that disdains the laws of thinking. There is no liberty that does not involve the observance of law. Nevertheless, you have, every man has, as much right as I have to read God's Word, to think what truths are in that Word, and to use every part of the mind in reasoning upon those truths. Sometimes men say that faith requires us to lay aside our reason. I beg your pardon, it never does. I will tell you what I think about faith and reason. It is about these as it is about birds that both run and fly. A turkey that runs around in the woods never rises suddenly. It first runs on the ground till it gains sufficient momentum to enable it to rise and fly. Now I think that reason is like legs that run on the ground; and as soon as you have come to the end of the earth, if you need more, and you have faith, lift your wings, and you can fly. But one follows the other. Faith never can be said to be coincident with reason. Reason is that faculty which knows things so far as they can be known; and up to the point to which they can be found out, you are free to use it; and, when you get to the end of knowing, if you have faith, then fly. All beyond is the region of faith. Faith is that which takes cognizance of things that are not within the sphere of knowing. And a part of Christian liberty is the right of free thinking and free believing.

If there are infidels here that have been accustomed to carp at religion, and that say that they have a right of free investigation, I beg to inform them that they have not that right any more than every Christian has it. You have the liberty to think: we have the liberty to think. We are responsible for the laws of thought: you are responsible for the laws of thought. We all stand on one ground in that regard. And as far as the liberty of believing is concerned, we all have that. You may frame a doctrine different from mine, and you have a right to your doctrine, and I have a right to mine. You have a right to use your liberty of believing, though I do not always respect the way in which men use their liberty of believing. You have a right to investigate, to think, to believe, and to frame doctrines; but you are bound to do these things according to certain laws of investigation, of thought, of belief, and of doctrine, that have been unfolded and established.

A word more, perhaps, is required respecting this declaration that you have a right to use every part of your mind. There are old castles and old mansions that have some rooms that the children are not allowed to go into. They are haunted rooms. The children have lived ten or fifteen years without ever having entered those rooms, except, perhaps, occasionally at broad noonday. They would not go into them at night for all the world, because they are haunted.

Now the mind has haunted rooms; and on Sunday I reason in this place, with my causality, my comparison, my analogical powers, without disturbing anybody; but the moment that, in reasoning, I with mirth drive right toward a great truth, filled full of benignity toward men, and reverence toward God, men hear sounds proceeding from those rooms. If I am largely endowed with the organ of mirthfulness, what did God put it into me for but that it might be a help to me in reasoning? But the moment I begin to use it, men look toward the haunted rooms, and say, "I positively heard sounds that seemed like laughter"; and they begin to exclaim against the desecration of the Sabbath!

Now, I declare the liberty of God's people to use every faculty of their mind on Sunday as well as on week-days. A man has as much right to smile on Sunday as on Monday. He has as much right to laugh, if he has a good reason for laughing, in the church as out of it. It is foolish to laugh in either place without a good reason; and if you have a good reason, it is foolish not to laugh! It is every person's liberty to use every faculty that God put into his mind according to its laws, for a good purpose.

The like is true in respect to imagination. Because this has been employed so much in the service of sin, men think that it is not fit to be employed in the service of God. But if it has been perverted, we must consecrate it, and lift it up to higher uses. And how blessed is that liberty from God to the human mind of using every one of the faculties according to the law that is in it!

There is also the liberty of worship which Christ has restored to us; and that is absolute. Why, you may be a Quaker; God is willing, and I am willing, if you are. Do not you want to be one? Well, you may be a Presbyterian, if your conscience wants it, and your heart wants it; I am willing, and God is willing. Do not you like it? Then you may be a Methodist. If you do not like that, you may be a Baptist. If you do not like that, you may come here and be all together. If you do not want any of these nor all of them, what do you want? You are at liberty to choose the denomination that suits you best.

When you are grown to manhood, and when, conscious of the purity of your intent, when, full of honor — when, revering moral sentiment as if it were a religion, you at last find one that is to be your companion for life, and when, drawing near, your heart would speak to her, who shall give a liturgy or ritual in which to utter the words of love? Who shall prescribe to you the mode of expressing devotion? Your soul finds its own channel, and employs its own words; and no man may step between you and her whom you love to say, "Speak thus, and only thus."

And if it be so when we meet our mere companions and equals, how much more is this royalty of liberty when the soul goes rolling back toward God, and would fain express its sense of love and gratitude in the presence of divine realities! Who shall tell the soul how to speak to God? Who shall tell my child how to come and throw its arms about me? What tyrannic schoolmaster shall stand in the door when my daughter would rush to me after a long separation, with sobs and silence to say, "I love"; or with laughter and glee to say, "I love"; or with words well-measured and outpoured to say, "I love"? The soul asks no interpreter; it is its own interpreter; and no man may stand in its way and say to God what it wants to say. This would be an intrusion. If men ask your help in matters of this kind, you may give it; but your help must not be their tyrant.

There is also in this same gift of religion the liberty of beauty and of taste. A great many persons have felt that it was wicked for a Christian to dress beautifully. Do not misunderstand me. You have a right to use your rights and liberties as you please, when you please to subordinate them to others' benefits. Then it is perfectly right. And if, in accordance with this condition, a man in his own judgment says, "I do love beauty, and I will have it in my dwelling and on my person," in the name of the Lord Jesus Christ I rebuke those who pronounce it to be wicked, and I say to them, "Get thee behind me, Satan; thou art an offence unto me; for thou savorest not of the things that be of God." There is a royal liberty of all to follow every faculty in their mind according to the law that God put into that faculty, and not according to the law of society or of public sentiment. Of course there are many ethical questions of how far or how much; and these are legitimate questions; but that persons may enjoy beauty, robe themselves in it, surround themselves by it, and adorn their houses with it, I maintain. Though every man, in his own place and circumstances, must determine how much of that liberty he shall dispense with or retain for the sake of others, the liberty is there; and no man can call you to account for it. And not only are men to allow you to enjoy that liberty, but they are bound to respect your employment of it, and they have no right to point to you and say, "He is a Christian, and yet he dresses in those jewels and feathers and trappings." It is because you are a Christian that you have a right, if you can afford it, to dress in silks and satins and diamonds. A man has a right to do what he pleases in this regard, subject to God, and not to you, little godling.

The time is coming when men must learn this. The first lesson of Christianity was a lesson of self-denial. Heretofore men have been obliged to learn how to live in abnegation. But the world is not always going to be in a state in which this will be necessary. The day is rapidly coming when intelligence, art, and abundance will everywhere exist. And men must learn how to be rich, and be Christians too. They must learn how to be the admirers and creators and dispensers of beauty, and yet be Christians. And although there is a royal sphere of Christian life in self-denial which we never shall be done with, in one place and another, — though there will be abnegation in every Christian life, — yet intelligence and art and abundance will belong to Christian life, and men must learn to be Christians in these things. And when a man says to me, "I cannot understand how it is that you, being a Christian, possess yourself of so many things that are beautiful, and merely beautiful, while around about you is a world lying in wickedness," I reply that it is because I choose to raise up a higher idea for men to aim at in social life. If the notions of some men were carried out on this subject, we should dress, as John did, in camel's hair, and live in wildernesses and caves, and have insects for food.

And that which is true of beauty and taste is also true of art, of music, of wealth, and of the occupations and pursuits of life.

But mark, that this is not the liberty of doing just as a man pleases as between himself and God. It is just the contrary. Every man, as between himself and God, is bound to do the things that are indicated by the law that he has received in himself, and outside of himself. But as respects your fellow-men around about you, it is your liberty, so far as they interfere with you, and attempt to hinder you, to carry out the law of God as it has been manifested to you, to the fullest extent.

It is this obedience to law that makes such liberty safe, and gives society such benefits from it. If it was a liberty that gave a man the right to do anything that he pleased, it might be dangerous. It would then be what is called licentiousness in the Bible. But where it consists in the right of a man to follow out divine laws as they are written in him, then the more broad that liberty is, the more perfectly regulated and ordered and safe will the man's life be. A *little* liberty in men may be dangerous. Then give them more. It is said that a little learning is dangerous. Yes, a little learning is; but a little intelligence is not. There is a great difference between intelligence and learning. A little intelligence is safe; a little more is safer yet; a little more is still safer; and the more a man has of it the better he is. For intelligence does not consist in the facts that a man knows. It consists in the power of knowing. It is the educated faculty in man. And so it is in respect to liberty. Liberty is meant for man, and man is meant for liberty; and the more you can make him understand the law of God that is in him, the more you can drive him up to a full obedience to, and to a complete use of, the law that is written in him, the more safe he will be. A man will be a better father, a better husband, a better brother, a better neighbor, a better citizen, and a better Christian, the more liberty he has. Liberty is the breath of the soul. It is that by which God meant that we should live. Men live just in proportion as they are free; and they come short of true living just in proportion as they are cramped and confined and imprisoned. And how few there are that live, in the large sense of the term! Nevertheless, we are called to the royal gift of liberty in Jesus Christ.

But remember that there is something more. "Only use not liberty for an occason to the flesh." Do not think that this liberty is for your own profit and benefit. Do not be stingy because you have the riches of liberty; "but by love serve one another," — become slaves to each other. By compulsion, no man should be a slave; but without compulsion, and under the drawings of love, every man should be. Do you want to see a slave? Do not go down to those paradisiacal lying places in the South, to see the happy slave. I will point you to one.

The day is drawing to a close. Through all the hours of it a slave has been moving about the house; and now, as twilight comes on, hear the slave singing a hymn. And what is it that this angelic choir is singing to? It is a little nothing, called a baby. And who is this slave, fit to be an angel in royalty of gifts, and in richness of cultivation? Why, it is Mrs. Browning, the poetess, noble in understanding, versed in the lore of ages, deep in nature, full of treasure such as no king, no court, and no palace ever had. She sings. And when the little child is uneasy she serves it. When the child tires of the pillow and the cradle, it makes a pillow of her. And when she is weary, if the child does not wish to go, she still holds it. And when at last it will lie down, she still wakes for fear that the child will awake. And in every single hour of the night she hears its call. Not a whimper or sound from the child escapes her notice. And she is up before the morning star. And, though weary, all day again this slave serves this little baby, — this little uncrowned despot of the heart!

Ah! there is no slave out of heaven like a loving woman; and of all loving women there is no such slave as a mother. And how royal, next to God himself, are slaves! But remember what kind they must be. "By love serve one another." That is the coin that buys them. It is love, and it is giving one's self for another's benefit and to another's life in the fulness of love, that makes true slavery. How beautiful are those slaves that are slaves through love! Not the Greek Slave could be compared with them. No ideal that we can form can approach to the glory of their nature. No measure can be found by which to estimate the value of one that is a slave through love to another's uses.

It is a serious responsibility that goes with liberty; if you have it, you must use it in the fear of God for the good of others as well as for your own good.

May God give us liberty, all of us, in Jesus Christ, and may he teach us to use that liberty as Christ himself used it, "who, being in the form of God, thought it not robbery to be equal with God, but made himself of no reputation, and took upon him the form of a servant, and was made in the likeness of men; and, being found in fashion as a man, humbled himself, and became obedient unto death, even the death of the cross." And then may God highly exalt us as he exalted him, and give us, as he gave him, a name which is above every name, because our liberty has been used for others, and not for ourselves alone.

XVIII.

THE SOUTHERN BABYLON.*

"And after these things I saw another angel come down from heaven, having great power; and the earth was lightened with his glory. And he cried mightily with a strong voice, saying, Babylon the great is fallen, is fallen, and is become the habitation of devils, and the hold of every foul spirit, and a cage of every unclean and hateful bird. For all nations have drunk of the wine of the wrath of her fornication, and the kings of the earth have committed fornication with her, and the merchants of the earth are waxed rich through the abundance of her delicacies. And I heard another voice from heaven, saying, Come out of her, my people, that ye be not partakers of her sins, and that ye receive not of her plagues. For her sins have reached unto heaven, and God hath remembered her iniquities. Reward her even as she rewarded you, and double unto her double according to her works: in the cup which she hath filled, fill to her double. How much she hath glorified herself, and lived deliciously, so much torment and sorrow give her; for she saith in her heart, I sit a queen, and am no widow, and shall see no sorrow. Therefore shall her plagues come in one day, death and mourning and famine; and she shall be utterly burned with fire: for strong is the Lord God who judgeth her." — Rev. xviii. 1-8.

THE Book of Revelation is not to be studied as we study a star in the system of astronomy, with exact and mathematical calculation, but as we gaze upon a light or beacon set to teach us the general direction in which we are to lay our course. It is an illumination which God has lit up in the later days of the world to fill us

* January 4, 1863, the first Sabbath of the new year.

in times of despondency with courage and cheer and hope.

The term *Babylon*, borrowed from a real city, is employed here, as in other places, often figuratively. And without straining a point at all, it may be said that it is the kingdom of despotism, the kingdom of oppression, on earth, that is meant by the term *Babylon.* It is more specific than the term *kingdom of darkness;* for it seems to refer to a speciality of despotism. The violation of the eternal principles of justice for the injury and destruction of men, — this seems to be that which is grouped and included under that term *Babylon.* Nay, it is even more full and specific than that. It is the violation of human rights by the despotic selfishness of commerce that is included in and intended by the term *Babylon.* For although it was not the genius of the Hebrew mind to generalize philosophically as we do, to state a general truth in generic terms; and though accordingly there is no specific statement to this effect, yet, if you take the particulars that go to make up the declaration here respecting Babylon, you shall find that it is so. A great community, banded, fed, prospered, and made rich, through commerce, by unlawful means, involving the waste and the destruction of the rights, the purity, and the lives of the poor and of the needy, — such a community is a Babylon.

If you ask, then, "What is this Babylon?" it is the symbol of the injustice and the oppression practised by the commerce of the world. The spirit of modern times is commercial. Commerce is a great divine instrumentality in civilizing and Christianizing the world. Comprehensively regarded, it may be said to be a Christian agency. As a general tendency, it is doing more good to the world than we can calculate or imagine. And yet those that are conducting the commerce of the world are, to a very great extent, in their private and special operations respecting it, oppressors. For the first contact of the commercial spirit is apt to produce oppression. The commerce of the world is conducted by the strong; and usually it operates against the weak. And there is no Christianity yet that can restrain large numbers of men under such circumstances. The strength that intelligence gives, the very power which Christianity has wrought, the facility of practical life, and the fertility of thought and feeling that has been bred in us by many generations, have made us keen, potent, victorious, in the conflicts of commerce throughout the world, without at the same time making us so humane as to feel that we are burdened with the responsibility of all those whom our commerce regards.

And the world is full of this spirit. Commerce is a gigantic power. And the selfishness of commerce is a very fortress of sin. It is wrought into all nations. The conflict of the Gospel with the spirit of selfishness in commerce is to constitute a solemn part of the history of the coming times of the world.

If you ask, further, "Where is Babylon?" I reply, "In no one place, in no one age; but in every age, and in every land where the energies and industries of nations are aroused to increase wealth regardless of the welfare of mankind,—there is Babylon." "The kingdom of God,—where is that?" In no one place; for *the kingdom of God* is a term that signifies the movement of a moral force. And wherever there is progressive goodness, wherever there is rectitude and justice, there is the kingdom of God. And wherever there is injustice, wherever there is the spirit of traffic and of gain, wherever there is the power and the practice of increasing one's own strength at the expense of the welfare of others, there is the other kingdom, or that part of the kingdom of darkness which is called in the Revelation "Babylon." It is, then, the symbol of a moral movement.

This is the great form of wickedness in our day. Once the world was warlike, and the populations of the earth were destroyed by war and its attendant evils, by famine, by pestilence, and by the executioner's axe; but like numbers of men are now destroyed by coal-mines, by factories, by overtaxing labors in cities and on plantations. And all the wastes and destructions of men that aforetime have been through governments, are now through firms and companies, in the main; for Babylon is the modern dynasty of the Devil.

Against this the whole spirit and tendency of Christianity utters its solemn protest. Man is sacred, — not fabrics, not metals, not buildings, not cities, but mankind. This is to become the fanaticism, or at least the enthusiasm, of modern civilization, — the sacredness of mankind; and those who are the weakest are to become the special objects of Divine care; and we are to accept that. While hitherto, in the earlier periods of this world's struggle, the strong have had the advantage in life, as that struggle progresses, and God is bringing moral things to their victorious periods, we shall begin to see that he takes care of the weakest and the lowest. We are beginning to see it already.

A judgment is decreed against this special wickedness; and it is so determined that God does not leave it even to his own voluntary government of providence, but infixes it into the course of nature, and establishes it by natural law. It has been made apparent, and it becomes more and more apparent, that any course which builds up national wealth and national power at the expense of the poor and the needy, works in at the same time an element of decline, of weakness, and of death itself.

The whole future progress of Christianity requires the overthrow of such a wrong. The essence of Christianity is good-will to the poor and to the needy. It must destroy, therefore, every system whose essence is the neglect, the misuse, the degradation, and the destruction of the poor and the needy. However long delayed, however much soever seemingly overthrown, God has determined that there yet shall be victory of Christianity over this form of Satan.

Hence the solemnity and the full meaning of our text in its exhortation to every one to come out from such wickedness.

"I heard another voice from heaven, saying, Come out of her, my people, that ye be not partakers of her sins, and that ye receive not of her plagues."

Every man that means to stand safely, every man that means to be recognized and owned of God, is summoned carefully to separate himself from all courses and tendencies and parties and sides that are seeking their success by wasting or destroying God's poor and God's needy.

I propose, from this stand-point, on this the first Sabbath of January, — for that day stands lifted higher, it seems to me, as a watch-tower, than all the other Sabbaths, — to look upon the world, and summarily to consider the present condition of nations with reference to this peculiar triumph of the Gospel, — the deliverance of the poor from the exactions and oppressions of tyrannic and despotic commerce.

I. Look upon that continent, dark and mysterious, of Africa. But little light falls there. Its interior is possessed by populations immense but ignorant, debased by superstition, practising many outrages among themselves and upon themselves, and yet susceptible of civilization and of an eminent future. It is the fashion of many persons to deride and to despise the African people, as a stock incapable of civilization. I have no manner of doubt that there are some elements of civilization that are more eminent in one nationality than in another, but I count it as little less than blasphemous to say of a whole continent of people that God has made, that they are unsusceptible of that development and civilization which is the common property and lot of the whole human family. I regard the African race as destined to a future, — if not such a one as belongs to European races, yet one that shall be signal for its own light and its own glory.

Some efforts are making for this benighted continent. Travellers are exploring its territory; and every year they are bringing us more and more accurate and extended information concerning it. Missions have lit tapers, at last, along the coast. Colonies there are, one or two; and although they are green spots on the great continent, they are just such green spots as in this winter night you shall find of mistletoe in the boughs of old oak-trees. There is one little handful of mistletoe to a whole great barren tree; and as that hangs in the bough of the tree, so these one or two colonies hang in the boughs of that vast continent. And commerce is hovering around about it, like a sea-gull, off and on, seeking food.

Yet, withal, but little is yet accomplished; and we may say that darkness still broods where for ages darkness has not been irradiated. Africa and its countless millions may be said to be yet buried in a midnight for which there seems to be no preparation of morning. But a morning shall come, though its star has not yet dawned. God, that holds the stars in his right hand, will in his own time roll them above the horizon; and there shall be a bright and morning star for Africa.

II. Look at Asia. The prevalent condition of its population is one of abasement and oppression. The unnumbered millions of people that dwell in Asia are low, debased, oppressed, wasting and wasted. India and China have been appropriated by the commerce of Europe, and chiefly of Great Britain. For more than a hundred and fifty years, the commerce of England has fed on the people of Asia. England has fed on the spoils of commercial oppression. All her Christianity is not to-day strong enough to roll an opium-pill into the sea! All her love of liberty and Christianity combined is not to-day strong enough to break a thread of cotton! And of all the nations of time, of all the kingdoms on the earth, there is not one that stands so centrally the very Babylon of Babylons, made rich and strong by grinding people and eating them up, as England.

And yet there are some signs of movement even in

Asia: there are some in India, some in China, and some in Japan. There are there some preparations for a growth of civilization; but it belongs to another generation. There are to be great revolutions and great changes in prosperous empires before the latter-day glory is to come, if great moral truths and equities are to be illustrated in latter-day glory. There is but little of promise in Asia.

III. Let us turn, then, to Europe. What is its condition with reference to the enfranchisement of its millions of common people? I note with pleasure and joy the signs of revived national life in the group of Mediterranean nations. Spain is showing signs of renewed life. Italy has electrified the world by springing from her dust and standing up again clothed and in her right mind. Greece is also beginning to assert her national life. And Turkey herself, though a sick and feeble and perishing nation in her political forms, has under her political forms a stock as noble, I believe, as there is on the face of the earth. For although every Turk that has touched public life has found in it about the same effect which it has wrought in Occidental nations, and has been corrupted by it, if you go outside of state and government employment, you shall find that the common people of Turkey are a noble common people. And there is hope for them. In regard to all this group of nations along the Mediterranean, it is a popular and commercial regeneration that is taking place, and not a governmental regeneration. The people of all these kingdoms have asserted their rights; and in so far as they have been gained, they have been gained *by* them, and not *for* them. It is an initiative and prophetic, rather than a settled and accomplished thing. Southern Europe looks toward a brighter future. There is hope for her common people.

And as for Middle Europe, including Austria, Germany, Denmark, and Scandinavia, it may be said that there is a reactionary and conservative state of government in this long line of nations, but that there is a slow amelioration of the common people, which is important rather for what it promises than for what it yet is. It seems to me that the progress of the Germanic race may more fitly be compared to the motion of its glaciers on the Tyrol mountains than to the growth of the harvests of our populous plains and valleys, where the seed is sown, and comes up, and grows, and ripens, and is ready for the sickle, in one year. The German mind is like a frozen river lying aslant upon the mountains, which moves, but which moves so slowly that men disputed for a whole generation as to whether it did move or not, — a question which could be settled only by driving stakes and taking observations from month to month. But it moves. And as the glaciers are making channels in the sides of the mountains, and abrading the rocks, and melting the ice, and flowing down, and making soil in the valleys below, so the Germanic and central nations of Europe are moving and preparing for a glorious future.

Russia presents the most noble attitude of any nation in Europe. The whole national life is undergoing a change in the direction of restoring rights to the common people. If we had been called to single out that nation which would most signally illustrate the spirit of Christian democracy, the last one that we should have mentioned would have been Russia. And yet she is the first in this thing. "The last shall be first."

This is not the work of the people; it is not the work of commerce. The most remarkable feature in this movement of the vast Russian Empire, of the enfranchisement of its serfs, is that it is the work of the government; and that it is the work of a government the most concentrated and autocratic that has been known in the history of the world. And the Czar of Russia stands, beyond all question, the emancipator of the nineteenth century. Crown the head, then, of this Cæsar. Pluck leaves from the tree of life and immortal blossoms, and put a wreath around about his head, who, standing in a place that has made men before him hard and cruel and selfish, has been moved by the Spirit of God to take his position in the forefront of modern progress, and emancipate the myriad slaves of his vast empire. The whole resources of that kingdom are now embarked in this gigantic reformation. It is the only instance of the kind in Europe. There is not another movement like it there. Every other king in Europe of whom we know anything is fearing and dreading a popular enfranchisement. All the other governments of Europe may now be said to be resisting the encroachments of the common people, and seeking to build new dikes and levees and dams to keep the people within some bounds. And Russia only stands, by her government, and through her autocrat, her Czar, giving liberty to her slaves.

Not in Italy, that old land of republics and of early civilization; not in Germany, that land of Reformation, — the seed-ground and granary of modern liberty; not in France, for an age inoculating the world with the virus of democracy, which never takes at home; not in England, the land of the Puritan, and the sturdy defender of popular rights; — but in Russia, a synonyme for all that is despotic, is now going on God's drama of emancipation, the most illustrious act of modern times.

If we look to Western Europe, France and England are both of them retrograding; not in wealth, — they were never so rich; not in material civilization, — they were never building so many roads and so many ships, and making so many improvements. In both, commerce is the instrument that is strongest, and is most influencing government and the intermediate classes between the government and the lowest class. And the spirit of commerce in England and France is not only selfish, but tending to be despotic, and to violate the natural rights of man. The war of France to-day in Mexico is a most signal illustration of the commerce of France; and that war seeks to violate every right of a nation for no other reason than a commercial reason.

I shall not speak of England and her position, for the simple reason that there is bad blood enough, — and there has been reason enough for bad blood! My convictions are such, and they are so fixed in my very nature, that if I speak at all I shall speak strongly; and I do not wish to deepen and strengthen any impressions, which are already deep enough and strong enough, between our kindred on the other side of the water and ourselves here. God will judge her, and history will judge her.

From Europe, turn we to the other continent that is left, — America. Unmentioned in our inventory of American States is one which has in it perhaps as bright a promise as any other on the continent, — Canada. The umbilical cord which connects this unweaned child with her unfertilizing mother ought to be cut! It is high time it was cut! And with a territory second to none, with climates as favorable as our own, with two oceans as much as we, and with the beginning of a population than which no nation could desire to have a better, I know not why Canada is not yet to take her place among the great nations of the time and the world. In so far as her present is concerned, it may be torpid in spots, and inert, but in all its activities it is forward and healthful and Christian. God bless Canada, and give her a glorious and illustrious future. And as she bears her meteor flag westward, it shall be her glory, above any nation that dwells upon this hemisphere, to carry a banner that in her hands has never been held over the head of a slave. And when her cities shall be built, and her ports shall be opened on the Pacific coast, and her commerce shall extend from ocean to ocean, clear across this hemisphere, she shall be the free nation of the North, and the mother of freedom. Again, God bless Canada!

Before I speak of our own affairs, let me dismiss the residue of the earth, by saying that South America seems to me like an hour-glass that has just so many sands in it, which run from this orb down into that, and then, by revolution, is turned upside down, when the same sands run back again. She has been shifting about once in ten years ever since I was born, and I do not know how long the same process had been going on when I was born. I suppose from the beginning of the world. As she was, she is still,—and I know not but that she will be so to the end of time. The signs of her future are not many, nor are they very encouraging.

In looking upon our own country, the external appearance is sad. Civil war is always a spectacle of sadness. The conflict of brethren, the horrible loss of life, and the attendant sufferings that hover about the movements of armies, and that belong to campaigns,—if you look upon these outward things, you shall mourn, and say, "It is a time of darkness, of thick darkness, when there is no light even upon the mountains"; but if you look at the condition of the country, not externally, not from within, it is noble. For there is just now a conflict for the government of this continent between two giant forces,—the spirit of Christian liberty and democracy, and the spirit of aristocratic oppression. And the spectacle which is before God and angels and faith-seeing men, is this spectacle of the last great battle of the Lord God Almighty on this continent between these two great forces; the one importing, in its heart, in its principles, and in its inevitable victories, the welfare of the common people to the very bottom; and the other importing, in its heart, in its principles, and in its intent, the subjugation of the common people; the one, by every single element that belongs to it, by its whole Christianity, by all its antecedents, by every single one of the institutions that it has established, living for the education and the elevation of the ignorant and the poor, and for the strengthening of the weak; and the other, by every radical element of its existence, and by its avowed and declared purposes, taking the poor and the weak and the ignorant, as the vintner takes the cluster, to crush it, that he may drink the wine that runs from it. These two great opposing forces are now in conflict on this continent.

We love to read, in Milton, of the fight of angels, good and bad. We love, in poetic descant, to imagine God blowing his great trumpet, and summoning all the good and all the evil into conflict; but there never was portrayed in Milton, or in any fiction, a conflict so sublime as that which is taking place in our land and in our time. You and I, and your children and mine, are witnessing the illustrious parts of the conflict between the great cause of God in modern civilization and the cause of the Devil.

The present stage of this conflict, I think, is the sublimest that it has yet attained. If the very conception is sublime, thus far the outworking of it has been. At last the government of the United States stands straight again.

In our Western forests, where mighty tempestuous winds rend and cast down trees one upon another, now and then, in its fall during a storm, some great tree overlays the stem of another tree, and holds it down, and it learns to grow crooked; until another storm comes and shakes off the entangling load, when the bent tree is left to seek its original straightness, which, little by little, and year by year, it at last recovers, so that the crook is all gone, and it once more holds out its branches to the free heaven alike on every side.

Just so, at last, the government of these United States has righted itself. Slavery, that bent it and held it down so long, has rolled off, and left it to extend every leaf and every branch alike North and South and East and West, to the spirit of liberty. The President of these United States — to be accused, certainly, of no haste; to be charged with no rashness in judgment; led by no vain confidence in his own intuitions; after long and painful deliberation, and an anxious seeking for some other way — has been constrained to issue his Proclamation for the emancipation of the slaves of the States that are in rebellion against this government. And I consider that to be the event of this century in the West. There are two great facts in this world, and there are but two. All other facts besides these are as dust. They are, first, the autocrat of Russia, standing in the far Eastern hemisphere, and against his nobles, employing the whole military resources and wealth of that great empire for the enfranchisement of his serfs; and second, the President of this Occidental republic, standing in the midst of war and darkness, and sending forth the light of that Proclamation by which he declares the liberty of three millions of slaves on this continent. These two events are like two mountains of Calvary lifted up. All the rest that is doing in the world is low and dim in the comparison.

The moral recognition which the President was pleased to give in the issuing of this military order is most becoming. It seems to me that it could not have been omitted in his Proclamation. After so many ages of Christianity in the world, after such a career as that of this nation, if the President of the

United States had not based his action, at least in part, on considerations of justice and rectitude, he would have violated the very spirit of the age in which he lives. And I thank God, in his behalf, that he was led to take that step; and that, though he took it as the Commander-in-chief of our armies, he yet took it because it was just, as well as necessary. For I tell you, you are not fit to be free, nor to be the conservators of the freedom of other men, until the time comes when you shall be able to say, in the fulness of your heart, in respect to every man on the globe, black or white, that liberty is his right, — not our benefit, not our advantage, but his right. And although the occasion of giving men back their natural rights is a military necessity, it is none the less a glorious triumph, that through that we recognize the divine truth of the natural right of every man to his own life, and his own liberty, and to the pursuit of happiness.

This Proclamation, I know, may not set one slave free to-day or to-morrow, — for the Proclamation is but an arrow. The army is the bow. An arrow without a bow is a poor thing. This Proclamation without an army might effect but little; but with an army it may produce important results. And as to that, the Lord God of love is also the Lord God of hosts. The God of justice is the God of battles. And since we have conformed to the decrees of eternal justice, may we not believe that now He that leads the armies of the heaven and of the earth will give us victory? I believe that he will.

Although there may not be to-day nor to-morrow the emancipation of any considerable number of slaves, although the freedom of those in bondage is something that is yet to be earned, we have emancipated a good deal. Though we may not have set free one slave, we have set this government free, and we have set this great nation free; and that is a great deal. You and I have no longer the responsibility of the slavery of three millions of men by our relations to a government which indorses their servitude. We have been bending under our own indorsements, like merchants who have lent their name to paper enough to sweep their whole property; and now we are like those same merchants when at last their paper is all gathered up, and their name is cancelled, and there is not the scratch of a pen against them.

There is one feature in the Proclamation to which I desire to call your attention, and that is the declaration of the Commander-in-Chief of the armies of these United States that the slaves set free should be employed in the military service of the government. I thank God for that. It is a most potent step. The moment a man is declared to be free, that moment he becomes a citizen: not with all the political rights and duties known to a citizen; but he becomes a citizen. A man may be a citizen, and yet not be like every other one. A woman is a citizen; but she does not vote nor bear office under the government. A child is a citizen; and still a child has no part in forming public policy. And a slave is a citizen, if he is born in this country, and if he is declared to be free. He may not be a citizen empowered to vote, or entitled to office; but he is a citizen entitled to his life, to his liberty, and to the pursuit of happiness. He is a citizen entitled to self-defence, and to the privilege of fighting for his own country.

When the President, recognizing the liberty of these oppressed people, declares that they shall be protected and received into the army, and allowed to hold forts and perform other military service, he has taken a second great step over and above the declaration of their freedom; for it prevents the motives for an irregular and savage warfare on their part, should they be provoked to any such folly. It provides a way in which whatever resistance they may please to make against their oppressors may be under the direction of the military authorities of this nation.

Nobody can predict the future except in a very general way; but I anticipate now a conflict more terrific than anything that we have yet had. I have never been one that supposed such a proclamation would alarm Southern men. The day for doing things with moral effect was allowed to pass by. God had a plan in it; and since that has come to pass which I saw coming to pass, since our mistakes have been overruled, as they have been, for the furtherance of the great cause of God in liberty, I am not disposed to complain, as at times I did complain. It is very evident that the whole period of popular enthusiasm, and the whole time for striking down the rebellion when in the gristle, was wasted. The counsels that for a long time prevailed and controlled the movements of our armies were counsels which subsequent events have proved to have been foolish, and which it has been found necessary to cut up by the roots and cast away. And diplomacy is now occupied in unsaying what diplomacy was twelve months ago occupied in saying. But that is all past; that has gone by. What the future is to be I cannot tell; but I suppose that this Proclamation will be met by a counter proclamation of the President of the so-called Confederate States. We cannot but acknowledge that, whatever may be their faults, the South have not found themselves wanting in fidelity to their own ideas, in manliness in the defence of their territory, nor in a head to guide them skilfully and bravely. And if this Proclamation is not met with a proclamation that more than matches it on the part of Mr. Davis, it will be the first time that he has been found stumbling in this conflict.

And then, when it is proclamation against proclamation, government against government, and people against people, there will be no such thing as compromise, there will be no chance for amicable settlement, — as for a long time there has not been. And you must lie down and let them walk over your necks, or they must lie down and you must walk over their necks. We may just as well look at it as it is. We may just as well understand the literal truth, and prepare ourselves for the one thing or the other.

I believe that there are many honest men who think that this matter might yet be compromised. There are many honest men who are overturing backwards and forwards, and trying to bring about a friendly adjustment of the case. But making overtures to the Southern government is just about such a piece of wisdom as it would be for a Sunday-school child to sit by the cage of a boa-constrictor in Van Amburg's menagerie, and try to make him recite the ten commandments! May all that they have accomplished by their mediations do them good. I give them the credit of being honest men ; but they are very simple, to say the least. The South do not mean compromise. They have taken their ear of corn, and husked it, and there is no husk left. They have shelled it, and there is no cob left. Their cause is clear kernel and meal, nothing else. And we may as well husk our ear now, and see everything in the grit and grain, and put our absoluteness against their absoluteness, and go forward with the old war-cry, *God and Justice*, and let that prevail which God pleases to make triumphant. I am willing to take the risk. I am willing to have one more battle-field, illustrious above every other; because never since the sun shone, never since governments were ordained, has there been an issue so absolute, so perpendicular, so crystalline, so devoid of all side issues, as this issue between absolute liberty and absolute slavery; between aristocracy and democracy; between the spirit of Christianity and the infidelity of oppression. Never before was there an issue so clear on both sides; and let it be settled. Let no man stand between these combatants; for the war must be fought out. You have gone to the expense, you have heaped up your treasure, you have sent forth your sons, you have mustered your armies, and you can never do it again so cheaply and with so little bloodshed as now. Therefore, in the name of God, in the name of Christ, in the name of the Holy Ghost, for the sake of humanity, and for the love of mankind, let this conflict go on till victory is declared on one side or the other.

But, whatever we may say or do, brethren, I believe that we are going on the Gulf-Stream of a Divine decree. I believe that we, as a nation, are being swept down a course that has been appointed from the foundation of the world, and that the counsels of eternity are guiding that movement by which we are dancing like bubbles on the waves of the sea. Therefore it is rather to urge you to joyful consent, than because I think you can withdraw yourselves from this movement, that I now speak. For it has been wisely said, that in times of revolution single men are nothing at all; that great principles and causes take their course, and no man can hinder or resist them. If a man were being swept down the Niagara River, it would make very little difference, in so far as his rescue was concerned, what his struggles or his thoughts were. Once in the stream, he must go over the precipice, and take his chances. And we must go down the cataract of war. It is not in the power of any limber-backed, shallow-pated fool to stop the career of God's decrees.

What, then, are our duties at this time, as a Christian people ? It seems to me that our first duty consists in such a preparation of heart and mind that we can walk with God, and look at the events that are taking place, not from the low stand-point of the passions, or of self-interest, but from the stand-point of truth and righteousness. We ought to stand on the high platform on which God stands, and from thence behold the course of Divine Providence.

And then, next, we should be chastened, it seems to me, in our griefs and in our sorrows. God sends mourning into every house. Again that has come to pass which took place ages since. We are the modern Egypt; and the millions in the house of bondage we have refused to let go, until, as of old, the first-born has fallen in almost every family in the North. And the outcry that is heard in all our land is the outcry of grief and sorrow at the death of, O how many young! how many noble! how many heroic!

You have sent your children in honor before you, but you have not lost one of them. And, of the young and fair that went forth from the college, from the academy, from the law-office, from their many vocations, and grasped the sword and musket, and entered into the service of their dearly beloved country, methinks I see one and another, in their bright ascension, standing to look on the bodies dripping on fields of gore, and to chide the grief that sees the outside, and not, through that, the reality and glory of their heavenly state. You mourn not as those that have no hope, for the fallen.

We ought also to understand that, in the victory of our government, which we may hope impends, there is to be laid upon the Church a very solemn responsibility for the care of these millions of poor and helpless creatures. It is going to be a very serious thing for a man to be a philanthropist and a Christian from this time forward; and we ought not to spend our enthusiasm merely in patriotic descant: we ought to begin to pray, and to ask God what is our duty toward those that are about to be rolled as a responsibility upon the conscience and the heart of the Church. We must think betimes of these things, and prepare ourselves for them beforehand.

Moreover, it is the duty of all, and I solemnly enjoin it upon every young man and maiden, to stand up now, at home and abroad, in season and out of season, and with a holy and chastened enthusiasm, for those great principles of Christian liberty which have been imperilled, and which lie at the root of this moral struggle.

There is one thing that commands my admiration, whether it be in man or bird or beast, — and that is, fidelity to an avowed object, and a readiness to suffer for it.

It befell me, when I lived in the West, to be disquieted by the screeching of blue-jays around my house, and I determined that I would make way with the nuisance. Accordingly, day by day, I took my gun, and dropped them one after another. And I noticed, from time to time, how tenacious they were of life, and how violently every one of them fought when wounded. One day I picked up a bird that I had shot, and I was forcibly impressed with the heroism that he displayed. He would not die. He would not give up. He fought me with claw and bill, and gleamed upon me with his bright, kingly eye. And the thought came over me of his pluck, and courage, and unflinching spirit, and I said to him, "You deserve to live, and for your sake I will never shoot another of your kind," — and I never did. I admired the temper of that unvanquished bird.

And — let me confess the weakness — I admire, even in a bad cause, the heroic spirit, the indomitable courage, that we behold in Southern women, in Southern men, and in Southern boys. They are on the wrong side; but they put us to shame by their utter enthusiasm for the most accursed cause that ever the sun was permitted to shine on. They have embraced it, and have given their heart and life to it, and they are willing to suffer for it. And now, shall we, for the sake of that cause which is the hope of nations, for the sake of that cause which was cradled in the bosom of ages, for the sake of that cause which bears prophecies of good-will to all the world, — shall we, for the sake of all that unites earth to heaven and makes man godlike, for the sake of God and justice, and for the sake of sweet and ever-blooming liberty, have no enthusiasm and no courage? I command every young man in my presence to let no man daunt him; to let no man deter him from an outspoken and enthusiastic love of liberty and right. And I command every maiden to crown with her smiles, and to give preference to only those men who are enough men to avow their enthusiasm for liberty. Since to our hands is committed this priceless boon, on us rests the responsibility of vindicating the natural rights of men, of showing courage and enthusiasm for them, and of rebuking, with the utmost scorn and indignation that a Christian heart may feel, those miserable manlings, those wretched homunculi, that stand in the midst of the blessings of liberty to be ashamed of liberty, and to call it a sentimentalism and a philanthropism. Let these isms, and all the manikins that belong to them, go; and do you stand enthusiasts and glorious triumphers for God in human rights.

Meanwhile, shall I draw aside the veil? Shall I point out what is coming? Shall I open up the future? I will read, rather, the words of the sublime prophecy. Listen to the doom that is to be theirs, who, for pelf and selfish commerce, are determined to oppress the poor and the needy. It is the Word of God.

"And the kings of the earth, who have committed fornication, and lived deliciously with her, shall bewail her, and lament for her," — they are doing it already; they want a mediation; they are very anxious to have peace,— "when they shall see the smoke of her burning, standing afar off for the fear of her torment, saying, Alas, alas, that great city Babylon, that mighty city! for in one hour is thy judgment come. And the merchants of the earth shall weep and mourn over her; for no man buyeth their merchandise any more; the merchandise of gold and silver and precious stones, and of pearls, and fine linen, and purple, and silk, and scarlet, and all thyine-wood, and all manner vessels of ivory, and all manner vessels of most precious wood, and of brass, and iron, and marble, and cinnamon, and odors, and ointments, and frankincense, and wine, and oil, and fine flour, and wheat, and beasts, and sheep, and horses, and chariots, and slaves, and souls of men."

That is the commerce of the South.

"And the fruits that thy soul lusteth after are departed from thee, and all things which were dainty and goodly are departed from thee, and thou shalt find them no more at all. The merchants of these things, which were made rich by her, shall stand afar off, for the fear of her torment, weeping and wailing, and saying, Alas, alas, that great city that was clothed in fine linen, and purple, and scarlet, and decked with gold, and precious stones, and pearls! For in one hour so great riches is come to nought. And every ship-master, and all the company in ships, and sailors, and as many as trade by sea, stood afar off, and cried when they saw the smoke of her burning, saying, What city is like unto this great city! And they cast dust on their heads, and cried, weeping and wailing, saying, Alas, alas, that great city, wherein were made rich all that had ships in the sea, by reason of her costliness! for in one hour is she made desolate. Rejoice over her, thou heaven, and ye holy apostles and prophets; for God hath avenged you on her. And a mighty angel took up a stone like a great millstone, and cast it into the sea, saying, Thus with violence shall that great city Babylon be thrown down, and shall be found no more at all."

So may slavery perish, and those that uphold it!

www.ingramcontent.com/pod-product-compliance
Lightning Source LLC
LaVergne TN
LVHW021122110826
845150LV00005B/924

* 9 7 8 1 4 2 5 5 5 0 8 9 9 *